PRESENTED TO:

_____

FROM:

_____

DATE:

_____

LOUISA MAY ALCOTT'S CHRISTMAS TREASURY

The Complete Christmas Collection

Edited by Stephen W. Hines
Illustrations by C. Michael Dudash

RIVER
OAK
PUBLISHING

Louisa May Alcott's Christmas Treasury
The Complete Christmas Collection
ISBN 1-58919-950-2
Copyright © 2002 by Stephen W. Hines

Published by RiverOak Publishing
P.O. Box 55388
Tulsa, Oklahoma 74155

Book design by Koechel Peterson & Associates
Edited by Stephen W. Hines
Illustrations by C. Michael Dudash

Contents

Introduction

Some readers today have a problem with happy endings. Louisa May Alcott did not. Her own life was one of early trial followed by fabulous success and years of acclaim, honor, and happiness. The improbable became probable in Louisa May Alcott's life story, and she did not see why it should not be so for others.

By all accounts, Bronson Alcott, Louisa's father, belonged in another world—a world of the spirit where the tawdry concerns of making a living would not intrude on his philosophy of mental wellness and idealism. Mr. Alcott had both feet planted firmly in the air.

Bronson was not incapable of making a decent living for his family; but he thought his best way of making that decent living was beneath him. He was a good carpenter, but such work was beneath a philosopher and teacher who wished to experience truth through nature more than he wanted to give his children milk—for that would be stealing from the cow. Bronson was very particular about his soul, and about not stealing from cows.

Thus was started the famous Alcott sinking fund. It was famous to friends and acquaintances because it was sinking and always in need of additional supply—mostly from the helping hand of Ralph Waldo Emerson, who shared many sympathies with Bronson Alcott but who was not actually afraid of making a living.

Emerson's generosity kept the humble little Alcott brood from starving, and Louisa May never forgot his lessons in practical charity. All of her life she revered Emerson and gave generously to family and friends herself. She had a passing interest in philosophy but a deeper interest in good deeds and charity that led to transformed lives.

When Louisa became rich after the publication of *Little Women*, she promptly paid all her family's debts to Emerson and others. The Alcotts would not sink again. Nor would Louisa May forget the assistance her family had received.

It is no wonder then that so many of her stories feature practical charity and happy endings. Such was the shape of her life. Do not reject charity, nor look down upon it, but be worthy of it; and if you rise to a higher station, do not forget to show charity to others.

And at what better time of the year could charity be shown than at Christmas. Even the poor and the humble can give gifts to each other, and thoughtless people become thoughtful at Christmastime. The novelist Charles Dickens had shown this to be so in his classic *A Christmas Carol,* a story that no doubt greatly influenced Louisa May Alcott.

Certainly, it is true that the keeping of Christmas, particularly in Alcott's native state of Massachusetts, was not common in the early life of that colony. For many years its celebration was banned under the Puritans because of ancient associations with a pagan Roman festival: *Natalis Invicti Solis* (Birth of the Unconquered Sun).

Fortunately, by the time Louisa May Alcott took up the pen, there were no such strictures on the holiday. There can be little doubt that Dickens set the example of Christmas stories that were to follow, to which Louisa May Alcott added her own powerful touch as a writer.

Certainly, there is a wonder to Christmas, and people are called upon to raise themselves to a higher standard of behavior. For the virtuous there is sure to be a blessed reward. The path from self to selflessness—this is the path of happiness. All who follow it may experience the joy of Christmas. Now who would wish to argue with such sentiments? For Miss Alcott, her Christmas stories were a true biography of her own life.

Merry Christmas.

The Quiet Little Woman

*P*atty stood at the window looking thoughtfully down at a group of girls playing in the yard below. All had cropped heads, all wore brown gowns with blue aprons, and all were orphans like herself. Some were pretty and some plain, some rosy and gay, some pale and feeble, but all seemed to be happy and having a good time in spite of many hardships.

More than once, one of the girls nodded and beckoned to Patty, but she shook her head decidedly and continued to stand listlessly watching and thinking to herself with a child's impatient spirit—

Oh, if someone would only come and take me away! I'm so tired of living here, and I don't think I can bear it much longer.

Poor Patty might well wish for a change; she had been in the orphanage ever since she could remember. And though everyone was very kind to her, she was heartily tired of the place and longed to find a home.

At the orphanage, the children were taught and cared for until they were old enough to help themselves, then they were adopted or went to work as servants. Now and then, some forlorn child was claimed by family. And once the relatives of a little girl named Katy proved to be rich and generous people who came for her in a fine carriage, treated all the other girls in honor of the happy day, and from time to time, let Katy visit them with arms full of gifts for her former playmates and friends.

Katy's situation made a great stir in the orphanage, and the children never tired of talking about it and telling it to newcomers as a sort of modern-day fairy tale. For a time, each hoped to be claimed in the same way, and listening to stories of what they would do when their turn came was a favorite amusement.

By and by, Katy ceased to come, and gradually new girls took the places of those who had left. Eventually, Katy's good fortune was forgotten by all but Patty. To her, it remained a splendid possibility, and she comforted her loneliness by dreaming of the day her "folks" would come for her and bear her away to a future of luxury and pleasure, rest and love. But year after year, no one came for Patty, who worked and waited as others were chosen and she was left to the many duties and few pleasures of her dull life.

People who came for pets chose the pretty, little ones; and those who wanted servants took the tall, strong, merry-faced girls, who spoke up brightly and promised to learn to do anything required of them. Patty's pale face, short figure with one shoulder higher than the other, and shy ways limited her opportunities. She was not ill now, but looked so, and was a sober, quiet little woman at the age of thirteen.

The good matron often recommended Patty as a neat, capable, and gentle little person, but no one seemed to want her, and after every failure, her heart grew heavier and her face sadder, for the thought of spending the rest of her life there in the orphanage was unbearable.

No one guessed what a world of hopes and thoughts and feelings lay hidden beneath that blue pinafore, what dreams this solitary child enjoyed, or what a hungry, aspiring young soul lived in her crooked little body.

But God knew, and when the time came, He remembered Patty and sent her the help she so desperately needed. Sometimes when we least expect it, a small cross proves a lovely crown, a seemingly unimportant event becomes a lifelong experience, or a stranger becomes a friend.

It happened so now, for as Patty said aloud with a great sigh, "I don't think I can bear it any longer!" a hand touched her shoulder and a voice said gently—

"Bear what, my child?"

The touch was so light and the voice so kind that Patty answered before she had time to feel shy.

"Living here, ma'am, and never being chosen as the other girls are."

"Tell me all about it, dear. I'm waiting for my sister, and I'd like to hear your troubles," the kindly woman said, sitting down in the window seat and drawing Patty beside her. She was not young or pretty or finely dressed. She was instead a gray-haired woman dressed in plain black, but her eyes were so cheerful and her voice so soothing that Patty felt at ease in a minute and nestled up to her as she shared her little woes in a few simple words.

"You don't know anything about your parents?" asked the lady.

"No, ma'am. I was left here as a baby without even a name pinned to me, and no one has come to find me. But I shouldn't wonder if they did come even now, so I keep ready all the time and work as hard as I can so they won't be ashamed of me, for I guess my folks is respectable," Patty replied, lifting her head with an air of pride that made the lady ask with a smile:

"What makes you think so?"

"Well, I heard the matron tell the lady who chose Nelly Brian that she always thought I came of high folks because I was so different from the others, and my ways was nice, and my feet so small—see if they ain't"—and slipping them out of the rough shoes she wore, Patty held up two slender, little feet with the arched insteps that tell of good birth.

Miss Murray—for that was her name—laughed right out loud at the innocent vanity of the poor child, and said heartily, "They are small, and so are your hands in spite of work. Your hair is fine, your eyes are soft and clear, and you are a good child I'm sure, which is best of all."

Pleased and touched by the praise that is so pleasant to us all, yet half ashamed of herself, Patty blushed and smiled, put on her shoes, and said with unusual animation—

"I'm pretty good, I believe, and I know I'd be much better if I could only get out. I do so long to see trees and grass, and sit in the sun, and listen to the birds. I'd work real hard and be happy if I could live in the country."

"What can you do?" asked Miss Murray, stroking Patty's smooth head and looking down into the wistful eyes fixed upon her.

Modestly, but with a flutter of hope in her heart, Patty recited her domestic accomplishments. It was a good list for a thirteen-year-old, for Patty had been working hard for so long that she had become unusually clever at all sorts of housework as well as needlework.

As she ended, she asked timidly, "Did you come for a girl, ma'am?"

"My sister-in-law, Mrs. Murray, did, but she found one she likes and is going to take her on trial." Her answer caused the light to fade from Patty's eyes and the hope to die in her heart.

"Who is it, please?" she asked.

"Lizzie Brown, a tall, nice-looking girl of fourteen."

"You won't like her, I know, for Lizzie is a real—" There Patty stopped short, turned red, and looked down as if ashamed to meet the keen, kind eyes fixed on her.

"A real what?"

"Please, ma'am, don't ask. It was mean of me to say that, and I mustn't go on. Lizzie can't help being good with you, and I am glad she has a chance to go away."

Aunt Jane Murray asked no more questions, but she noted the little glimpse of character, and tried to brighten Patty's mood by talking about something of interest to her.

"Suppose your 'folks,' as you say, never come for you, and you never find your fortune as some girls do, can't you make friends and fortune for yourself?"

"How can I?" questioned Patty, wonderingly.

"By cheerfully taking whatever comes, by being helpful and affectionate to all, and by wasting no time dreaming about what may happen, but bravely making each day a comfort and a pleasure to yourself and others. Can you do that?"

"I can try, ma'am," answered Patty, meekly.

"I wish you would, and when I come again, you can tell me how you are doing. I believe you will succeed, and when you do, you will have found for yourself a fine fortune and confident certainty of your friends. Now I must go. Cheer up, deary, your turn will come one day."

With a kiss that won Patty's heart, Miss Murray went away, casting more than one look of pity at the small figure sobbing in the window seat, with a blue pinafore over her face.

13

This disappointment was doubly hard for Patty because Lizzie was not a good girl and to her mind, did not deserve such good fortune. Besides, Patty had taken a great fancy to the lady who spoke so kindly to her.

For a week after this, she went about her work with a sad face, and all her daydreams were of living with Miss Jane Murray in the country.

Monday afternoon, as Patty stood sprinkling clothes for ironing, one of the girls burst in, saying all in a breath—

"Patty! Someone has come for you at last, and you are to go right up to the parlor. It's Mrs. Murray. She brought Liz back 'cause she told fibs and was lazy. Liz is as mad as hops, for it is a real nice place with cows and pigs and chickens and children, and the work ain't hard and she wanted to stay. Do hurry, and don't stand staring at me that way."

"It can't be me—no one ever wants me—it's some mistake—" stammered Patty, who was so startled and excited that she did not know what to say or do.

"It's no mistake," the girl insisted. "Mrs. Murray won't have anyone but you, and the matron says you are to come right up. Go along—I'll finish here. I'm so glad you have your chance at last!" And with a good-natured hug, the girl pushed Patty out of the kitchen.

In a few minutes, Patty came flying back in a twitter of delight to report that she was leaving at once and must say good-bye. Everyone was pleased, and when the flurry was over, the carriage drove away with the happiest little girl you have ever seen riding inside, for at last someone did want her. Patty had found a place.

During the first year Patty lived with the Murrays, they found her to be industrious, docile, and faithful—and yet she was not happy and had not found with them all she expected. They were kind to her, providing plenty of food and not too much work. They clothed her comfortably, let her go to church, and did not scold her very often. But no one showed that they loved her, no one praised her efforts, no one seemed to think that she had any hope or wish beyond her daily work; and no one saw in the shy, quiet little maiden a lonely, tenderhearted girl longing for a crumb of the love so freely given to the children of the home.

The Murrays were busy people with a large farm to care for. The master and his oldest son were hard at it all summer. Mrs. Murray was a brisk, smart housewife who "flew 'round" herself and expected others to do the same. Pretty Ella, the daughter, was about Patty's age and busy with her school, her little pleasures, and all the bright plans young girls love and live for. Two or three small lads rioted about the house making much work and doing very little.

One of these boys was lame, and this fact seemed to establish a sort of friendly understanding between him and Patty. In truth, he was the only one who ever expressed any regard for her. She was very good to him, always ready to help, always patient with his fretfulness, and always quick to understand his sensitive nature.

"She's only a servant, a charity girl who works for her board and wears my old clothes. She's good enough in her place, but of course she can't expect to be like one of us," Ella once said to a young friend—and Patty heard her.

"Only a servant. . . ." That was the hard part, and it never occurred to anyone to make it softer, so Patty plodded on, still hoping and dreaming about friends and fortune.

Had it not been for Aunt Jane, the child might not have gotten on at all. But Miss Murray never forgot her, even though she lived twenty miles away and seldom came to the farm. She wrote once a month and never failed to include a little note to Patty, which she fully expected would be answered.

Patty wrote a neat reply, which was very stiff and short at first. But after a time, she quite poured out her heart to this one friend who sent her encouraging words, cheered her with praise now and then, and made her anxious to be all Miss Jane seemed to expect. No one in the house took much notice of this correspondence, for Aunt Jane was considered "odd," and Patty posted her replies with the stamps her friend provided. This was Patty's anchor in her little sea of troubles, and she clung to it, hoping for the day when she had earned such a beautiful reward that she would be allowed to go and live with Miss Murray.

Christmas was coming, and the family was filled with great anticipation; for they intended to spend the day at Aunt Jane's and bring her home for dinner and a dance the next day. For a week beforehand, Mrs. Murray flew 'round with more than her accustomed speed, and Patty trotted about from morning till night, lending a hand to all the most disagreeable jobs. Ella did the light, pretty work, and spent much time fussing over her new dress and the gifts she was making for the boys.

When everything was done at last, Mrs. Murray declared that she would drop if she had another thing to do but go to Jane's and rest.

Patty had lived on the hope of going with them, but nothing was said about it. At last, they all trooped gaily away to the station, leaving her to take care of the house and see that the cat did not touch one of the dozen pies carefully stored in the pantry.

Patty kept up bravely until they were gone, then she sat down like Cinderella, and cried and cried until she could cry no more. It certainly did seem as if she were never to have any fun, and no fairy godmother came to help her. The shower of tears did her good, and she went about her work with a meek, patient face that would have touched a heart of stone.

All the morning she worked to finish the odd jobs left for her to do, and in the afternoon, as the only approach to the holiday she dared venture, Patty sat at the parlor window and watched other people go to and fro, intent on merrymaking in which she had no part.

Her only pleasant little task was that of arranging gifts for the small boys. Miss Jane had given her a bit of money now and then, and out of her meager store, the loving child had made presents for the lads—poor ones certainly, but full of goodwill and the desire to win some affection in return.

The family did not return as early as she had expected, which made the evening seem very long. Patty got out her treasure box and, sitting on the warm kitchen hearth, tried to amuse herself while the wind howled outside and the snow fell fast.

When Aunt Jane welcomed the family, her first word, as she emerged from a chaos of small boys' arms and legs, was "Why, where is Patty?"

"At home, of course; where else would she be?" answered Mrs. Murray.

"Here with you. I said 'all come' in my letter; didn't you understand it?"

"Goodness, Jane, you didn't mean to bring her, too, I hope."

"Yes, I did, and I'm quite disappointed. I'd go and get her myself if I had the time."

Miss Jane knit her brows and looked vexed, and Ella laughed at the idea of a servant girl going on holiday with the family.

"It can't be helped now, so we'll say no more and make it up to Patty tomorrow if we can." Aunt Jane smiled her own pleasant smile and kissed the little lads all 'round as if to sweeten her temper as soon as possible.

They had a capital time, and no one observed that Aunty, now and then, directed the conversation to Patty by asking a question about her or picking up on every little hint dropped by the boys concerning her patience and kindness.

At last, Mrs. Murray said, as she sat resting with a cushion at her back, a stool at her feet, and a cup of tea steaming deliciously under her nose, "Afraid to leave her there in charge? Oh, dear, no. I've entire confidence in her, and she is equal to taking care of the house for a week if need be. On the whole, Jane, I consider her a pretty promising girl. She isn't very quick, but she is faithful, steady, and honest as daylight."

"High praise from you, Maria; I hope she knows your good opinion of her."

"No, indeed! It wouldn't do to pamper a girl's pride by praising her. I say, 'Very well, Patty' when I'm satisfied, and that's quite enough."

"Ah, but you wouldn't be satisfied if George only said, 'Very well, Maria' when you had done your very best to please him in some way."

"That's a different thing," began Mrs. Murray, but Miss Jane shook her head, and Ella said, laughing—

"It's no use to try to convince Aunty on that point; she has taken a fancy to Pat and won't see any fault in her. She's a good enough child, but I can't get anything out of her; she is so odd and shy."

"I can! She's first rate and takes care of me better than anyone else," said Harry, the lame boy, with sudden warmth. Patty had quite won his selfish little heart by many services.

"She'll make Mother a nice helper as she grows up, and I consider it a good speculation. In four years, she'll be eighteen, and if she goes on doing so well, I won't begrudge her wages," added Mr. Murray, who sat nearby with a small son on each knee.

"She'd be quite pretty if she were straight and plump and jolly. But she is as sober as a deacon, and when her work is done, she sits in a corner watching us with big eyes as shy and mute as a mouse," said Ned, the big brother, lounging on the sofa.

"A dull, steady-going girl, suited for a servant and no more," concluded Mrs. Murray, setting down her cup as if the subject were closed.

"You are quite mistaken, and I'll prove it!" Aunt Jane announced, jumping up so energetically that the boys laughed and the elders looked annoyed. Pulling out a portfolio, Aunt Jane untied a little bundle of letters, saying impressively—

"Now listen, all of you, and see what has been going on with Patty this year."

Then Miss Jane read the little letters one by one, and it was curious to see how the faces of the listeners first grew attentive, then touched, then self-reproachful, and finally filled with interest and respect and something very like affection for little Patty.

These letters were pathetic, as Aunty read them to listeners who could supply much that the writer generously left unsaid, and the involuntary comments of the hearers proved the truth of Patty's words.

"Does she envy me because I'm pretty and gay and have a good time? I never thought how hard it must be for her to see me have all the fun and she all the work. She's a girl like me, and

I might have done more for her than give her my old clothes and let her help me get dressed for parties," said Ella hastily as Aunt Jane laid aside one letter in which poor Patty told of many "good times and she not in 'em."

"Sakes alive! If I'd known the child wanted me to kiss her now and then as I do the rest, I'd have done it in a minute!" said Mrs. Murray, with sudden softness in her sharp eyes as Aunt Jane read this little bit—

"I am grateful, but, oh! I'm so lonely, and it's so hard not to have any mother like the other children. If Mrs. Murray would only kiss me good night sometimes, it would do me more good than pretty clothes or nice food."

"I've been thinking I'd let her go to school ever since I heard her showing Bob how to do his lessons. But Mother didn't think she could spare her," broke in Mr. Murray apologetically.

"If Ella would help a little, I guess I could allow it. Anyway, we might try for awhile, since she is so eager to learn," added his wife, anxious not to seem unjust in Jane's eyes.

"Well, Joe laughed at her as much as I did when the boys hunched up their shoulders the way she does," cried conscious-stricken Bob, who had just heard a sad little paragraph about her crooked figure and learned that it came from lugging heavy babies at the orphanage.

"I cuffed 'em both for it, and I have always liked Patty," said Harry, in a moral tone, which moved Ned to say—

"You'd be a selfish little rascal if you didn't, when she slaves so for you and gets no thanks for it. Now that I know how it tires her poor little back to carry wood and water, I shall do it myself, of course. If she'd only told me, I'd have done it all the time."

And so it went until the letters were done and they knew Patty as she was. Each felt sorry that he or she had not found her out before. Aunt Jane freed her mind on the subject, but the others continued to discuss it until quite an enthusiastic state of feeling set in, and Patty was in danger of being killed with kindness.

It is astonishing how generous and clever people are when once awakened to duty, a charity, or a wrong. Now everyone was eager to repair past neglect, and if Aunt Jane had not wisely restrained them, the young folks would have done something absurd.

They laid many nice little plans to surprise Patty, and each privately resolved not only to give her a Christmas gift but also to do the better thing by turning over a new leaf for the new year.

All the way home, they talked over their various projects, and the boys kept bouncing into the seat with Aunt Jane to ask advice about their funny ideas.

"It must have been rather lonesome for the poor little soul all day. I declare, I wish we'd taken her along!" said Mrs. Murray, as they approached the house through the softly falling snow.

"She's got a jolly good fire all ready for us, and that's a mercy, for I'm half frozen," said Harry, hopping up the step.

"Don't you think if I touch up my blue merino, it would fit Patty and make a nice dress along with one of my white aprons?" whispered Ella, as she helped Aunt Jane out of the sleigh.

"I hope the child isn't sick or scared. It's two hours later than I expected to be home," added Mr. Murray, stepping up to peep in at the kitchen window, for no one came to open the door and no light but the blaze of the fire shone out.

"Come softly and look in," he whispered, beckoning to the rest. "It's a pretty little sight even if it is in a kitchen."

Quietly creeping to the two low windows, they all looked in, and no one said a word, for the lonely little figure was both pretty and pathetic when they remembered the letters lately read. Patty lay flat on the old rug, fast asleep with one arm pillowed under her head. In the other arm lay Puss in a cozy bunch, as if she had crept there to be sociable since there was no one else to share Patty's long vigil. A row of slippers, large and small, stood warming on the hearth, two little nightgowns hung over a chair, the teapot stood in a warm nook, and through the open door, they could see the lamp burning brightly in the sitting room, the table ready, and all things in order.

"Faithful little creature! She's thought of every blessed thing, and I'll go right in and wake her with a good kiss!" cried Mrs. Murray, darting for the door.

But Aunt Jane drew her back, begging her not to frighten the child by any sudden, unexpected demonstrations of affection. So they all went softly in—so softly that tired Patty did not wake, even though Puss pricked up her ears and opened her moony eyes with a lazy purr.

"Look here!" whispered Bob, pointing to the poor little gifts half tumbling out of Patty's apron. She had been pinning names on them when she fell asleep, and now her secret was known too soon.

No one laughed at the presents, and with a look of tender pity, Ella covered the few humble treasures in Patty's box. As she laid back, she remembered what she had once called "rubbish," how full her own boxes were with the pretty things girls love, and how easy it would have been to add to Patty's pitiful store.

No one exactly knew how to awaken the sleeper, for she was something more than a servant in their eyes now. Aunt Jane settled the matter by stooping down and taking Patty in her arms. The big eyes opened at once and stared up at the face above. Then a smile so bright, so glad, shone all over the child's face as she clung to Aunt Jane, crying joyously—

"Is it really you? I was so afraid you wouldn't come that I cried myself to sleep."

Never before had any of them seen such love and happiness in Patty's face, heard such a glad, tender sound in her voice, or guessed what an ardent soul dwelt in her quiet body.

She was herself again in a minute, and jumping up, slipped away to see that everything was ready should anyone want supper after the cold drive.

Soon the family went off to bed, and there was no time to let out the secret. Patty was surprised by the kind good nights everyone sent her way, but she thought no more of it than to feel that Miss Jane brought a warmer atmosphere to the home.

23

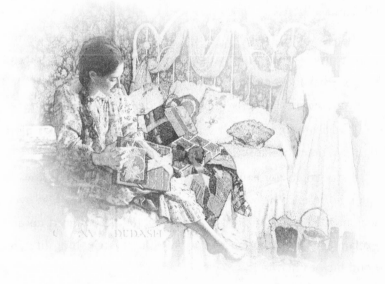

Patty's surprise began early the next day, for the first thing she saw upon opening her eyes was a pair of new stockings crammed full of gifts hanging at the foot of her bed and several parcels lying on the table.

What a good time she had opening the delightful bundles. She laughed and cried at the droll things the boys gave and the comfortable and pretty things the elders sent. Such a happy child was she that when she tried to say her prayers, she couldn't find words beautiful enough to express her gratitude for so much kindness!

A new Patty went downstairs that morning—a bright-faced girl with smiles on the mouth that used to be so sad and silent, confidence in the timid eyes, and the magic of the heartiest goodwill to make her step light, her hand skillful, her labor a joy, and service no burden.

They do care for me, after all, and I never will complain again, she thought with a glad flutter at her heart and sudden color in her cheeks as everyone welcomed her with a friendly, "Merry Christmas, Patty!"

It was the merriest Christmas ever, and when the bountiful dinner was spread and Patty stood ready to wait, you can imagine her feelings as Mr. Murray pointed to a seat near Miss Jane and said in a fatherly tone that made his gruff voice sweet—

"Sit down and enjoy it with us, my girl; nobody has more right to it, and we are all one family today."

Patty could not eat much, her heart was so full, but it was a splendid feast to her, and when toasts were drunk she was overwhelmed by the honor Harry did her, for he bounced up and exclaimed: "Now we must drink to 'Our Patty'—long life and good luck to her!"

That really was too much, and she fairly ran away to hide her blushes in the kitchen and work off her excitement washing dishes.

More surprises came that evening. When she went to put on her clean calico smock, she found the pretty blue dress and white apron laid ready on her bed along with a note that read, "With Ella's love."

"It's like a fairy story that keeps getting nicer and nicer since the godmother came," whispered Patty, as she glanced shyly at Aunt Jane.

"Christmas is the time for all sorts of pleasant miracles," answered Aunt Jane, smiling back at her little maiden, who looked so neat and blithe in her new dress and happy face.

Patty thought nothing further in the way of bliss could happen to her that night, but it did when Ned, anxious to atone for his past neglect, pranced up to her as a final dance was forming and said heartily—

"Come, Patty, everyone is to dance this one, even Harry and the cat!" And before she could collect her wits enough to say "No," she was leading off and flying down the middle with the young master, in great style.

That was the crowning honor, for she was a girl with all a girl's innocent hopes, fears, desires, and delights, and it had been rather hard to stand by while all the young neighbors were frolicking together.

When everyone was gone, the tired children asleep, and the elders on their way up to bed, Mrs. Murray suddenly remembered she had not covered the kitchen fire. Aunt Jane said she would do it, and went down so softly that she did not disturb faithful Patty, who had also gone to see that all was safe.

Aunt Jane stopped to watch the little figure standing on the hearth alone, looking into the embers with thoughtful eyes. If Patty could have seen her future there, she would have found a long life spent in glad service to those she loved and who loved her. Not a splendid future, but a useful, happy one—"only a servant" perhaps, yet a good and faithful woman, blessed with the confidence, respect, and affection of those who knew her genuine worth.

As a smile broke over Patty's face, Miss Jane said with an arm round the little blue-gowned figure—

"What are you dreaming and smiling about, deary? The friends that are to come for you someday, with a fine fortune in their pockets?"

"No, Ma'am, I feel as if I've found my folks. I don't want any finer fortune than the love they've given me today. I'm trying to think how I can deserve it, and smiling because it's so beautiful and I'm so happy," answered Patty, looking up at her first friend with full eyes and a glad glance that made her lovely.

The Quiet Little Woman—

The world of Patty, the orphan girl, was one with which Louisa May Alcott was quite familiar. Louisa's mother had been one of the first paid social workers in the United States, and all of the Alcott family had a strong sense of social obligation. By the standards of their day, they would have been regarded as quite progressive in their views, and many times they showed themselves ready to help those in need even as they had been helped in their impecunious days.

Nevertheless, Louisa May Alcott would have found it strange indeed if anyone had suggested to her that there could be a general scheme for helping all in need regardless of an individual's efforts and personal morality. She herself had put forth Herculean efforts to write enough stories, including some rather gaudy thrillers, to pull the Alcott family out of debt. Naturally, she came to believe that individual effort made a difference.

In all her writing, Louisa's characters exhibit virtue and vice within a context of personal responsibility. Characters like poor Patty may indeed need a helping hand from someone like Aunt Jane—especially at Christmastime—but Patty must help too. She has powers of her own and a will of her own that she must draw on to accept her lot and find happiness where she can.

No one could tell Miss Alcott about the nature of poverty and privation because she knew of it firsthand, and she also knew that there really were people in the world who had earned, or were worthy of, a second chance, while there were others, like the bad maid Lizzie Brown, who "deserved nothing" and squandered her chance at a good life.

Perhaps we today need to learn a lesson from Miss Alcott and from Patty. All too often we are told there is no limit to what we can do and what personal peace, comfort, and satisfaction we may achieve—if only hindrances to opportunity could be swept from our path, perhaps by the church, perhaps by a social organization, perhaps by the mercy of the government itself, regardless of whether we are worthy of the opportunity or not.

But for Patty and Louisa May, moral character cannot be excluded as a factor in our own well-being and in what we make of ourselves and of our opportunities. As we awaken morally to what is charitable, truthful, and good, we awaken our own souls to moral transformation. If we have been dealt a bad hand by life, the virtue of accepting what has been dealt to us strengthens us to our challenge. Others have overcome through worthy endeavors; so can we.

Christmas is a good time to ponder these truths. Charity is a theme of the season, yet how charity is received is important too.

As Louisa May Alcott knew from her own observations, moral good is rewarded, often in this life, and surely in the world to come. Vice, on the other hand, gives us no aid in battling against the odds of going upstream. Most success and even peace are achieved by overcoming, and goodness helps us rise to our occasion and opportunity, no matter how rarely they might come.

True, it has been observed that sometimes the unworthy do prosper, but even that cannot take away from the satisfaction of virtue. For virtue itself is a reward, a prosperity to the soul, to be enjoyed equally by both the humble and the great.

A Hospital Christmas

Adapted by Stephen W. Hines

"Merry Christmas!" "Merry Christmas!" "Merry Christmas, and lots of 'em, Ma'am!" echoed from every side as Miss Hale entered her ward in the gray December dawn. No wonder the greetings were hearty, that thin faces brightened, and eyes watched for the coming of this small luminary more eagerly than for the rising of the sun.

When the patients had awakened that morning, each man found that, in the silence of the night, some friendly hand had laid a little gift beside his bed. Very humble little gifts they were, but well chosen and thoughtfully bestowed by one who made the blithe anniversary pleasant even in a hospital and sweetly taught the lesson of the hour—Peace on Earth, Goodwill to Man.

"I say, Ma'am, these are just splendid. I've dreamt about such for a week, but I never thought I'd get 'em," cried one poor fellow surveying a fine bunch of grapes with as much satisfaction as if he had found a fortune.

"Thank you kindly, Miss, for the paper and the fixings. I hated to keep borrowing, but I hadn't any money," said another, eyeing his gift with happy anticipations of the home letters with which the generous pages should be filled.

"They are dreadful soft and pretty, but I don't believe I'll ever wear 'em out; my legs are so wimbly there's no go in 'em," whispered a fever patient looking sorrowfully at the swollen feet ornamented with a pair of carpet slippers gay with roses and evidently made for his special need.

"Please hang my posy basket on the gas burner in the middle of the room where all the boys can see it. It's too pretty for one alone."

"But then you can't see it yourself, Joe, and you are fonder of such things than the rest," said Miss Hale, taking both the little basket and the hand of her pet patient, a lad of twenty, dying of rapid consumption.

"That's the reason I can spare it for a while, because I shall feel 'em in the room just the same, and they'll do the boys good. You pick out the one you like best for me to keep and hang up the rest till by and by, please."

She gave him a sprig of mignonette, and he smiled as he took it, for it reminded him of her in her sad-colored gown. Although Miss Hale was quiet and unobtrusive, she had created a gratitude in the hearts of those about her that was like the fresh scent of a flower to the lonely lad who never had known womanly tenderness and care until he found them in a hospital. Joe's prediction was verified; the flowers did do the boys good. All welcomed them with approving glances, and all felt their refining influence more or less keenly, from cheery Ben, who paused to fill the cup inside with fresher water, to surly Sam, who stopped growling as his eye rested on a geranium very like the one blooming in his sweetheart's window when they parted a long year ago.

"Now, as this is to be a merry day, let us begin to enjoy it at once. Fling up the window, Ben, and Barney, go for breakfast while I finish washing faces and settling bedclothes."

With which directions the little woman fell to work with such infectious energy that, in fifteen minutes, thirty gentlemen with clean faces and hands were partaking of refreshments with as much appetite as their various conditions would permit. Meantime the sun came up, looking bigger, brighter, and jollier than usual, as he is apt to do on Christmas days. Not a snowflake chilled the air that blew in as blandly as if winter had relented and wished the "boys" the compliments of the season in his mildest mood. A festival smell pervaded the whole house, and appetizing rumors of turkey, mince pie, and oysters for dinner circulated through the wards. When breakfast was done, the wounds dressed, directions for the day delivered, and as many of the disagreeables as possible were over, the fun began. In any other place, that would have been considered a very quiet morning, but to the weary invalids prisoned in that room, it was quite a whirl of excitement. None were dangerously ill but Joe, and all were easily amused since weakness, homesickness, and ennui made every trifle a joke or an event.

In came Ben, looking like a "Jack in the Green," with his load of hemlock and holly. Such of the men as could get about and had a hand to lend, lent it, and soon, under Miss Hale's directions, a green bough hung at the head of each bed suspended from the gas burners and nodding over the fireplace, while the finishing effect was designed to be a cross and crown at the top and bottom of the room. Great was the interest, many were the mishaps, and frequent was the laughter that attended this performance. Wounded men, when convalescent, are particularly jovial.

When "Daddy Mills," as one venerable volunteer was irreverently christened, expatiated learnedly upon the difference between "spruce, hemlock, and pine," how they all listened, each thinking of some familiar wood still pleasantly haunted by boyish recollections of stolen nuts, maple syrup, and squirrel nests. When quiet Hayward amazed the company by coming out strong in a most unexpected direction and telling with much effect the story of a certain "fine old gentleman" who supped on hemlock tea and died directly, what commendations were bestowed upon the unfortunate fellow in language more hearty than classical, as a twig of the historical tree was passed 'round like a new style of refreshment, that inquiring parties might satisfy themselves regarding the flavor of the Socratic draught. When Barney the buffoon essayed a grand ornament above the door, and relying upon one insufficient nail, descended to survey his success with the proud exclamation, "Look at the neatness of that job, gentle-men"—at which point the whole thing tumbled down about his ears—how they all shouted. But poor Pneumonia Ned, having lost his voice, could only make ecstatic demonstrations with his legs.

When Barney cast himself and his hammer despairingly upon the floor, and Miss Hale, stepping into a chair, pounded stoutly at the traitorous nail and performed some miracle with a bit of string that made all fast, what a burst of applause arose from the beds. When a gruff Dr. Bangs came in to see what all the noise was about, the same intrepid lady not only boldly explained but also stuck a bit of holly in his button hole. Not only that, but she wished him a merry Christmas with such a face full of smiles that the crabbed old doctor felt himself giving in very fast and bolted out again, calling Christmas a humbug. He predicted that over the thirty emetics he would have to pre-scribe on the morrow, but indignant denials followed him down the hallway. And when all was done, everybody agreed with Joe when he said, "I think we are coming to Christmas in great style; things look so green and pretty, I feel as I was settin' in a bower."

Pausing to survey her work, Miss Hale saw Sam looking as black as any thundercloud. He bounced over on his bed the moment he caught her eye, but she followed him up and, gently covering the cold shoulder he evidently meant to show her, peeped over it, asking, with unabated gentleness:

"What can I do for you, Sam? I want to have all the faces in my ward bright ones today."

"My box ain't come; they said I should have it two, three days ago. Why don't they do it, then?" growled Ursa Major.

"It is a busy time, you know, but it will come if they promised, and patience won't delay it, I assure you."

"My patience is used up, and they are a mean set of slow coaches. I'd get it fast enough if I wore an officer's straps. As I don't, I'll bet I shan't see it till the things ain't fit to eat, the news is old, and I don't care a hang about it."

"I'll see what I can do; perhaps before the hurry of dinner begins someone will have time to go for it."

"Nobody ever does have time here, but folks who would give all they are worth to be stirring 'round. You can't get it, I know. It's my luck, so don't you worry, Ma'am."

Miss Hale did not worry, but worked, and in time a messenger was found, provided with the necessary money, pass, and directions, and dispatched to hunt up the missing Christmas box. Then she paused to see what came next, not that it was necessary to look for a task, but to decide which, out of many, was most important to do first.

"Why, Turner, crying again so soon? What is it now? The light head or the heavy feet?"

"It's my bones, Ma'am. They ache so I can't lay easy any way, and I'm so tired I just wish I could die and be out of this misery," sobbed the poor ghost of a once strong and cheery fellow. Miss Hale's kindly hand wiped his tears away and gently rubbed the weary shoulders.

"Don't wish that, Turner, for the worst is over now; and all you need is to get your strength again. Make an effort to sit up a little; it is quite time you tried. A change of posture will help the ache wonderfully and make this 'dreadful bed,' as you call it, seem very comfortable when you come back to it."

"I can't, Ma'am, my legs ain't a bit of use, and I ain't strong enough even to try."

"You never will be if you don't try. Never mind the poor legs; Ben will carry you. I've got the matron's easy chair all ready and can make you very cozy by the fire. It's Christmas Day, you know; why not celebrate it by overcoming the despondency that slows your recovery and prove that illness has not taken all the manhood out of you?"

"It has, though. I'll never be the man I was, and may as well lie here till spring, for I shall be no use if I do get up."

If Sam was a growler, this man was a whiner, and few hospital wards are without both. But knowing that much suffering had soured the former and pitifully weakened the latter, their nurse had patience with them and still hoped to bring them 'round again. As Turner whimpered out his last dismal speech, she bethought herself of something which, in the hurry of the morning, had slipped her mind till now.

"By the way, I've got another present for you. The doctor thought I'd better not give it yet, lest it should excite you too much; but I think you need excitement to make you forget yourself, and that when you find how many blessings you have to be grateful for, you will make an effort to enjoy them."

"Blessings, Ma'am? I don't see 'em."

"Don't you see one now?" And drawing a letter from her pocket, she held it before his eyes. His listless face brightened a little as he took it, but gloomed over again as he said fretfully:

"It's from my wife, I guess. I like to get her letters, but they are always full of grievings and groanings over me, so they don't do me much good."

"She does not grieve and groan in this one. She is too happy to do that, and so will you be when you read it."

"I don't see why—hey?—why you don't mean— "

"Yes I do!" cried the little woman, clapping her hands and laughing so delightedly that the Knight of the Rueful Countenance was betrayed into a broad smile for the first time in many weeks. "Is not a splendid little daughter a present to rejoice over and be grateful for?"

"Hooray! Hold a bit—it's all right—I'll be out again in a minute."

After this remarkably spirited outburst, Turner vanished under the bedclothes, letter and all. Whether he read, laughed, or cried in the seclusion of that cotton grotto was unknown; but his nurse suspected that he did all three. When he reappeared he looked as if, during that pause, he had dived into his "sea of troubles" and fished up his old self again.

"What *will* I name her?" was his first remark, delivered with such vivacity that his neighbors began to think he was getting delirious again.

"What is your wife's name?" asked Miss Hale, gladly entering into the domesticities that were producing such a salutary effect.

"Her name's Ann, but neither of us like it. I'd fixed on George, because I wanted my boy called after me; and now you see I ain't a bit prepared for this young woman." Very proud of the young woman he seemed, nevertheless, and perfectly resigned to the loss of the expected son and heir.

"Why not call her Georgiana then? That combines both her parents' names and is not a bad one in itself."

"Now that's just the brightest thing I ever heard in my life!" cried Turner, sitting bolt upright in his excitement, though half an hour before he would have considered it an utterly impossible feat. "Georgiana Butterfield Turner—it's a tip-top name, Ma'am, and we can call her Georgie just the same. Ann will like that; it's so genteel. Bless them both! Don't I wish I was at home." And down he lay again, despairing.

"You can be before long, if you choose. Get your strength up, and off you go. Come, begin at once—drink your beef broth and sit up for a few minutes, just in honor of the good news, you know."

"I will, by George! No, by Georgiana! That's a good one, ain't it?" and the whole ward was electrified by hearing a genuine giggle from the veteran sad sack.

Down went the detested beef broth, and up scrambled the determined drinker with many groans and a curious jumble of chuckles, staggers, and fragmentary repetitions of his first, last, and only joke. But when fairly settled in the great rocking chair, with the gray flannel gown comfortably on and the new slippers getting their inaugural scorch, Turner forgot his bones and swung to and fro before the fire, feeling amazingly well and looking very like a trussed fowl being roasted in the primitive fashion.

The languid importance of the man and the irrepressible satisfaction of the parent were both laughable and touching things to see, for the happy soul could not keep the glad tidings to himself. A hospital ward is often a small republic, beautifully governed by pity, patience, and the mutual sympathy that lessens mutual suffering. Turner was no favorite; but more than one honest fellow felt his heart warm towards him as they saw his dismal face kindle with fatherly pride and heard the querulous quaver of his voice soften with fatherly affection, as he said, "My little Georgie."

"He'll do now, Ma'am. This has given him the boost he needed, and, in a week or two, he'll be off our hands."

Big Ben made the remark with a beaming countenance, and Big Ben deserves a word of praise, because he never said one for himself. He was an ex-patient promoted to an attendant's place, which he filled so well that he was regarded as a model for all the rest to copy. Patient, strong, and tender, he seemed to combine many of the best traits of both man and woman. He appeared to know by instinct where the soft spot was to be found in every heart, and how best to help sick body or sad soul. No one would have guessed this to have seen him lounging in the hall during one of the short rests he allowed himself.

He was a brawny, six-foot fellow in red shirt, blue trousers tucked into his boots, and an old cap, visor always up, and under it a roughly bearded, coarsely featured face, whose prevailing expression was one of great gravity and kindliness, though a humorous twinkle of the eye at times betrayed the man, whose droll sayings often set the boys in a roar. "A good-natured, clumsy body" would have been the verdict passed upon him by a causal observer, but watch him in his ward and see how great a wrong that hasty judgment would have done him.

Unlike his predecessor, who helped himself generously when the meals came up and carelessly served out rations for the rest, leaving even the most helpless to bungle for themselves or wait till he was done, Ben often left nothing for himself or took cheerfully such cold bits as remained when all the rest were served; so patiently feeding the weak, being hands and feet to the maimed, and being such a pleasant provider for all that, as one of the boys said, "It gives a relish to the vittles to have Ben fetch 'em." If one were restless, Ben carried him in his strong arms; if one were undergoing the sharp torture of the surgeon's knife, Ben held him with a touch as firm as kind; if one were homesick, Ben wrote letters for him with great hearty blots and dashes under all the affectionate or important words.

More than one poor fellow read his fate in Ben's pitying eyes and breathed his last breath away on Ben's broad breast—always a quiet pillow till its work was done—then he would heave a sigh of genuine grief as his big hand softly closed the tired eyes and made another comrade ready for the last review. Our Civil War showed us many Bens, because the same power of human pity that makes women brave also makes men tender; and each is the more womanly or the more manly for these revelations of unsuspected strength and sympathies.

At twelve o'clock, dinner was the prevailing idea in Ward number three, and when the door opened, every man sniffed as savory odors broke loose from the kitchens and went roaming about the house. Now this Christmas dinner had been much talked of; for certain charitable and patriotic persons had endeavored to provide every hospital in Washington with materials for this time-honored feast. Some mistake in the list sent to headquarters, some unpardonable neglect of orders, or some premeditated robbery, caused the long-expected dinner in Wilson Hospital to prove a dead failure; but to which of these causes it was attributable was never known. The deepest mystery enveloped the sad situation.

The full weight of the dire disappointment was mercifully lightened by premonitions of the impending blow. Barney was often missing, for the attendants were to dine *en masse* after the patients were done. Therefore a speedy banquet for the latter parties was ardently desired, and he probably devoted his energies to goading on the cooks. From time to time he appeared in the doorway, flushed and breathless, made some thrilling announcement, and vanished, leaving ever-increasing appetite, impatience, and expectation behind him.

Dinner was to be served at one. At half-past twelve Barney proclaimed, "There ain't no vegetables but squash and pitaters." A universal groan arose, and several indignant parties on a short allowance of meat consigned the defaulting cook to a warmer climate than the tropical one he was then enjoying. At twenty minutes to one, Barney increased the excitement by whispering, ominously, "I say, the puddings aren't very good."

"Fling a pillow at him and shut the door, Ben," roared one irascible being, while several others *not* fond of puddings received the fact with equanimity. At quarter to one, Barney piled up the agony by adding the bitter information, "There isn't but two turkeys for this ward, and they's little fellers."

Anxiety instantly appeared in every countenance, and intricate calculations were made as to how far the two fowls would go when divided among thirty men. Also friendly warnings were administered to several of the feebler gentlemen not to indulge too freely, if at all, for fear of relapses from overeating. Once more did the bird of evil omen return, for at ten minutes to one, Barney croaked through the keyhole, "Only half of the pies has come, gentlemen." That capped the climax, for the masculine palate has a predilection for pastry, and mince pie was the sheet anchor to which all had clung when other hopes went down.

Even Ben looked dismayed; not that he expected anything but the perfume and pickings for his share, but he had set his heart on having the dinner, an honor to the institution and a memorable feast for the men so far away from home, and all that usually makes the day a festival among the poorest. He looked pathetically grave as Turner began to fret, Sam began to swear under his breath, Hayward to sigh, Joe to wish it was all over, and the rest to vent their emotions with a freedom that was anything but inspiring. At that moment, Miss Hale came in with a great basket of apples and oranges in one hand, and several useful looking bottles in the other.

"Here is our dessert, boys! A kind friend remembered us, and we will drink her health in her own cider."

A feeble smile circulated around the room, and, in some sanguine bosoms, hope revived again. Ben briskly emptied the basket while Miss Hale whispered to Joe:

"I knew you would be glad to get away from the confusion of this next hour to enjoy a breath of fresh air and dine quietly with Mrs. Burton 'round the corner, wouldn't you?"

"Oh, Ma'am, so much! The noise, the smells, the fret and flurry make me sick just to think of! But how can I go? That dreadful ambulance 'most killed me last time, and I'm weaker now."

"My dear boy, I have no thought of trying that again till our ambulances are made fit for the use of weak and wounded men. Mrs. Burton's carriage is at the door, with her motherly self inside, and all you have got to do is to let me bundle you up and Ben carry you out."

With a sigh of relief Joe submitted to both these processes, and when his nurse watched his happy face as the carriage slowly rolled away, she felt well repaid for the little sacrifice of rest and pleasure so quietly made; for Mrs. Burton had come to carry her, not Joe, away.

"Now, Ben, help me to make this unfortunate dinner go off as well as we can," she whispered. "On many accounts it is a mercy that the men are spared the temptations of a more generous meal. Pray don't tell them so, but make the best of it, as you know very well how to do."

"I'll try my best, Miss Hale, but I'm no less disappointed, because some of 'em, being no better than children, have been living on the thoughts of it for a week; and it comes hard to give it up."

If Ben had been an old-time patriarch, and the thirty boys his sons, he could not have spoken with a more paternal regret, or gone to work with a better will. Putting several small tables together in the middle of the room, he left Miss Hale to make a judicious display of plates, knives, and forks, while he departed for the banquet. Presently he returned, bearing the youthful turkeys and the vegetables in his tray, followed by Barney, carrying a plum pudding baked in a milk pan and six very small pies. Miss Hale played a lively march as the procession approached, and, when the viands were arranged, with the red and yellow fruit prettily heaped up in the middle, it really did look like a dinner.

"Here's richness! Here's the delicacies of the season and the comforts of life!" said Ben, falling back to survey the table with as much apparent satisfaction as if it had been a lord mayor's feast.

"Come, hurry up, and give us our dinner; what there is of it!" grumbled Sam.

"Boys," continued Ben, beginning to cut up the turkeys, "these noble birds have been sacrificed for the defenders of their country. They will go as far as ever they can, and when they can't go any further, we shall endeavor to supply their deficiencies with soup or ham, oysters having given out unexpectedly. Put it to a vote. Both have been provided on this joyful occasion, and a word will fetch either."

"Ham! Ham!" resounded from all sides. Soup was an every-day affair, and therefore repudiated with scorn; but ham, being a rarity, was accepted as a proper reward of merit and a tacit acknowledgement of their wrongs.

The "noble birds" did go as far as possible, and were handsomely assisted by their fellow martyr. The pudding was not as good as could have been desired, but a slight exertion of fancy made the crusty knobs do duty for raisins. The pies were small, yet a laugh added flavor to the mouthful apiece; for when Miss Hale asked Ben to cut them up, that individual regarded her with an inquiring aspect as he said, in his drollest tone:

"I wouldn't wish to appear stupid, Ma'am, but when you mention 'pies,' I presume you allude to these trifles. 'Tarts' or 'patties' would meet my views better, in speaking of the third course of this lavish dinner. As such, I will do my duty by 'em, hoping that the appetites are to match."

Carefully dividing the six pies into twenty-nine diminutive wedges, he placed each in the middle of a large clean plate and handed them about with the gravity of an undertaker. Dinner had restored good humor to many; this hit at the pies put the finishing touch to it. And from that moment, an atmosphere of jollity prevailed. Healths were drunk in cider; apples and oranges flew about as an impromptu game of ball was got up; Miss Hale sang a Christmas carol; and Ben gamboled like a sportive giant as he cleared dishes away. Pausing in one of his prances to and fro, he beckoned the nurse out, and when she followed, handed her a plate heaped up with good things from a better table than she ever sat at now.

"From the matron, Ma'am. Come right in here and eat it while it's hot; they are most through in the dining room, and you'll get nothing half so nice," said Ben, leading the way into his pantry and pointing to a sunny window seat.

"Are you sure she meant it for me and not for yourself, Ben?"

"Of course she did! Why, what should I do with it, when I've just been feastin' sumptuous in this very room?"

"I don't exactly see what you have been feasting on," said Miss Hale, glancing 'round the tidy pantry as she sat down.

"Havin' eat up the food and washed up the dishes, it naturally follows that you don't see, Ma'am. But if I go off in a fit by and by, you'll know what it's owin' to," answered Ben, vainly endeavoring to look like a man suffering from overeating.

"Such kind fibs are not set down against one, Ben, so I will eat your dinner; for if I know you, you will throw it out the window to prove that you can't eat it."

"Thankee, Ma'am, I'm afraid I should," said Ben, looking very much relieved as he polished his last pewter fork and hung his towels up to dry.

A pretty general siesta followed the excitement of dinner, but by three o'clock the public mind was ready for amusement, and the arrival of Sam's box provided it. He was asleep when it was brought in and quietly deposited at his bed's foot, ready to surprise him on awaking. The advent of a box was a great event, for the fortunate receiver seldom failed to "stand treat," and next best to getting things from one's own home was the getting them from some other boy's home. This was an unusually large box, and all felt impatient to have it opened, though Sam's exceeding crustiness prevented the indulgence of great expectations. Presently he roused, and the first thing his eye fell upon was the box with his own name sprawling over it in big black letters. As if it were merely the continuance of his dream, he stared stupidly at it for a moment, then rubbed his eyes and sat up, exclaiming:

"Hullo! That's mine!"

"Ah! Who said it wouldn't come? Who hadn't the faith of a grasshopper? And who don't half deserve it for being a Barker by nature as by name?" cried Ben, emphasizing each question with a bang on the box as he waited, hammer in hand, for the arrival of the ward master, whose duty it was to oversee the opening of such matters, lest contraband articles should do mischief to the owner or his neighbors.

"Ain't it a jolly big one? Knock it open, and don't wait for anybody or anything!" cried Sam, tumbling off his bed and beating impatiently on the lid with his one hand.

In came the ward master, off came the cover, and out came a motley collection of apples, socks, doughnuts, paper, pickles, photographs, pocket-handkerchiefs, gingerbread, letters, jelly, newspapers, tobacco, and cologne. "All right; glad it's come. Don't kill yourself," said the ward master as he took a hasty survey and walked off again. Drawing the box nearer the bed, Ben delicately followed, and Sam was left to brood over his treasures in peace.

At first all the others, following Ben's example, made elaborate pretenses of going to sleep, being absorbed in books, or being utterly uninterested in the outer world. But very soon curiosity got the better of politeness, and one by one they all turned 'round and stared. They might have done so from the first, for Sam was perfectly unconscious of everything but his own affairs, and, having read the letters, looked at the pictures, unfolded the bundles, turned everything inside out and upside down, tasted all the eatables, and made a spectacle of himself with jelly, he paused to get his breath and find his way out of the confusion he had created. Presently he called out:

"Miss Hale, will you come and right up my duds for me?" adding, as her woman's hands began to bring matters straight, "I don't know what to do with 'em all. Some won't keep long, and it will take pretty steady eating to get through 'em in time, supposin' appetite holds out."

"How do the others manage with their things?"

"You know they give 'em away, but I'll be hanged if I do, because they are always callin' names and pokin' fun at me. Guess they won't get anything out of me now."

The old, morose look came back as he spoke, for it had disappeared while reading the home letters, touching the home gifts. Still busily folding and arranging, Miss Hale quietly observed:

"We all know how much you have suffered, and all respect you for the courage with which you have borne your long confinement and your loss; but don't you think you have given the boys some cause for making fun of you, as you say? You used to be a favorite and can be again, if you will only put off these crusty ways, which will grow upon you faster than you think. Better lose both arms than cheerfulness and self-control, Sam."

Pausing to see how her little lecture was received, she saw that Sam's better self was waking up and added yet another word, hoping to help a mental ailment as she had done with so many physical ones. Looking up at him with her kind eyes, she said, in a lowered voice:

"This day, on which the most perfect life began, is a good day for all of us to set about making ourselves readier to follow that divine example. Troubles are helpers if we take them kindly, and the bitterest may sweeten us for all our lives. Believe and try this, Sam, and when you go away from us, let those who love you find that two battles have been fought, two victories won."

Sam made no answer but sat thoughtfully picking at the half-eaten cookie in his hand. Presently he stole a glance about the room, and, as if all helps were waiting for him, his eye met Joe's. From his solitary corner by the fire and the bed, he would seldom leave again until he went to his grave. The boy smiled back at him so heartily, so happily, that something gushed warm across Sam's heart as he looked down upon the faces of mother, sister, sweetheart, scattered 'round him, and remembered how poor his comrade was in all such tender ties, and yet how rich in that beautiful contentment, which, "having nothing, yet hath all." The man had no words in which to express this feeling, but it came to him and did him good, as he proved in his own way. "Miss Hale," he said, a little awkwardly, "I wish you'd pick out what you think each would like and give 'em to the boys."

He got a smile in answer that drove him to his cookie as a refuge. His lips trembled, and he felt half proud, half ashamed to have earned such bright approval.

"Let Ben help you. He knows better than I. But you must give them all yourself; it will so surprise and please the boys. And then tomorrow we will write a capital letter home telling what a jubilee we made over their fine box."

At this proposal Sam half repented; but as Ben came lumbering up at Miss Hale's summons, he laid hold of his new resolution as if it was a sort of shower bath to which he held the string, one pull of which would finish the baptism. Dividing his most cherished possession, which (alas for romance!) was the tobacco, he bundled the larger half into a paper, whispering to Miss Hale:

"Ben ain't exactly what you'd call a ministering angel to look at, but he is amazin' near one in his ways, so I'm goin' to begin with him."

Up came the "ministering angel," in red flannel and cowhide boots; and Sam tucked the little parcel into his pocket, saying, as he began to rummage violently in the box:

"Now jest hold your tongue and lend a hand here about these things."

Ben was so taken aback by this proceeding that he stared blankly till a look from Miss Hale enlightened him. Taking his cue, he played his part as well as could be expected on so short a notice. Clapping Sam on the shoulder—not the bad one as Ben was always thoughtful of those things—he exclaimed heartily:

"I always said you'd come 'round when this poor arm of yours got a good start; and here you are jollier 'n ever. Lend a hand! So will I, a pair of 'em. What's to do? Pack these traps up again?"

"No; I want you to tell what *you'd* do with 'em if they were yours. Free, you know, as free as if they really was."

Ben held on to the box a minute as if this second surprise rather took him off his legs; but another look from the prime mover in this resolution steadied him, and he fell to work as if Sam had been in the habit of being "free with his things."

"Well, let's see. I think I'd put the clothes and such into this smaller box that the bottles come in, and stand it under the table, handy. Here's newspapers—pictures in 'em, too! I should make a circulatin' library of 'em; they'll be a real treat. Pickles? Well, I guess I should keep them on the winder here as a kind of a relish dinnertimes or to pass along to them as longs for 'em. Cologne? That's a dreadful handsome bottle, ain't it? That, now, would be fust-rate to give away to somebody as was very fond of it—a kind of delicate attention, you know—if you happen to meet such a person anywheres."

Ben nodded towards Miss Hale, who was absorbed in folding pocket-handkerchiefs. Sam winked expressively and patted the bottle as if congratulating himself that it *was* handsome, and that he *did* know what to do with it. The pantomime was not elegant, but as much real affection and respect went into it as if he had made a set speech and presented the gift upon his knees.

"The letters and photographs I should probably keep under my pillow for a spell; the jelly I'd give to Miss Hale to use for the sick ones; the cake stuff and that pot of jam I'd stand treat with for tea, since dinner wasn't all we could have wished. The apples I'd keep to eat and fling at Joe when he was too bashful to ask for one, and the tobacco I would *not* go lavishin' on folks that have no business to be enjoyin' luxuries when many a poor fellow is dyin' of want down to Charlestown. There, sir! That's what *I'd* do if anyone was so clever as to send me a jolly box like this."

Sam was enjoying the full glow of his shower bath by this time. As Ben designated the various articles, he set them apart. And when the inventory ended, he marched away with the first installment: two of the biggest, rosiest apples for Joe and all the pictorial papers. Pickles are not usually regarded as tokens of regard, but as Sam dealt them out one at a time—for he would let nobody help him, and his single hand being the left, was as awkward as it was willing—the boys' faces brightened. A friendly word accompanied each pickle, which made the sour gherkins as welcome as sweetmeats.

With every trip, the donor's spirits rose. Ben circulated freely between times, and, thanks to him, not an allusion to the past marred the satisfaction of the present. Jam, soda biscuits, and cake were such welcome additions to the usual bill of fare that when supper was over, a vote of thanks was passed, and speeches were made. Being true Americans, the ruling passion found vent in the usual "Fellow citizens!" and allusions to the "Star-spangled Banner." After which, Sam subsided, feeling himself a public benefactor and a man of mark.

A perfectly easy, pleasant day throughout would be almost an impossibility in any hospital, and this one was no exception to the general rule. So, at the usual time, Dr. Bangs went his rounds leaving the customary amount of discomfort, discontent, and dismay behind him. A skillful surgeon and an excellent man was Dr. Bangs, but not a sanguine or conciliatory individual. Many cares and crosses caused him to regard the world as one large hospital and his fellow beings all more or less dangerously wounded patients in it. He saw life through the bluest of blue spectacles and seemed to think that the sooner people quitted it, the happier for them. He did his duty by the men, but if they recovered, he looked half disappointed and congratulated them with cheerful prophecies that there would come a time when they would wish they hadn't. If one died, he seemed relieved and surveyed him with pensive satisfaction, saying heartily:

"He's comfortable, now, poor soul, and well out of this miserable world. Thank God!"

But for Ben's presence, the sanitary influences of the doctor's ward would have been small, and Dante's doleful line might have been written on the threshold of the door:

WHO ENTERS HERE LEAVES HOPE BEHIND.

Ben and the doctor perfectly understood and liked each other, but never agreed and always skirmished over the boys as if manful cheerfulness and medical despair were fighting for the soul and body of each one.

"Well," began the doctor, looking at Sam's arm, or rather at all that was left of that member after two amputations, "we shall be ready for another turn at this in a day or two if it don't mend faster. Tetanus sometimes follows such cases, but that is soon over; and I should not object to a case of it by way of variety." Sam's hopeful face fell, and he set his teeth as if the fatal symptoms were already felt.

"If one kind of lockjaw was not fatal, it wouldn't be a bad thing for some folks I could mention," observed Ben, covering the well-healed stump as carefully as if it were a sleeping baby— adding, as the doctor walked away, "There's a sanguinary old sawbones for you! Why, bless your buttons, Sam, you are doing splendid, and he goes on that way because there's no chance of his having another cut at you! Now he's bothering Turner, jest as we've blowed a spark of spirit into him. If ever there was a born extinguisher, it's Bangs!"

Ben rushed to the rescue, and not a minute too soon; for Turner, who now labored under the delusion that his recovery depended solely upon his getting out of bed every fifteen minutes, was sitting by the fire, looking up at the doctor, who pleasantly observed, while feeling his pulse:

"So you are getting ready for another fever, are you? Well, we've grown rather fond of you and will keep you six weeks longer if you have your heart set on it."

Turner looked nervous, for the doctor's jokes were always grim ones; but Ben took the other hand in his and gently rocked the chair as he replied, with great politeness:

"This robust convalescent of ours would be happy to oblige you, sir, but he has a pressin' engagement up to Jersey for next week and couldn't stop on no account. You see Miss Turner wants a careful nurse for little Georgie, and he's a goin' to take the place."

Feeling himself on the brink of a laugh as Turner simpered with a ludicrous mixture of pride in his baby and fear for himself, Dr. Bangs said, with unusual sternness and a glance at Ben:

"You take the responsibility of this step upon yourself, do you? Very well; then I wash my hands of Turner. Only, if that bed is empty in a week, don't lay the blame of it at my door."

"Nothing shall induce me to do it, sir," briskly responded Ben. "Now then, turn in my boy and sleep your best, for I wouldn't but disappoint that cheerfulest of men for a month's wages; and that's liberal, as I ain't likely to get it."

"How is this young man after the rash dissipations of the day?" asked the doctor, pausing at the bed in the corner after he had made a lively progress down the room, hotly followed by Ben.

"I'm first-rate, sir," panted Joe, who always said so, though each day found him feebler than the last. Everyone was kind to Joe, even the gruff doctor, whose manner softened and who was forced to frown heavily to hide the pity in his eyes.

"How's the cough?"

"Better, sir. Being weaker, I can't fight against it as I used to do, so it comes rather easier."

"Sleep any last night?"

"Not much. But it's very pleasant lying here when the room is still and no light but the fire. Ben keeps it bright; and when I fret, he talks to me and makes the time go telling stories till he gets so sleepy he can hardly speak. Dear old Ben! I hope he'll have someone as kind to him when he needs it as I do now."

"He will get what he deserves by and by, you may be sure of that," said the doctor, as severely as if Ben merited eternal condemnation.

A great drop splashed down upon the hearth as Joe spoke; but Ben put his foot on it, and turned about as if defying anyone to say he shed it.

"Of all the perverse and reckless women whom I have known in the course of a forty years' practice, this one is the most per-verse and reckless," said the doctor, abruptly addressing Miss Hale, who just then appeared bringing Joe's "posey-basket" back. "You will oblige me, Ma'am, by sitting in this chair with your hands folded for twenty minutes. The clock will then strike nine, and you will go straight up to your bed."

Miss Hale demurely sat down, and the doctor ponderously departed, sighing regretfully as he went through the room, as if disappointed that the whole thirty were not lying at death's door. But on the threshold he turned about, exclaimed, "Good night, boys! God bless you!" and vanished as precipitately as if a trapdoor had swallowed him up.

Miss Hale was a perverse woman in some things; for instead of folding her tired hands, she took a rusty-covered volume from the mantelpiece, and sitting by Joe's bed, began to read aloud. One by one all other sounds grew still; one by one the men composed themselves to listen; and one by one the words of the sweet old Christmas story came to them as the woman's quiet voice went reading on. If any wounded spirit needed balm, if any hungry heart asked food, if any upright purpose, newborn aspiration, or sincere repentance wavered for want of human strength, all found help, hope, and consolation in the beautiful and blessed influences of the book, the reader, and the hour.

The bells rung nine, the lights grew dim, the day's work was done; but Miss Hale lingered beside Joe's bed. His face wore a wistful look, and he seemed loath to have her go.

"What is it, dear?" she said. "What can I do for you before I leave you to Ben's care?"

He drew her nearer, and whispered earnestly:

"It's something that I know you'll do for me, because I can't do it for myself, not as I want it done, and you can. I'm going pretty fast now, Ma'am. And when—when someone else is lying here, I want you to tell the boys—everyone, from Ben to Barney—how much I thanked 'em, how much I loved 'em, and how glad I was that I had known 'em, even for such a little while."

"Yes, Joe, I'll tell them all. What else can I do, my boy?"

"Only let me say to you what no one else must say for me, that all I want to live for is to try and do something in my poor way to show you how I thank you, Ma'am. It isn't what you've said to me; it isn't what you've done for me alone that makes me grateful. It's because you've taught me many things without knowing it, showed me what I ought to have been before, if I'd had anyone to tell me how, and made this such a happy, home-like place, I shall be sorry when I have to go."

Poor Joe! It must have fared hardly with him all those twenty years, if a hospital seemed homelike and a little sympathy, a little care, could fill him with such earnest gratitude. He stopped a moment to lay his cheek upon the hand he held in both of his, then hurried on as if he felt his breath beginning to give out:

"I dare say many boys have said this to you, Ma'am, better than I can, because I don't say half I feel. But I know that none of 'em ever thanked you as I thank you in my heart, or ever loved you as I'll love you all my life. Today I hadn't anything to give you, I'm so poor; but I wanted to tell you this, on the last Christmas I shall ever see."

It was a very humble kiss he gave that hand, but the fervor of a first love warmed it, and the sincerity of a great gratitude made it both a precious and pathetic gift to one who, half unconsciously, had made this brief and barren life rich and happy at its close. Always womanly and tender, Miss Hale's face was doubly so as she leaned over him, whispering:

"I have had my present, now. Good night, Joe."

What Polly Found in Her Stocking

With the first pale glimmer,
Of the morning red,
Polly woke delighted
And flew out of bed.
Out the door she hurried,
Never stopped for clothes,
Though Jack Frost's cold fingers
Nipped her little toes.
There it hung! The stocking,
Long and blue and full;
Down it quickly tumbled
With a hasty pull.
Back she capered, laughing,
Happy little Polly;
For from out the stocking
Stared a splendid dolly!
Next, what most she wanted,

In a golden nut,
With a shining thimble,
Scissors that would cut;
Then a book all pictures,
"Children in the Wood."
And some scarlet mittens
Like her scarlet hood.
Next a charming jump rope,
New and white and strong;
(Little Polly's stocking
Though small was very long,)
In the heel she fumbled,
"Something soft and warm,"
A rainbow ball of worsted
Which could do no harm.
In the foot came bonbons,
In the toe a ring,
And some seeds of mignonette
Ready for the spring.
There she sat at daylight
Hugging close dear dolly;
Eating, looking, laughing,
Happy little Polly!

Rosa's Tale

"**N**ow, I believe everyone has had a Christmas present and a good time. Nobody has been forgotten, not even the cat," said Mrs. Ward to her daughter, as she looked at Pobbylinda, purring on the rug, with a new ribbon round her neck and the remains of a chicken bone between her paws.

It was very late, for the Christmas tree was decorated, the little folks in bed, the baskets and bundles left at poor neighbors' doors, and everything ready for the happy day which would begin as the clock struck twelve. They were resting after their mother's words reminded Belinda of one good friend who had received no gift that night.

"We've forgotten Rosa! Her mistress is away, but she shall have a present nevertheless. As late as it is, I know she would like some apples and cake and a Merry Christmas from the family."

Belinda jumped up as she spoke, and having collected such remnants of the feast as a horse would relish, she put on her hood, lighted a lantern, and trotted off to the barn to deliver her Christmas cheer.

As she opened the door of the loose box in which Rosa was kept, Belinda saw Rosa's eyes shining in the dark as she lifted her head with a startled air. Then, recognizing a friend, the horse rose and came rustling through the straw to greet her late visitor. She was evidently much pleased with the attention and gratefully rubbed her nose against Miss Belinda. At the same time, she poked her nose suspiciously into the contents of the basket.

Miss Belinda well knew that Rosa was an unusually social beast and would enjoy the little feast more if she had company, so she hung up the lantern, and sitting down on an inverted bucket, watched her as she munched contentedly.

"Now really," said Miss Belinda, when telling her story afterwards, "I am not sure whether I took a nap and dreamed what follows, or whether it actually happened; for strange things do occur at Christmastime, as everyone knows.

"As I sat there, the town clock struck twelve, and the sound reminded me of the legend, which affirms that all dumb animals are endowed with speech for one hour after midnight on Christmas Eve, in memory of the animals who lingered near the manger when the blessed Christ Child was born.

"I wish this pretty legend were true and our Rosa could speak, if only for an hour. I'm sure she has an interesting history, and I long to know all about it.

"I said this aloud, and to my utter amazement the bay mare stopped eating, fixed her intelligent eyes upon my face, and answered in a language I understood perfectly well—'You shall indeed know my history, for whether the legend you mention is true or not, I do feel that I can confide in you and tell you all that I feel,' sweet Rosa told me.

"'I was lying awake listening to the fun in the house, thinking of my dear mistress so far away across the ocean and feeling very sad, for I heard you say that I was to be sold. That nearly broke my heart, for no one has ever been so kind to me as Miss Merry; and nowhere shall I be taken care of, nursed, and loved as I have been since she bought me. I know I'm getting old and stiff in the knees. My forefoot is lame, and sometimes I'm cross when my shoulder aches; but I do try to be a patient, grateful beast. I've gotten fat with good living, my work is not hard, and I dearly love to carry those who have done so much for me. I'll carry them about until I die in the harness if they will only keep me.'

"I was so astonished by Rosa's speech that I tumbled off the pail on which I was sitting and landed in the straw staring up at Rosa, as dumb as if I had lost the power she had gained. She seemed to enjoy my surprise, and added to it by letting me hear a genuine horse laugh—hearty, shrill, and clear—as she shook her pretty head and went on talking rapidly in the language which I now perceived to be a mixture of English and the peculiar dialect of the horse country.

"'Thank you for remembering me tonight, and in return for the goodies you bring I'll tell my story as quickly as I can, for I have often longed to recount the trials and triumphs of my life. Miss Merry came last Christmas Eve to bring me sugar, and I wanted to speak, but it was too early and I could not say a word, though my heart was full.'

"Rosa paused an instant, and her fine eyes dimmed as if with tender tears at the recollection of the happy year, which followed the day she was bought from the drudgery of a livery stable to be a lady's special pet. I stroked her neck as she stooped to sniff affectionately at my hood, and eagerly said—

"'Tell away, dear. I'm full of interest, and understand every word you say.'

"Thus encouraged, Rosa threw up her head, and began once again to speak with an air of pride, which plainly proved what we had always suspected, that she belonged to a good family.

"'My father was a famous racer, and I am very like him; the same color, spirit, and grace, and but for the cruelty of man, I might have been as renowned as he. I was a happy colt, petted by my master, tamed by love, and never struck a blow while he lived. I won one race for him, and my future seemed so promising that when he died, I brought a great price.

"'I mourned the death of my master, but I was glad to be sent to my new owner's racing stable, where I was made over by everyone. I heard many predictions that I would be another Goldsmith Maid or Flora Temple. Ah, how ambitious and proud I was in those days! I was truly vain in regard to my good blood, my speed, and my beauty; for indeed, I was handsome then, though you may find it difficult to believe now.' Rosa sighed regretfully as she stole a look at me, and turned her head in a way that accentuated the fine lines about her head and neck.

"'I do not find it hard to believe at all,' I answered. 'Miss Merry saw them, though you seemed to be nothing more than a skeleton when she bought you. The Cornish blacksmith who shod you noted the same. It is easy to see that you belong to a good family by the way you hold your head without a checkrein and carry your tail like a plume,' I said, with a look of admiration.

"'I must hurry over this part of my story because, though brilliant, it was very brief, and ended in a way that made it the bitterest portion of my life,' continued Rosa. 'I won several races, and everyone predicted that I would earn great fame. You may guess how high my reputation was when I tell you that before my last, fatal trial, thousands were bet on me, and my rival trembled at the thought of racing against me.

" 'I was full of spirit, eager to show my speed, and sure of success. Alas, how little I knew of the wickedness of human nature then, how dearly I bought the knowledge, and how completely it has changed my whole life! You do not know much about such matters, of course, and I won't digress to tell you all the tricks of the trade; only beware of jockeys and never bet.

" 'I was kept carefully out of everyone's way for weeks and only taken out for exercise by my trainer. Poor Bill! I was fond of him, and he was so good to me that I never have forgotten him, though he broke his neck years ago. A few nights before the great race, as I was enjoying a good sleep carefully tucked away in my stall, someone stole in and gave me a dish of warm mash. It was dark, and I was but half awake. I ate it like a fool, even though I knew by instinct that it was not Bill who left it for me.

" 'I was a trusting creature then, and used to all sorts of strange things being done to prepare me to race. For that reason, I never suspected that something could be wrong. Something was very wrong, however, and the deceit of it has caused me to be suspicious of any food ever since. You see, the mash was dosed in some way; it made me very ill and nearly allowed my enemies to triumph. What a shameful, cowardly trick.

" 'Bill worked with me day and night, trying desperately to prepare me to run. I did my best to seem well, but there was not time for me to regain my lost strength and spirit. My pride was the only thing that kept me going. "I'll win for my master, even if I die in doing it," I said to myself. When the hour came, I

61

pranced to my place trying to look as well as ever, though my heart was heavy and I trembled with excitement. "Courage, my lass, and we'll beat them in spite of their dark tricks," Bill whispered, as he sprang into place.

"'I lost the first heat but won the second, and the sound of the cheering gave me strength to walk away without staggering, though my legs shook under me. What a splendid minute that was when, encouraged and refreshed by my faithful Bill, I came on the track again! I knew my enemies began to fear. I carried myself so bravely that they fancied I was quite well, and now, excited by that first success, I was mad with impatience to be off and cover myself with glory.

"'Rosa looked as if her 'splendid moment' had come again, for she arched her neck, opened wide her red nostrils, and pawed the straw with one little foot. At the same time, her eyes shone with sudden fire, and her ears were pricked up as if to catch again the shouts of the spectators on that long ago day.

"'I wish I had been there to see you!' I exclaimed, quite carried away by her ardor.

"'I wish you had indeed,' she answered, 'for I won. I won! The big, black horse did his best, but I had vowed to win or die, and I kept my word. For I beat him by a head, and as quickly as I had done so, I fell to the ground as if dead. I might as well have died then and there. I heard those around me whispering that the poison, the exercise, and the fall had ruined me as a racer.

"'My master no longer cared for me and would have had me shot if kind Bill had not saved my life. I was pronounced good for nothing, and Bill was able to buy me cheaply. For quite a long time, I was lame and useless, but his patient care did wonders. And just as I was able to be of use to him, he was killed.

" 'A gentleman in search of a saddle horse purchased me because my easy gait and quiet temper suited him; for I was meek enough now, and my size allowed me to carry his delicate daughter.

" 'For more than a year, I served little Miss Alice, rejoicing to see how rosy her pale cheeks became, how upright her feeble figure grew, thanks to the hours she spent with me. My canter rocked her as gently as if she were in a cradle, and fresh air was the medicine she needed. She often said she owed her life to me, and I liked to think so; for she made my life a very easy one.

" 'But somehow my good times never lasted long, and when Miss Alice went west, I was sold. I had been so well treated that I looked as handsome and happy as ever. To be honest though, my shoulder never was strong again, and I often had despondent moods, longing for the excitement of the race track with the instinct of my kind; so I was glad when, attracted by my spirit and beauty, a young army officer bought me, and I went to the war.

" 'Ah! You never guessed that, did you? Yes, I did my part gallantly and saved my master's life more than once. You have observed how martial music delights me, but you don't know that it is because it reminds me of the proudest hour of my life. I've told you about the saddest—now listen as I tell you about the bravest and give me a pat for the courageous act that won my master his promotion though I got no praise for my part of the achievement.

" 'In one of the hottest battles, my captain was ordered to lead his men on a most perilous mission. They hesitated; so did he, for it was certain to cost many lives, and, brave as they were, they paused an instant. But, I settled the point. Wild with the sound of drums, the smell of powder, and the excitement of the hour, I rebelled. Though I was sharply reined in, I took the bit between my teeth and dashed straight ahead into the midst of the fight. Though he tried, my rider could do nothing to stop me. The men, thinking their captain was leading them on, followed cheering loudly and carrying all that was before them.

"'What happened just after that I never could remember, except that I got a wound here in my neck and a cut on my flank. The scar is there still, and I'm proud of it, though buyers always consider it a blemish. When the battle was won, my master was promoted on the field, and I carried him up to the general as he sat among his officers under the torn flags.

"'Both of us were weary and wounded. Both of us were full of pride at what we had done, but he received all the praise and honor. I received only a careless word and a better supper than usual.

"'It seemed so wrong that no one knew or appreciated my courageous action. Not a one seemed to care that it was the horse, not the man, who led that fearless charge. I did think I deserved at least a rosette—others received much more for far less dangerous deeds. My master alone knew the truth of the matter. He thanked me for my help by keeping me always with him until the sad day when he was killed in a skirmish and lay for hours with no one to watch and mourn over him but his faithful horse.

"'Then I knew how much he loved and thanked me. His hand stroked me while it had the strength, his eye turned to me until it grew too dim to see, and when help came at last, I heard him whisper to a comrade, "Be kind to Rosa and send her safely home. She has earned her rest."

"'I had earned it, but I did not get it. When I arrived home, I was received by a mother whose heart was broken by the loss of her son. She did not live long to cherish me. The worst of my bad times were only beginning.

"'My next owner was a fast young man who treated me badly in many ways. At last the spirit of my father rose within me, and I ran away with my master and caused him to take a brutal fall.

"'To tame me down, I was sold as a carriage horse. That almost killed me, for it was dreadful drudgery. Day after day, I pulled heavy loads behind me over the hard pavement. The horses that pulled alongside me were far from friendly, and there was no affection to cheer my life.

"'I have often longed to ask why Mr. Bergh does not try to prevent such crowds from piling into those carriages. Now I beg you to do what you can to stop such an unmerciful abuse.

"'In snowstorms it was awful, and more than one of my mates dropped dead with overwork and discouragement. I used to wish I could do the same, for my poor feet, badly shod, became so lame I could hardly walk at times, and the constant strain on the upgrades brought back the old trouble in my shoulder worse than ever.

"'Why they did not kill me, I don't know. I was a miserable creature then, but there must be something attractive that lingers about me; for people always seem to think I am worth saving. Whatever can it be, ma'am?'

"'Now, Rosa, don't talk so. You know you are an engaging, little animal, and if you live to be forty, I'm sure you will still have certain pretty ways about you—ways that win the hearts of women, if not of men. Women sympathize with your afflictions, find themselves amused with your coquettish airs, and like your affectionate nature. Men, unfortunately, see your weak points and take a money view of the case. Now hurry up and finish. It's getting a bit cold out here.'

"I laughed as I spoke, and Rosa eyed me with a sidelong glance and gently waved her docked tail, which was her delight. The sly thing liked to be flattered and was as fond of compliments as a girl.

" 'Many thanks. I will come now to the most interesting portion of my narrative. As I was saying, instead of being knocked on the head, I was packed off to New Hampshire and had a fine rest among the green hills, with a dozen or so weary friends. It was during this holiday that I acquired the love of nature Miss Merry detected and liked in me when she found me ready to study sunsets with her, to admire new landscapes, and enjoy bright, summer weather.

" 'In the autumn, a livery stable keeper bought me, and through the winter, he fed me well. By spring, I was quite presentable. It was a small town, but a popular place to visit in the summertime. I was kept on the trot while the season lasted, mostly because ladies found me easy to drive. You, Miss Belinda, were one of the ladies, and I never shall forget, though I have long ago forgiven it, how you laughed at my odd gait the day you hired me.

" 'My tender feet and stiff knees made me tread very gingerly and amble along with short, mincing steps, which contrasted rather strangely with my proudly waving tail and high carried head. You liked me nevertheless because I didn't rattle you senseless as we traveled down the steep hills. You also seemed pleased that I didn't startle at the sight of locomotives and stood patiently while you gathered flowers and enjoyed the sights and sounds.

" 'I have always felt a regard for you because you did not whip me and admired my eyes, which, I may say without vanity, have always been considered unusually fine. But no one ever won my whole heart like Miss Merry, and I never shall forget the happy day when she came to the stable to order a saddle horse. Her cheery voice caught my attention, and when she said after looking at several showy beasts, "No, they don't suit me. This little one here has the right air," my heart danced within me and I looked 'round with a whinny of delight. "Can I ride her?" she asked, understanding my welcome. She came right up to me, patted me, peered into my face, rubbed my nose, and looked at my feet with an air of interest and sympathy that made me feel as if I'd like to carry her clear around the world.

"'Ah, what rides we had after that! What happy hours trotting merrily through the green woods, galloping over the breezy hills, and pacing slowly along quiet lanes, where I often lunched luxuriously on clover tops while Miss Merry took a sketch of some picturesque scene with me in the foreground.

"'I liked that very much. We had long chats at such times, and I was convinced that she understood me perfectly. She was never frightened when I danced for pleasure on the soft turf. She never chided me when I snatched a bite from the young trees as we passed through sylvan ways, never thought it any trouble to let me wet my tired feet in babbling brooks, and always kindly dismounted long enough to remove the stones that plagued me.

"'Then how well she rode! So firm yet light in the seat, so steady a hand on the reins, so agile a foot to spring on and off, and such infectious spirits. No matter how despondent or cross I might be, I felt happy and young again whenever dear Miss Merry was on my back.'

"Here Rosa gave a frisk that sent the straw flying and made me shrink into a corner. She pranced about the box, neighing so loudly that she woke the big, brown colt in the next stall and set poor Buttercup to lowing for her lost calf, which she had managed to forget about for a few moments in sleep.

"'Ah, Miss Merry never ran away from me! She knew my heels were to be trusted, and she let me play as I would, glad to see me lively. Never mind, Miss Belinda, come out and I'll behave as befits my years,' laughed Rosa, composing herself, and adding in a way so like a woman that I could not help smiling in the dark—

"'When I say "years," I beg you to understand that I am not as old as that base man declared, but just in the prime of life for a horse. Hard usage has made me seem old before my time, but I am good for years of service yet.'

"'Few people have been through as much as you have, Rosa, and you certainly have earned the right to rest.' I said consolingly, for her little whims and vanities amused me.

"'You know what happened next,' she continued, 'but I must seize this opportunity to express my thanks for all the kindness I've received since Miss Merry bought me, in spite of the ridicule and dissuasion of all her friends.

"'I know I didn't look a good bargain. I was very thin and lame and shabby, but she saw and loved the willing spirit in me. She pitied my hard lot and felt that it would be a good deed to buy me even if she never got much work out of me.

"'I shall always remember that, and whatever happens to me hereafter, I never shall be as proud again as I was the day she put my new saddle and bridle on me. I was led out, sleek, plump, and handsome with blue rosettes at my ears, my tail cut in the English style, and on my back, Miss Merry sat in her London hat and habit, all ready to head a cavalcade of eighteen horsemen and horsewomen.

"'We were the most perfect pair of all, and when the troop pranced down the street six abreast, my head was the highest, my rider the straightest, and our two hearts the friendliest in all the goodly company.

"'Nor is it pride and love alone that bind me to her. It is gratitude as well. She often bathed my feet herself, rubbed me down, watered me, blanketed me, and came daily to see me when I was here alone for weeks in the winter. Didn't she write to the famous friend of my race for advice, and drive me seven miles to get a good smith to shoe me well? Didn't she give me weeks of rest without shoes in order to save my poor, contracted feet? And am I not now fat and handsome, and barring the stiff knees, a very presentable horse? If I am, it is all owing to Miss Merry, and for that reason, I want to live and die in her service.

"'She doesn't want to sell me and only told you to do so because you didn't want to care for me while she is gone. Dear Miss Belinda, please keep me! I'll eat as little as I can. I won't ask for a new blanket, though this old army one is thin and shabby. I'll trot for you all winter and try not to show it if I am lame. I'll do anything a horse can, no matter how humble, in order to earn my living. Don't, I beg you, send me away among strangers who have neither interest nor pity for me!'

"Rosa had spoken rapidly, feeling that her plea must be made now or never. Before another Christmas, she might be far away and speech of no use to win her wish. I was greatly touched, even though she was only a horse. She was looking earnestly at me as she spoke and made the last words very eloquent by preparing to bend her stiff knees and lie down at my feet. I stopped her and answered with an arm about her neck and her soft nose in my hand—

"'You shall not be sold, Rosa! You shall go and board at Mr. Town's great stable, where you will have pleasant society among the eighty horses who usually pass the winter there. Your shoes

69

shall be taken off so that you might rest until March at least. Your care will be only the best, my dear, and I will come and see you. In the spring, you shall return to us, even if Miss Merry is not here to welcome you.'

"'Thanks, many, many thanks! But I wish I could do something to earn my board. I hate to be idle, though rest is delicious. Is there nothing I can do to repay you, Miss Belinda? Please answer quickly. I know the hour is almost over,' cried Rosa, stamping with anxiety. Like all horses, she wanted the last word.

"'Yes, you can,' I cried, as a sudden idea popped into my head. 'I'll write down what you have told me and send the little story to a certain paper I know of. The money I get for it will pay your board. So rest in peace, my dear. You will have earned your living after all, and you may rest knowing that your debt is paid.'

"Before she could reply, the clock struck one. A long sigh of satisfaction was all the response in her power. But, we understood each other now, and cutting a lock from her hair for Miss Merry, I gave Rosa a farewell caress and went on my way. I couldn't help wondering if I had made it all up or the charming beast had really broken a year's silence and freed her mind.

"However that may be, here is the tale. The sequel to it is that the bay mare has really gone to board at a first-class stable," concluded Miss Belinda. "I call occasionally and leave my card in the shape of an apple, finding Madam Rosa living like an independent lady, her large box and private yard on the sunny side of the barn, a kind ostler to wait upon her, and much genteel society from the city when she is inclined for company.

"What more could any reasonable horse desire?"

THE EDITOR'S NOTES

Rosa's Tale—

Aesop may have originated the talking animal story, but he was by no means its last practitioner. Fables and moral tales featuring animals were popular throughout the Middle Ages, and even the famous English poet Geoffrey Chaucer had a thing or two to say about a rooster in Canterbury.

No one knows the origin of the story of animals being endowed with speech on Christmas Eve as a reward for their silence while the baby Jesus slept in a manger, but "Rosa's Tale" shows the true mettle of a horse who is given one great opportunity to speak for herself about the mistreatment she has suffered at human hands.

Christmas is the season of thoughtfulness; Belinda's response to Rosa's story is surely appropriate to the season. "Rosa's Tale" is worthy of even the great Chaucer's ingenuity as a moral tale.

Mrs. Podgers' Teapot

"Ah, dear me, dear me; I'm a deal too comfortable!"
Judging from appearances, Mrs. Podgers certainly had
some cause for that unusual exclamation. To begin with,
the room was comfortable. It was tidy, bright, and warm—full of
cozy corners and capital contrivances for quiet enjoyment. The
chairs seemed to extend their plump arms invitingly; the old-
fashioned sofa was so hospitable that whoever sat down upon it
was slow to get up; the pictures, though portraits, did not stare
one out of countenance but surveyed the scene with an air of
tranquil enjoyment; and the unshuttered windows allowed the
cheery light to shine out into the snowy street through blooming screens of Christmas roses and white chrysanthemums.

The fire was comfortable; for it was neither hidden in a stove
nor imprisoned behind bars, but went rollicking up the wide
chimney with a jovial roar. It flickered over the supper table as if
curious to discover what savory foods were concealed under the
shining covers. It touched up the old portraits till they seemed
to wink; it covered the walls with comical shadows, as if the
portly chairs had set their arms akimbo and were dancing a jig.
The fire flashed out into the street with a voiceless greeting to
every passerby; it kindled mimic fires in the brass andirons and
the teapot simmering on the hob, and best of all, it shone its

brightest on Mrs. Podgers, as if conscious that it couldn't do a better thing.

Mrs. Podgers was comfortable as she sat there, buxom, blooming, and brisk, in spite of her forty years and her widow's cap. Her black gown was illuminated to such an extent that it couldn't look sombre. Her cap had given up trying to be prim long ago, and cherry ribbons wouldn't have made it more becoming as it set off her crisp, black hair and met in a coquettish bow under her plump chin. Her white apron encircled her trim waist, as if conscious of its advantages, and the mourning pin upon her bosom actually seemed to twinkle with satisfaction at the enviable post it occupied.

The sleek cat, purring on the hearth, was comfortable; so was the agreeable fragrance of muffins that pervaded the air, so was the drowsy tick of the clock in the corner. And if anything was needed to give a finishing touch to the general comfort of the scene, the figure pausing in the doorway supplied the want most successfully.

Heroes are always expected to be young and comely, also fierce, melancholy, or at least what novel readers call "interesting"; but I am forced to own that Mrs. Podger was none of these. Half the real beauty, virtue, and romance of the world gets put into humble souls, hidden in plain bodies. Mr. Jerusalem Turner was an example of this; and, at the risk of shocking sentimental readers, I must frankly state that he was fifty, stout, and bald, also that he used bad grammar, had a double chin, and was only the clerk in a prosperous grocery store. A hale and hearty old gentleman with cheerful brown eyes, a ruddy countenance, and curly gray hair sticking up all round his head, he had an air of energy and independence that was pleasant to behold. There he stood, beaming upon the unconscious Mrs. Podgers, softly rubbing his hands and smiling to himself with the air of a man enjoying the chief satisfaction of his life, as he was.

"Ah, dear me, dear me, I'm a deal too comfortable!" sighed Mrs. Podgers, addressing the teapot.

"Not a bit, Mum; not a bit."

In walked the gentleman, and up rose the lady, saying, with a start and an aspect of relief:

"Bless me, I didn't hear you! I began to think you were never coming to your tea, Mr. 'Rusalem."

Everybody called him Mr. 'Rusalem, and many people were ignorant that he had any other name. He liked it, for it began with the children, and the little voices had endeared it to him, not to mention the sound of it from Mrs. Podgers' lips for ten years.

"I know I'm late, Mum, but I really couldn't help it. Tonight's a busy time, and the lads are just good for nothing with their jokes and spirits, so I stayed to steady 'em and do a little job that turned up unexpected."

"Sit right down and have your tea while you can, then. I've kept it warm for you, and the muffins are done lovely."

Mrs. Podgers bustled about with an alacrity that seemed to give an added relish to the supper; and when her companion was served, she sat smiling at him with her hand on the teapot, ready to replenish his cup before he could ask for it.

"Have things been fretting of you, Mum? You looked down-hearted as I came in, and that ain't accordin' to the time of year, which is merry," said Mr. 'Rusalem, stirring his tea with a sense of solid satisfaction that would have sweetened a far less palatable draught.

"It's the teapot. I don't know what's got into it tonight, but, as I was waiting for you, it set me thinking of one thing and another, till I declare I felt as if it had up and spoke to me, showing me how I wasn't grateful enough for my blessings, but a deal more comfortable than I deserved."

While speaking, Mrs. Podgers' eyes rested on an inscription that encircled the corpulent little silver pot: *"To our Benefactor— They who give to the poor lend to the Lord."* Now one wouldn't think there was anything in the speech or the inscription to disturb Mr. 'Rusalem; but there seemed to be, for he fidgeted in his chair, dropped his fork, and glanced at the teapot with a very odd expression. It was a capital little teapot, solid, bright as hands could make it, and ornamented with a robust young cherub perched upon the lid, regardless of the warmth of his seat. With her eyes still fixed upon it, Mrs. Podgers continued meditatively:

"You know how fond I am of the teapot for poor Podgers' sake. I really feel quite superstitious about it; and when thoughts come to me, as I sit watching it, I have faith in them, because they always remind me of the past."

Here, after vain efforts to restrain himself, Mr. 'Rusalem broke into a sudden laugh, so hearty and infectious that Mrs. Podgers couldn't help smiling, even while she shook her head at him.

"I beg pardon, Mum; it's hysterical; I'll never do it again," panted Mr. 'Rusalem, as he got his breath and went soberly on with his supper.

It was a singular fact that whenever the teapot was particularly alluded to, he always behaved in this incomprehensible manner—laughed, begged pardon, said it was hysterical, and promised never to do it again. It used to trouble Mrs. Podgers very much, but she had grown used to it; and having been obliged to overlook many oddities in the departed Podgers, she easily forgave 'Rusalem his only one.

After the laugh there was a pause, during which Mrs. Podgers sat absently polishing up the silver cherub, with the memory of the little son who died two Christmases ago lying heavy at her heart, and Mr. 'Rusalem seemed to be turning something over in his mind as he watched a bit of butter sink luxuriously into the warm bosom of a muffin. Once or twice he paused as if listening. Several times he stole a look at Mrs. Podgers and presently said, in a somewhat anxious tone:

"You was saying just now that you was a deal too comfortable in order to realize your blessings?"

"Yes, I should. I'm getting lazy, selfish, and forgetful of other folks. You leave me nothing to do and make everything so easy for me that I'm growing young and giddy again. Now that isn't as it should be, 'Rusalem."

"It meets my views exactly, Mum. You've had your hard times, your worriments and cares, and now it's right to take your rest."

"Then why don't you take yours? I'm sure you've earned it drudging thirty years in the store, with more extra work than holidays for your share."

"Oh well, Mum, it's different with me, you know. Business is amusing; and I'm so used to it I shouldn't know myself if I was out of the store for good."

"Well, I hope you are saving up something against the time when business won't be amusing. You are so generous, I'm afraid you forget you can't work for other people all your days."

"Yes, Mum, I've put a little sum in a safe bank that pays good interest, and when I'm past work, I'll fall back and enjoy it."

To judge from the cheerful content of the old gentleman's face he was enjoying it already, and he looked about him with the air of a man who had made a capital investment and was in the receipt of generous dividends. Seeing Mrs. Podgers' bright eye fixed upon him, as if she suspected something and would have the truth out of him in two minutes, he recalled the conversation to the point from which it had wandered.

"If you would like to try how a little misery suits you, Mum, I can accommodate you, if you'll step upstairs."

"Good gracious, what do you mean? Who's up there? Why didn't you tell me before?" cried Mrs. Podgers, in a flutter of interest, curiosity, and surprise, as he knew she would be.

"You see, Mum, I was doubtful how you'd like it. I did it without stopping to think, and then I was afraid you'd consider it a liberty."

Mr. 'Rusalem spoke with some hesitation; but Mrs. Podgers didn't wait to hear him, for she was already at the door, lamp in hand, and would have been off had she known where to go, "upstairs" being a somewhat vague expression. The old gentleman led the way to the room he had occupied for thirty years, in spite of Mrs. Podgers' frequent offers of a better and brighter one. He was attached to it, small and dark as it was; for the joys and sorrows of more than half his life had come to him in that little room, and somehow, when he was there, it brightened up amazingly. Mrs. Podgers looked well about her but saw nothing new, and her conductor said, as he paused beside the bed:

"Let me tell you how I found it before I show it. You see, Mum, I had to step down the street just at dark, and passing the windows I give a glance in, as I've a bad habit of doing when the lamps is lighted and you a-setting there alone. Well, Mum, what did I see outside but a ragged little chap a-flattening his nose against the glass, and staring in with all his eyes. I didn't blame him much for it, and on I goes without a word. When I came back, I see him a-lying close to the wall, and mistrusting that he was up to some game that might give you a scare, I speaks to him. Well, he don't answer. I touches him; he don't stir. Then I picks him up, and seeing that he's gone in a fit or a faint, I makes for the store with a will. He come to rapid; and finding that he was most froze and starved, I fed and warmed and fixed him a trifle, and then tucked him away here; for he's got no folks to worry for him, and was too used up to go out again tonight. That's the story, Mum, and now I'll produce the little chap if I can find him."

With that, Mr. 'Rusalem began to grope about the bed, chuckling, yet somewhat anxious, for not a vestige of an occupant appeared, till a dive downward produced a sudden agitation of the clothes, a squeak, and the unexpected appearance out at the foot of the bed of a singular figure that dodged into a corner with one arm up, as if to ward off a blow, while a sleepy little voice exclaimed beseechingly, "I'm up, I'm up; don't hit me!"

"Lord, love the child; who'd think of doing that! Wake up, Joe, and see your friends," said Mr. 'Rusalem, advancing cautiously.

At the sound of his voice, down went the arm, and Mrs. Podgers saw a boy of nine or ten, arrayed in a flannel garment that evidently belonged to Mr. 'Rusalem; for though none too long, it was immensely broad, and the voluminous sleeves were pinned up, showing a pair of wasted arms, chapped with cold and mottled with bruises. A large blue sock still covered one foot The other was bound up as if hurt. A tall cotton nightcap, garnished with a red tassel, looked like a big extinguisher on a small candle; and from under it, a pair of dark, hollow eyes glanced sharply with a shrewd, suspicious look that made the little face more pathetic than the marks of suffering, neglect, and abuse, which told the child's story without words. As if quite reassured by 'Rusalem's presence, the boy shuffled out of his corner, saying coolly, as he prepared to climb into his nest again:

"I thought it was the old one when you grabbed me. Ain't this bed a first-rater, though?"

Mr. 'Rusalem lifted the composed young personage into the middle of the big bed, where he sat bolt upright, surveying the prospect from under the coverlet with an equanimity that quite took the good lady's breath away. But Mr. 'Rusalem fell back and pointed to him, saying, "There he is, Mum," with as much pride and satisfaction as if he had found some rare and valuable treasure; for the little child was very precious in his sight. Mrs. Podgers really didn't know whether to laugh or cry, and settled the matter by plumping down beside the boy, saying cordially, as she took the grimy little hands into her own:

"He's heartily welcome, 'Rusalem. Now tell me all about it, my poor dear, and don't be afraid."

"Ho, I ain't afraid a you nor he. I ain't got nothin' to tell; only my name's Joe, and I'm sleepy."

"Who is your mother, and where do you live, deary?" asked Mrs. Podgers, haunted with the idea that some woman must be anxious for the child.

"Ain't got any. We don't have 'em where I lives. The old one takes care of me."

"Who is the old one?"

"Granny. I works for her, and she lets me stay alonger her."

"Bless the dear! What work can such a mite do?"

"Heaps a things. I sifts ashes, picks rags, goes beggin', runs arrants, and sometimes the big fellers lets me sell papers. That's fun; only I gets knocked 'round, and it hurts, you'd better believe."

"Did you come here begging, and, being afraid to ring, stand outside looking in at me enjoying myself, like a selfish creeter as I am?"

"I forgot to ask for the cold vittles a-lookin' at warm ones, and thinkin' if they was mine what I'd give the little fellers when I has my tree."

"Your what, child?"

"My Christmas tree. Look a-here, I've got it, and all these to put on it tomorrer."

From under his pillow the boy produced a small branch of hemlock, dropped from some tree on its passage to a gayer festival than little Joe's; also an old handkerchief which contained his treasures—only a few odds and ends picked up in the streets: a gnarly apple, half a dozen nuts, two or three dingy bonbons, gleaned from the sweepings of some store, and a bit of cheese, which last possession he evidently prized highly.

"That's for the old one; she likes it, and I kep it for her, 'cause she don't hit so hard when I fetch her goodies. You don't mind, do you?" he said, looking inquiringly at Mr. 'Rusalem, who blew his nose like a trumpet and patted the big nightcap with a fatherly gesture more satisfactory than words.

"What have you kept for yourself, dear?" asked Mrs. Podgers, with an irrepressible sniff, as she looked at the poor little presents and remembered that they "didn't have mothers" where the child lived.

"Oh, I had my treat alonger him," said the boy, nodding toward 'Rusalem, and adding enthusiastically, "Wasn't that prime! It was real Christmasy a settin' by the fire, eating lots and not bein' hit."

Here Mrs. Podgers broke down; and, taking the boy in her arms, sobbed over him as if she had found her lost Neddy in this sad shape. The little lad regarded her demonstration with some uneasiness at first. But there is a magic about a genuine woman that wins its way everywhere, and soon the outcast nestled to her, feeling that this wonderful night was getting more "Christmasy" every minute.

Mrs. Podgers was herself again directly; and seeing that the child's eyelids were heavy with weakness and weariness, she made him comfortable among the pillows and began to sing the lullaby that used to hush her little son to sleep. Mr. 'Rusalem took something from his drawer and was stealing away, when the child opened his eyes and started up, calling out as he nodded, till the tassel danced on his preposterous cap:

"I say! Good night, good night!"

Looking much gratified, Mr. 'Rusalem returned, shook the little hand extended to him, kissed the grateful face, and went away to sit on the stairs with tear after tear dropping off the end of his nose as he listened to the voice that, after two years of silence, sung the air this simple soul thought the loveliest in the world. At first, it was more sob than song, but soon the soothing music flowed on unbroken, and the wondering child, for the first time within his memory, fell asleep in the sweet shelter of a woman's arms.

When Mrs. Podgers came out, she found Mr. 'Rusalem intent on stuffing another parcel into a long gray stocking already full to overflowing.

"For the little chap, Mum. He let fall that he'd never done this sort of thing in his life, and, as he hadn't any stockings of his own, poor dear, I took the liberty of lending him one of mine," explained Mr. 'Rusalem, surveying the knobby article with evident regret that it wasn't bigger.

Mrs. Podgers said nothing, but looked from the stocking to the fatherly old gentleman who held it; and if Mrs. Podgers had obeyed the impulse of her heart, she would have forgotten decorum and kissed him on the spot. She didn't, however, but went briskly into her own room, whence she presently returned with red eyes and a pile of small garments in her hands. Having nearly exhausted his pincushion in trying to suspend the heavy stocking, Mr. 'Rusalem had just succeeded as she appeared. He saw what she carried, watched her arrange the little shirt, jacket, and trousers, the half-worn shoes and tidy socks, beside the bed, with motherly care, with an expression which caused Mr. 'Rusalem to dart downstairs and compose himself by rubbing his hair erect, and shaking his fist in the painted face of the late Podgers.

An hour or two later the store was closed, the room cleared, Mrs. Podgers in her armchair on one side of the hearth with her knitting in her hand, Mr. 'Rusalem in his armchair on the other side with his newspaper on his knee, both looking so cozy and comfortable that anyone would have pronounced them a contented couple on the spot. Ah, but they weren't, you see, and that spoilt the illusion, to one party at least. Both were rather silent, both looked thoughtfully at the fire, and the fire gave them both excellent counsel, as it seldom fails to do when it finds any kindred warmth and brightness in the hearts and souls of those who study it. Mrs. Podgers kindled first and broke out suddenly with a nod of great determination.

83

"'Rusalem, I'm going to keep that boy, if it's possible!"

"You shall, Mum, whether it's possible or not," he answered, nodding back at her with equal wisdom.

"I don't know why I never thought of such a thing before. There's a many children suffering for mothers, and heaven knows I'm wearying for some little child to fill my Neddy's place. I wonder if you didn't think of this when you took that boy in; it would be just like you!"

Mr. 'Rusalem shook his head, but looked so guilty, that Mrs. Podgers was satisfied, called him "a thoughtful dear," within herself, and kindled still more.

"Between you and Joe and the teapot, I've got another idea into my stupid head, and I know you won't laugh at it. That loving little soul has tried to get a tree for some poor babies who have no one to think of them but him, and even remembered the old one, who must be a wretch to hit that child, and hit hard, too; I know by the looks of his arms. Well, I've a great longing to go and give him a tree—a right good one, like those Neddy used to have; to get in 'the little fellers' he tells of, give them a good dinner, and then a regular Christmas party. Can't it be done?"

"Nothing could be easier, Mum," and Mr. 'Rusalem, who had been taking counsel with the fire till he quite glowed with warmth and emotion, nodded, smiled, and rubbed his hands, as if Mrs. Podgers had invited him to a Lord Mayor's feast or some equally gorgeous jollification.

"I suppose it's the day, and thinking of how it came to be, that makes me feel as if I wanted to help everybody, and makes this Christmas so bright and happy that I never can forget it," continued the good woman with a heartiness that made her honest face quite beautiful to behold.

If Mrs. Podgers had only known what was going on under the capacious waistcoat opposite, she would have held her tongue; for the more charitable, earnest, and tenderhearted she grew, the harder it became for Mr. 'Rusalem to restrain the declaration which had been hovering on his lips ever since old Podgers died. As the comely woman sat there talking in that genial way, and glowing with goodwill to all mankind, it was too much for Mr. 'Rusalem; and finding it impossible to resist the desire to know his fate, he yielded to it, gave a portentous hem, and said abruptly:

"Well, Mum, have I done it?"

"Done what?" asked Mrs. P., going on with her work.

"Made you uncomfortable, according to promise."

"Oh dear, no, you've made me very happy and will have to try again," she answered, laughing.

"I will, Mum."

As he spoke, Mr. 'Rusalem drew his chair nearer, leaned forward, and looking straight at her, said deliberately, though his voice shook a little:

"Mrs. Podgers, I love you hearty; would you have any objections to marrying me?"

Not a word said Mrs. Podgers; but her knitting dropped out of her hand, and she looked as uncomfortable as she could desire.

"I thought that would do it," muttered Mr. 'Rusalem, but went on steadily, though his ruddy face got paler and paler, his voice huskier and huskier, and his heart fuller and fuller every word he attempted.

"You see, Mum, I have took the liberty of loving you ever since you came, more than ten years ago. I was eager to make it known long before this, but Mr. Podgers spoke first, and then it was no use. It come hard for a time, but I learned to give you up, though I couldn't learn not to love you, being as it was impossible. Since Podgers died, I've turned it over in my mind frequent, but felt as if I was too old and rough and poor in every way to ask so much. Lately, the wish has growed too strong for me, and tonight it won't be put down. If you want a trial, Mum, I should be that I'll warrant, for do my best, I could never be all I'm wishful of being for your sake. Would you give it name, and if not agreeable, we'll let it drop, Mum; we'll let it drop."

If it hadn't been for the teapot, Mrs. Podgers would have said yes at once. The word was on her lips, but as she looked up, the fire flashed brightly on the teapot (which always occupied the place of honor on the sideboard, for Mrs. P. was intensely proud of it), and she stopped to think, for it reminded her of something. In order to explain this, we must keep Mr. 'Rusalem waiting for his answer a minute.

Rather more than ten years ago, old Podgers happened to want a housekeeper and invited a poor woman to fill that post in his bachelor establishment. He never would have thought of marrying her, though the young woman was both notable and handsome, if he hadn't discovered that his partner loved her. Whereupon, the perverse old fellow immediately proposed, lest he should lose his housekeeper, and was accepted from motives of gratitude. Mrs. Podgers was a dutiful wife, but not a very happy one; for the world said that Mr. P. was a hard, miserly man, and his wife was forced to believe the world in the right, till the teapot changed her opinion.

There happened to be much suffering among the poor one year, owing to the burning of the mill, and contributions were solicited for their relief. Old Podgers, though a rich man, refused to give a penny, but it was afterwards discovered that his private charities exceeded many more ostentatious ones, and the word "miserly" was changed to "peculiar." When times grew prosperous again, the workmen, whose families had been so quietly served, clubbed together, got the teapot, and left it at Mr. Podgers' door one Christmas Eve. But the old gentleman never saw it, for sudden apoplexy struck and took him off that very afternoon.

In the midst of her grief, Mrs. Podgers was surprised, touched, and troubled by this revelation; for she had known nothing of the affair till the teapot came. Womanlike, she felt great remorse for what now seemed like blindness and ingratitude; she fancied she owed him some atonement, and remembering how often he had expressed a hope that she wouldn't marry again after he was gone, she resolved to gratify him.

The buxom widow had had many opportunities of putting off her widow's clothes, but she had refused all offers without regret till now. The teapot reminded her of Podgers and her vow; and though her heart rebelled, she thought it her duty to check the answer that sprung to her lips, and slowly, but decidedly, replied:

"I'm truly grateful to you, 'Rusalem, but I couldn't do it. Don't think you'd ever be a trial, for you're the last man to be that to any woman. It's a feeling I have that it wouldn't be kind to Podgers. I can't forget how much I owe him, how much I wronged him, and how much I can please him by staying as I am, for his frequent words were, 'Keep the property together, and don't marry, Jane.' "

"Very well, Mum, then we'll let it drop and fall back into the old ways. Don't fret yourself about it. I shall bear up, and—" There Mr. 'Rusalem's voice gave out, and he sat frowning at the fire, bent on bearing up manfully, though it was very hard to find that Podgers dead as well as Podgers living was to keep from him the happiness he had waited for so long. His altered face and broken voice were almost too much for Mrs. P., and she found it necessary to confirm her resolution by telling it. Laying one hand on his shoulder, she pointed to the teapot with the other, saying gently:

"The day that came and I found out how good he was, too late to beg his pardon and love him for it, I said to myself, 'I'll be true to Podgers till I die, because that's all I can do now to show my repentance and respect.' But for that feeling and that promise, I couldn't say no to you, 'Rusalem, for you've been my best friend all these years, and I'll be yours all my life, though I can't be anything else, my dear."

For the first time since its arrival, the mention of the teapot did not produce the accustomed demonstration from Mr. 'Rusalem. On the contrary, he looked at it with a momentary expression of indignation and disgust, strongly suggestive of an insane desire to cast the precious relic on the floor and trample on it. If any such temptation did assail him, he promptly curbed it and looked about the room with a forlorn air that made Mrs. Podgers hate herself, as he meekly answered:

"I'm obliged to you, Mum; the feeling does you honor. Don't mind me. It's rather a blow, but I'll be up again directly."

He retired behind his paper as he spoke, and Mrs. Podgers spoilt her knitting in respectful silence, till Mr. 'Rusalem began to read aloud as usual, to assure her that, in spite of the blow, he *was* up again.

In the gray dawn, the worthy gentleman was roused from his slumbers by a strange voice whispering shrilly in his ear:

"I say, there's two of 'em. Ain't it jolly?"

Starting up, he beheld a comical little goblin standing at his bedside with a rapturous expression of countenance and a pair of long gray stockings in its hands. Both were heaping full, but one was evidently meant for Mr. 'Rusalem, for every wish, whim, and fancy of his had been guessed and gratified in a way that touched him to the heart. If it were not indecorous to invade the privacy of a gentleman's apartment, I could describe how there were two boys in the big bed that morning; how the old boy revelled in the treasures of his stocking as heartily as the young one; how they laughed and exclaimed, pulled each others nightcaps off, and had a regular pillow fight; how little Joe was dressed into his new clothes and strutted like a small peacock in them; how Mr. 'Rusalem made himself splendid in his Sunday best and spent ten good minutes in tying the fine cravat somebody had hemmed for him. But lest it should be thought improper, I will merely say that nowhere in the city did the sun shine on happier faces than these two showed Mrs. Podgers, as Mr. 'Rusalem came in with Joe on his shoulder, both wishing her a merry Christmas as heartily as if this were the first the world had ever seen.

Mrs. Podgers was as brisk and blithe as they, though she must have sat up one-half the night making presents for them and laid awake the other half making plans for the day. As soon as she had hugged Joe, toasted him red, and heaped his plate with everything on the table, she told them the order of her schedule.

"As soon as ever you can't eat anymore, you must order home the tree, 'Rusalem, and then go with Joe to invite the party, while I see to dinner and dress up the pine as well as I can in such a hurry."

"Yes, Mum," answered Mr. 'Rusalem with alacrity, though how she was going to do her part was not clear to him. But he believed her capable of working any miracle within the power of mortal woman; and having plans of his own, he soon trudged away with Joe prancing at his side, so like the lost Neddy, in the little cap and coat, that Mrs. Podgers forgot her party to stand watching them down the crowded street, with eyes that saw very dimly when they looked away again.

Never mind how she did it; the miracle was wrought, for Mrs. Podgers and her maid Betsey fell to work with a will. And when women set their hearts on anything, it is a known fact that they seldom fail to accomplish it. By noon everything was ready—the tree waiting in the best parlor, the dinner smoking on the table, and Mrs. Podgers at the window to catch the first glimpse of her coming guests.

A last thought struck her as she stood waiting. There was but one high chair in the house, and the big ones would be doubtless too low for the little people. Bent on making them as comfortable as her motherly heart could desire, she set about mending the matter by bringing out from Podgers' bookcase several fat old ledgers, and arranging them in the chairs. While busily dusting one of these, it slipped from her hands, and as it fell, a paper fluttered from among the leaves. She picked it up, looked at it, dropped her duster, and became absorbed. It was a small sheet filled with figures, and here and there short memoranda—not an interesting looking document in the least—but Mrs. Podgers stood like a statue till she had read it several times; then she caught her breath, clapped her hands, laughed and cried together, and put the climax to her extraordinary behavior by running across the room and embracing the astonished little teapot.

How long she would have gone on in this wild manner it is impossible to say, had not the jingle of bells and a shrill, small cheer announced that the party had arrived. Whisking the mysterious paper into her pocket and dressing her agitated countenance in smiles, she hastened to open the door before chilly fingers could find the bell.

Such a merry load as that was! Such happy faces looking out from under the faded hoods and caps! Such a hearty "Hurrah for Mrs. Podgers!" greeted her straight from the grateful hearts that loved her the instant she appeared! And what a perfect Santa Claus Mr. 'Rusalem made, with his sleigh full of bundles as well as children, his face full of sunshine, his arms full of babies whom he held up that they too might clap their little hands while he hurrahed with all his might! Even reindeers, or the immemorial

white beard and fur cap of Mr. Claus, could not have improved
the picture.

It was good to see Mrs. Podgers welcome them all in a way
that gave the shyest courage, made the poorest forget patched
jackets or ragged gowns, and caused them all to feel that this
indeed was a merry Christmas. It was better still to see Mrs.
Podgers preside over the table, dealing out turkey and pudding
with such a bounteous hand that the small feasters often paused,
in sheer astonishment, at the abundance before them, and then
fell to eating again with renewed energy, as if they feared to
wake up presently and find the whole meal a dream.

It was best of all to see Mrs. Podgers gather them about her
afterwards, hearing their little stories, learning their many wants,
and winning their young hearts by such gentle wiles that they
soon regarded her as some beautiful, benignant fairy, who had
led them from a cold, dark world into the land of innocent
delights they had imagined, longed for, yet never hoped to find.

Then came the tree, hung thick with bonbons, fruit and
toys, gay mittens and tippets, comfortable socks and hoods, and,
lower down, more substantial but less showy gifts; for Mrs.
Podgers had nearly exhausted the Dorcas basket that fortunately
chanced to be with her just then. There was no time for candles,
but, as if he understood the matter and was bent on supplying all
deficiencies, the sun shone gloriously on the little tree and made
it doubly splendid in the children's eyes.

It would have touched the hardest heart to watch the children, as they trooped in and stood about the wonderful tree.
Some seemed ready to go wild with delight; some folded their
hands and sighed with solemn satisfaction; others looked as if
bewildered by such unwonted and unexpected good fortune; and
when Mr. 'Rusalem told them how this fruitful tree had sprung up

from their loving playmate's broken bough, little Joe hid his face in Mrs. Podgers' gown and could find no vent for his great happiness but tears. It was not a large tree, but it took a long while to strip it; and even when the last gilded nut was gone, the children still lingered about it, as if they regarded it with affection as a generous benefactor and were loath to leave it.

Next they had a splendid round of games. I don't know what will be thought of the worthy souls, but Mr. 'Rusalem and Mrs. Podgers played with all their might. Perhaps the reason why he gave himself up so freely to the spirit of the hour was that his disappointment was very heavy; and, according to his simple philosophy, it was wiser to soothe his wounded heart and cheer his sad spirit with the sweet society of little children than to curse fate and reproach a woman.

What was Mrs. Podgers' reason it is impossible to tell, but she behaved as if some secret satisfaction filled her heart so full that she was glad to let it bubble over in this harmless fashion. Both tried to be children again, and both succeeded capitally, though now and then their hearts got the better of them. Mr. 'Rusalem tossed all the little lads up to the ceiling and caught them; he kissed all the little girls, and, that no one might feel slighted, kissed Mrs. Podgers also.

When they played "Open the Gates," and the two grown people stood hand in hand while the mirthful troops marched under the tall arch, Mrs. Podgers never once looked Mr. 'Rusalem in the face, but blushed and kept her eyes on the ground, as if she was a bashful girl playing games with some boyish sweetheart. The children saw nothing of all this, and— bless their innocent little hearts!—they wouldn't have understood it if they had. But it was perfectly evident that the gray-headed gentleman and the mature matron had forgotten all about their years and were in their teens again, for true love is gifted with immortal youth.

When weary with romping, they gathered 'round the fire, and Mr. 'Rusalem told fairy tales, as if his dull ledgers had preserved these childish romances like flowers between their leaves and kept them fresh in spite of time. Mrs. Podgers sung to them, and made them sing with her, till passersby smiled and lingered as the childish voices reached them. Looking through the screen of roses, they caught glimpses of the happy little group singing in the ruddy circle of that Christmas fire.

It was a very humble festival, but with these poor guests came also Love and Charity, Innocence and Joy—the strong, sweet virtues that bless and beautify the world. And though eclipsed by many more splendid celebrations, I think the day was better and the blither for Mrs. Podgers' little party.

When it was all over—the grateful farewells and riotous cheers as the children were carried home, the twilight raptures of Joe, and the long lullaby before he could extinguish himself enough to go to sleep, the congratulations and clearing up—then Mr. 'Rusalem and Mrs. Podgers sat down to tea. But no sooner were they alone together than Mrs. P. fell into a curious flutter and did the oddest things. She gave Mr. 'Rusalem warm water instead of tea, passed the salt bowl when he asked for the sugar basin, burnt her fingers, laid her handkerchief on the tray, tried to put her fork in her pocket, and went on in such a way that Mr. 'Rusalem began to fear the day had been too much for her.

"You're tired, Mum," he said presently, hearing her sigh.

"Not a bit," she answered briskly, opening the teapot to add more water, but, seeming to forget her purpose, sat looking into its steamy depths as if in search of something. If it was courage,

she certainly found it, for all of a sudden she handed the mysterious paper to Mr. 'Rusalem, saying solemnly:

"Read that, and tell me if it's true."

He took it readily, put on his glasses, and bent to examine it,
but gave a start that caused the spectacles to fly off his nose, as
he exclaimed:

"Lord, bless me, he said he'd burnt it!"

"Then it *is* true? Don't deny it, 'Rusalem; it's no use, for I've
caught you at last!" And in her excitement, Mrs. Podgers slapped
down the teapot lid as if she had got him inside.

"I assure you, Mum, he promised to burn it. He made me
write down the sums, and so on, to satisfy him that I hadn't took
more'n my share of the profits. It was my own; and though he
called me a fool, he let me do as I liked, but I never thought it
would come up again like this, Mum."

"Of course you didn't, for it was left in one of the old ledgers
we had down for the dears to sit on. I found it, read it, and
understood it in a minute. It was you who helped the mill
people, and then hid behind Podgers because you didn't want to
be thanked. When he died and the teapot came, you saw how
proud I was of it—how I took comfort in thinking he did the
kind things; and for my sake you never told the truth, not even
last night, when a word would have done so much. Oh,
'Rusalem, how could you deceive me all these years?"

If Mr. 'Rusalem had desired to answer, he would have had no
chance, for Mrs. Podgers was too much in earnest to let anyone
speak but herself and hurried on, fearing that her emotion would
get the better of her before she had had her say.

"It was like you, but it wasn't right, for you've robbed yourself of the love and honor that was your due. You've let people
praise Podgers when he didn't deserve it; you've seen me take

pride in this because I thought he'd earned it; and you've only laughed at it all as if it was a fine joke to do generous things and never take the credit of 'em. Now I know what bank you've laid up your hard earnings in, and what a blessed interest you'll get by and by. Truly they who give to the poor lend to the Lord— and you don't need to have the good words written on silver, for you keep 'em always in your heart."

Mrs. Podgers stopped a minute for breath and felt that she was going very fast; for 'Rusalem sat looking at her with so much humility, love, and longing in his honest face that she knew it would be all up with her directly.

"You saw how I grieved for Neddy and gave me this mother- less boy to fill his place. You knew I wanted someone to make the house seem like home again, and you offered me the lovingest heart that ever was. You found I wasn't satisfied to lead such a selfish life, and you showed me how beautiful Charity could make it. You taught me to find duty waiting for me at my own door; and, putting by your own trouble, you've helped to make this day the happiest Christmas of my life."

If it hadn't been for the teapot, Mrs. Podgers would have given out here; but her hand was still on it, and something in the touch gave her steadiness for one more burst.

"I loved the little teapot for Podgers' sake; now I love it a hundred times more for yours, because you've brought its lesson home to me in a way I never can forget and have been my bene- factor as well as theirs, who shall soon know you as well as I do. 'Rusalem, there's only one way in which I can thank you for all this, and I do it with my whole heart. Last night you asked me for something, and I thought I couldn't give it to you. Now I'm sure I can, and if you still want it, why—"

Mrs. Podgers never finished that sentence; for, with an impetuosity surprising in one of his age and figure, Mr. 'Rusalem sprang out of his chair and took her in his arms, saying tenderly, in a voice almost inaudible, between a conflicting choke and chuckle: "My dear! My dear! God bless you!"

Peace from Heaven

In the rush of early morning,
When the red burns through the gray,
And the wintry world lies waiting
For the glory of the day,
Then we hear a fitful rustling
Just without upon the stair,
See two small white phantoms coming,
Catch the gleam of sunny hair.

Are they Christmas fairies stealing
Rows of little socks to fill?
Are they angels floating hither
With their message of goodwill?
What sweet spell are these elves weaving,
As like larks they chirp and sing?
Are these palms of peace from heaven
That these lovely spirits bring?

Rosy feet upon the threshold,
Eager faces peeping through,
With the first red ray of sunshine,
Chanting cherubs come in view:

Mistletoe and gleaming holly,
Symbols of a blessed day,
In their chubby hands they carry,
Streaming all along the way.

Well we know them, never weary
Of this innocent surprise;
Waiting, watching, listening always
With full hearts and tender eyes,
While our little household angels,
White and golden in the sun,
Greet us with the sweet old welcome,—
"Merry Christmas, everyone!"

A Country Christmas

"*D*ear Emily, I have a brilliant idea and at once hasten to share it with you. Three weeks ago I came up here to the wilds of Vermont to visit my old aunt, also to get a little quiet and distance in which to survey certain new prospects that have opened before me, and to decide whether I will marry a millionaire and become a queen of society or remain 'the charming Miss Vaughan and wait till the conquering hero comes.

"Aunt Plumy begs me to stay over Christmas, and I have consented, as I always dread the formal dinner with which my guardian celebrates the day.

"My brilliant idea is this. I'm going to make it a real old-fashioned frolic, and won't you come and help me? You will enjoy it immensely, I am sure, for Aunt is a character, Cousin Saul worth seeing, and Ruth a far prettier girl than any of the city rosebuds coming out this season. Bring Leonard Randal along with you to take notes for his new books; then it will be fresher and truer than the last, clever as it was.

"The air is delicious up here, society amusing, this old farmhouse full of treasures, and your bosom friend pining to embrace you. Just telegraph yes or no, and we will expect you on Tuesday. Ever yours, Sophie Vaughan"

"They will both come, for they are as tired of city life and as fond of change as I am," said the writer of the above, as she folded her letter and went to get it posted without delay.

Aunt Plumy was in the great kitchen making pies—a jolly old soul, with a face as ruddy as a winter apple, a cheery voice, and the kindest heart that ever beat under a gingham gown. Pretty Ruth was chopping the mince and singing so gaily as she worked that the four-and-twenty immortal blackbirds could not have put more music into a pie than she did.

Saul was piling wood into the big oven, and Sophie paused a moment on the threshold to look at him; for she always enjoyed the sight of this stalwart cousin, whom she likened to a Norse Viking, with his fair hair and beard, keen blue eyes, and six feet of manly height, with shoulders that looked broad and strong enough to bear any burden.

His back was toward her, but he saw her first and turned his flushed face to meet her, with the sudden lighting up it always showed when she approached.

"I've done it, Aunt, and now I want Saul to post the letter, so we can get a speedy answer."

"Just as soon as I can hitch up, cousin," and Saul pitched in his last log.

"Well, dear, I haven't the least mite of objection, as long as it pleases you. I guess we can stand it ef you city folk can. I presume to say things will look kind of sing'lar to 'em, but I suppose that's what they come for. Idle folks do dreadful queer things to amuse 'em," and Aunt Plumy leaned on the rolling pin to smile and nod with a shrewd twinkle of her eye, as if she enjoyed the prospect as much as Sophie did.

"I shall be afraid of them, but I'll try not to make you ashamed of me," said Ruth, who loved her charming cousin.

"No fear of that, dear. They will be the awkward ones, and you must set them at ease by just being your simple selves and treating them as if they were everyday people. Nell is very nice and jolly when she drops her city ways, as she must here. She will enter into the spirit of the fun at once, and I know you'll all like her. Mr. Randall is rather the worse for too much praise and petting, as successful people are apt to be, so a little plain talk and rough work will do him good. He is a true gentleman in spite of his airs and elegance, and he will take it all in good part, if you treat him like a man and not like a lion."

"I'll see to him," said Saul, who had listened with great interest to the latter part of Sophie's speech, evidently suspecting a lover and enjoying the idea of supplying him with a liberal amount of "plain talk and rough work."

"I'll keep 'em busy if that's what they need; for there will be a sight to do, and we can't get help easy up here. Our young men don't hire out much. Work to home till they marry and don't go gaddin' around getting their heads full of foolish notions and forgettin' all the useful things their mothers taught 'em."

Aunt Plumy glanced at Ruth as she spoke, and a sudden color in the girl's cheeks proved that the words hit certain ambitious fancies of this pretty daughter of the house of Basset.

"They shall do their parts and not be a trouble; I'll see to that, for you certainly are the dearest aunt in the world to let me take possession of you and yours in this way," cried Sophie, embracing the old lady with warmth.

Saul wished the embrace could be returned by proxy, as his mother's hands were too floury to do more than hover affectionately 'round the delicate face that looked so fresh and young beside her wrinkled one. As it could not be done, he fled temptation and "hitched up" without delay.

The three women laid their heads together in his absence, and Sophie's plan grew apace, for Ruth longed to see a real novelist and a fine lady, and Aunt Plumy, having plans of her own to further, said "Yes, dear," to every suggestion.

Great was the arranging and adorning that went on that day in the old farmhouse, for Sophie wanted her friends to enjoy this taste of country pleasures and knew just what additions would be indispensable to their comfort, what simple ornaments would be in keeping with the rustic stage on which she meant to play the part of prima donna.

Next day a telegram arrived accepting the invitation, for both the lady and the lion. They would arrive that afternoon, as little preparation was needed for this impromptu journey, the novelty of which was its chief charm to these blasé people.

Saul wanted to get out the double sleigh and span, for he prided himself on his horses; and a fall of snow came most opportunely to beautify the landscape and add a new pleasure to Christmas festivities.

But Sophie declared that the old yellow sleigh, with Punch, the farm horse, must be used, as she wished everything to be in keeping with simple ways. And Saul obeyed, thinking he had never seen anything prettier than his cousin when she appeared in his mother's old-fashioned cloak and blue silk pumpkin hood. He looked remarkably well himself in his fur coat, with hair and beard brushed till they shone like spun gold, a fresh color in his cheek, and the sparkle of amusement in his eyes, while excitement gave his usually grave face the animation it needed to be handsome.

Away they jogged in the creaking old sleigh, leaving Ruth, with a fluttering heart, to make herself pretty and Aunt Plumy to dish up a late dinner fit to tempt the most fastidious appetite.

"She has not come for us, and there is not even a stage to take us up. There must be some mistake," said Emily Herrick, as she looked about the shabby little station where they were set down.

"That is the never-to-be-forgotten face of our fair friend, but the bonnet of her grandmother, if my eyes do not deceive me," answered Randal, turning to survey the couple approaching in the rear.

"Sophie Vaughan, what do you mean by making such a spectacle of yourself?" exclaimed Emily, as she kissed the smiling face in the hood and stared at the quaint cloak.

"I'm dressed for my part, and I intend to keep it up. This is our host, my cousin, Saul Basset. Come to the sleigh at once; he will see to your luggage," said Sophie, painfully conscious of the antiquity of her array as her eyes rested on Emily's pretty hat and mantle and the masculine elegance of Randal's wraps.

They were hardly tucked in when Saul appeared with a valise in one hand and a large trunk on his shoulder, swinging both on to a wood sled that stood nearby as easily as if they had been handbags.

"That is your hero, is it? Well, he looks it: calm and comely, taciturn and tall," said Emily in a tone of approval.

"He should have been named Samson or Goliath, though I believe it was the small man who slung things about and turned out the hero in the end," added Randal, surveying the performance with interest and a touch of envy, for much pen work had made his own hands as delicate as a woman's.

"Saul doesn't live in a glass house, so stones won't hurt him. Remember, sarcasm is forbidden and sincerity the order of the day. You are country folks now, and it will do you good to try their simple, honest ways for a few days."

Sophie had no time to say more, for Saul came up and drove off with the brief remark that the baggage would "be along right away."

Being hungry, cold, and tired, the guests were rather silent during the short drive, but Aunt Plumy's hospitable welcome, and the savory fumes of the dinner awaiting them, thawed the ice and won their hearts at once.

"Isn't it nice? Aren't you glad you came?" asked Sophie, as she led her friends into the parlor, which she had redeemed from its primness by putting bright chintz curtains to the windows, hemlock boughs over the old portraits, a china bowl of flowers on the table and a splendid fire on the wide hearth.

"It is perfectly jolly, and this is the way I begin to enjoy myself," answered Emily, sitting down upon the homemade rug, whose red flannel roses bloomed in a blue list basket.

"If I may add a little smoke to your glorious fire, it will be quite perfect. Won't Samson join me?" asked Randal, waiting for permission, cigar case in hand.

"He has no small vices, but you may indulge yours," answered Sophie from the depths of a chair.

Emily glanced up at her friend, as if she caught a new tone in her voice, then turned to the fire again with a wise little nod, as if confiding some secret to the reflection of herself in the bright brass andiron.

"His Delilah does not take this form. I wait with interest to discover if he has one. What a daisy the sister is. Does she ever speak?" asked Randal, trying to lounge on the sofa where he was uncomfortably shifting about.

"Oh, yes, and sings like a bird. You shall hear her when she gets over her shyness. But no trifling, mind you, for it is a jealously guarded daisy and not to be picked by any idle hand," said

Sophie warningly, as she recalled Ruth's blushes and Randal's compliments at dinner.

"I should expect to be annihilated by the big brother if I attempted any but the 'sincerest' admiration and respect. Have no fears on that score, but tell us what is to follow the superb dinner—a spelling bee, hide and seek, a husking party, or a primitive pastime of some sort, I have no doubt."

"As you are new to our ways, I am going to let you rest this evening. We will sit about the fire and tell stories. Aunt is a master hand at that, and Saul has reminiscences of the war that are well worth hearing if we can only get him to tell them."

"Ah, he was there, was he?"

"Yes, all through it, and is known as Major Basset, though he likes his plain name best. He fought splendidly and had several wounds, though only a mere boy when he earned his scars and bars. I'm very proud of him for that," and Sophie looked so as she glanced at the photograph of a stripling in uniform set in the place of honor on the high mantelpiece.

"We must stir him up and hear these martial memories. I want some new incidents and shall book all I can get if I may."

Here Randal was interrupted by Saul himself, who came in with an armful of wood for the fire.

"Anything more I can do for you, cousin?" he asked, surveying the scene with a rather wistful look.

"Only come and sit with us and talk over war times with Mr. Randal."

"When I've foddered the cattle and done my chores, I'd be pleased to. What regiment were you in?" asked Saul, looking down from his lofty height upon the slender gentleman, who answered briefly:

"In none. I was abroad at the time."

"Sick?"

"No, busy with a novel."

"Took four years to write it?"

"I was obliged to travel and study before I could finish it. These things take more time to work up than outsiders would believe."

"Seems to me our war was a finer story than any you could find in Europe, and the best way to study it would have been to fit in it. If you want heroes and heroines, you'd have found plenty of 'em there."

"I have no doubt of it and shall be glad to atone for my seeming neglect of them by hearing about your own exploits, Major."

Randal hoped to turn the conversation gracefully, but Saul was not to be caught and left the room, saying, with a gleam of fun in his eye:

"I can't stop now. Heroes can wait; pigs can't!"

The girls laughed at this sudden descent from the sublime to the ridiculous, and Randal joined them, feeling his condescension had not been unobserved.

As if drawn by the merry sound, Aunt Plumy appeared, and being established in the rocking chair, fell to talking as easily as if she had known her guests for years.

"Laugh away, young folks. That's better for digestion than any of the medicines people use. Are you troubled with dyspepsia, dear? You didn't seem to take your supper very heartily, so I suppose you must be delicate," she said, looking at Emily, whose pale cheeks and weary eyes told the story of late hours and wasted time.

"I haven't eaten so much for years, I assure you, Mrs. Basset, but it was impossible to taste all your good things. I am not dyspeptic, thank you, but a little tired; for I've been working rather hard lately."

"Be you a teacher, or have you a 'profession,' as they call a trade nowadays?" asked the old lady in a tone of kindly interest, which prevented a laugh at the idea of Emily's being anything but a beauty and a belle. The others kept their composure with difficulty, and Emily answered demurely:

"I have no trade as yet, but I dare say I should be happier if I had."

"Not a doubt on it, my dear."

"What would you recommend, ma'am?"

"I should say dressmaking was rather in your line. Your clothes are very tasty, and do you credit if you made 'em your-self," and Aunt Plumy surveyed with feminine interest the simple elegance of the traveling dress which was the masterpiece of a French modiste.

"No, ma'am, I don't make my own things. I'm too lazy. It takes so much time and trouble to select them that I have only strength left to wear them."

"Housekeepin' used to be the favorite profession in my day. It's not fashionable now, but it needs a sight of trainin' to be perfect in all that's required; and I've an idee it would be a sight healthier and more useful than the paintin' and music and fancy work young women do nowadays."

"But everyone wants some beauty in their lives, and each one has a different sphere to fill, if one can only find it."

"It 'pears to me there's no call for so much art when nature's full of beauty for them that can see and love it. As for 'spheres' and so on, I've a notion if each of us did up our own little chores smart and thorough, we needn't go wandering 'round to set the world to rights. That's the Lord's job, and I presume to say He can do it without any advice of ourn," said Aunt Plumy in her plain-spoken way.

Something in the homely but true words seemed to rebuke the three listeners for wasted lives, and for a moment there was no sound but the crackle of the fire, the brisk click of the old lady's knitting needles, and Ruth's voice singing overhead as she made ready to join the party below.

"To judge by that sweet sound, you have done one of your 'chores' very beautifully, Mrs. Basset, and in spite of the follies of our day, succeeded in keeping one girl healthy, happy, and unspoiled," said Emily, looking up into the peaceful old face with her own lovely one full of respect and envy.

"I do hope so, for she's my ewe lamb, the last of four dear little girls; all the rest are in the burying ground 'side of father. I don't expect to keep her long and don't ought to regret when I lose her, for Saul is the best of sons; but daughters is more to mothers somehow, and I always yearn over girls that is left without someone left to keep 'em safe and warm in this world of tribulation!"

Aunt Plumy laid her hand on Sophie's head as she spoke with such a motherly look that both girls drew nearer, and Randal resolved to put Aunt Plumy in a book without delay.

Presently, Saul returned with little Ruth hanging on his arm and shyly nestling near him as he took the three-cornered leather chair in the chimney nook, while she sat on a stool close by.

"Now the circle is complete and the picture perfect. Don't light the lamps yet, please, but talk away and let me make a mental study of you. I seldom find so charming a scene to paint," said Randal, beginning to enjoy himself immensely, with a true artist's taste for novelty and effect.

"Tell us about your book, for we have been reading it as it comes out in the magazine and are much exercised about how it's going to end," began Saul, gallantly throwing himself into the breach, for a momentary embarrassment fell upon the women at the idea of sitting for their portraits before they were ready.

"Do you really read my poor serial up here and do me the honor to like it?" asked the novelist, both flattered and amused; for his work was of the artistic sort with microscopic studies of character and careful representations of modern life.

"Sakes alive, why shouldn't we?" cried Aunt Plumy. "We have some education, though we aren't real genteel. We've got a town library, kept up by the women, mostly, with fairs and tea parties and so on. We have the major magazines reg'lar, and Saul reads out the pieces while Ruth sews and I knit, my eyes bein' poor. Our winter is long, and evenin's would be kind of lonesome if we didn't have novels and newspapers to cheer us up."

"I am very glad I can help to beguile them for you. Now tell me what you honestly think of my work. Criticism is always valuable, and I should really like yours, Mrs. Basset," said Randal, wondering what the good woman would make of the delicate analysis and worldly wisdom on which he prided himself.

Short work, as Aunt Plumy soon showed him, for she rather enjoyed freeing her mind at all times and decidedly resented the insinuation that country folk could not appreciate literature as well as city people.

"I'm no great jedge about anything but naturalness in books, and it really does seem as if some of your men and women are dreadfully uncomfortable creatures. It 'pears to me it isn't wise to be always picking ourselves to pieces and pryin' into things that ought to come gradual by way of experience and the visitations of Providence. Flowers won't blow worth a cent ef you pull 'em open. Better wait and see what they can do alone. I do relish the smart sayin's, the odd ways of furrin parts, and the sarcastic slaps at folks' weak spots. But I knows, we can't live on spice cake and rouge cheeks, and I do feel as if books was more sustainin' ef they was full of everyday people and things, like good bread and butter. Them that goes to the heart and aren't soon forgotten is the kind I hanker for. Miss Terry's books now, and Miss Stowe's, and Dickens's Christmas pieces—them is real sweet and cheering, to my mind."

As the blunt old lady paused, it was evident she had produced a sensation, for Saul smiled at the fire, Ruth looked dismayed at this assault upon one of her idols; and the young ladies were both astonished and amused at the keenness of the new critic who dared express what they had often felt. Randal, however, was quite composed and laughed good-naturedly, though secretly feeling as if a pail of cold water had been poured over him.

"Many thanks, madam; you have discovered my weak point with surprising accuracy. But you see I cannot help 'picking folks to pieces,' as you have expressed it; that is my gift, and it has its attractions, as the sale of my books will testify. People like the 'spice bread,' and as that is the only sort my oven will bake, I must keep on in order to make my living."

"So a rum seller would say, but it's not a good trade to foller; and I'd chop wood 'fore I'd earn my livin' harmin' my feller man. 'Pears to me I'd let my oven cool a spell, and hunt up some homely, happy folks to write about. I'd write 'bout folks that don't borrow trouble and go lookin' for holes in their neighbors' coats, but take their lives brave and cheerful; and rememberin' we are all human, have pity on the weak and try to be as full of mercy, patience, and lovin'-kindness as Him who made us. That sort of a book would do a heap of good. It'd be real warmin' and strenghenin' and make them that read it love the man who wrote it, and remember him when he was dead and gone."

"I wish I could!" and Randal meant what he said, for he was as tired of his own style as a watchmaker might be of the magnifying glass through which he strains his eyes all day. He knew that the heart was left out of his work, and that both mind and soul were growing morbid with dwelling on the faulty, absurd, and metaphysical phases of life and character. He often threw down his pen and vowed he would write no more; but he loved ease, and the books brought money readily. He was accustomed to the stimulant of praise and missed it as the inebriate misses his wine, so that which had once been a pleasure to himself and others was fast becoming a burden and a disappointment.

The brief pause which followed his involuntary betrayal of discontent was broken by Ruth, who exclaimed, with a girlish enthusiasm that overpowered girlish bashfulness:

"I think all the novels are splendid! I hope you will write hundreds more, and I shall live to read 'em."

"Bravo, my gentle champion! I promise that I will write one more at least, and have a heroine in it whom your mother will both admire and love," answered Randal, surprised to find how grateful he was for the girl's approval, and how rapidly his trained fancy began to paint the background on which he hoped to copy this fresh, human daisy.

Abashed by her involuntary outburst, Ruth tried to efface herself behind Saul's broad shoulder, and he brought the conversation back to its starting point by saying in a tone of the most sincere interest:

"Speaking of the serial, I am very anxious to know how your hero comes out. He is a fine fellow, and I can't decide whether he is going to spoil his life marrying that silly woman, or do something grand and generous, and not be made a fool of."

"Upon my soul, I don't know myself. It is very hard to find new finales. Can't you suggest something, Major? Then I shall not be obliged to leave my story without an end, as people complain I am rather fond of doing."

"Well, no, I don't think I've anything to offer. Seems to me it isn't the sensational exploits that show the hero best, but some great sacrifice quietly made by a common sort of man who is noble without knowing it. I saw a good many such during the war, and often wish I could write them down, for it is surprising how much courage, goodness, and real piety is stowed away in common folks ready to show when the right time comes."

"Tell us one of them, and I'll bless you for a hint. No one knows the anguish of an author's spirit when he can't bring down the curtain on an effective tableau," said Randal, with a glance at his friends to ask their aid in eliciting an anecdote or reminiscence.

"Tell about the splendid fellow who held the bridge, like Horatio, till help came up. That was a thrilling story, I assure you," answered Sophie, with an inviting smile.

But Saul would not be his own hero, and said briefly:

"Any man can be brave when the battle fever is on him, and it only takes a little physical courage to dash ahead." He paused a moment with his eyes on the snowy landscape without, where twilight was deepening; then as if constrained by the memory that winter scene evoked, he slowly continued:

"One of the bravest things I ever knew was done by a poor fellow who has been a hero to me ever since, though I only met him that night. It was after one of the big battles of that last winter, and I was knocked over with a broken leg and two or three bullets here and there. Night was coming on, snow falling, and a sharp wind blew over the field where a lot of us lay, dead and alive, waiting for the ambulance to come and pick us up.

There was skirmishing going on not far off, and our prospects were rather poor between frost and fire.

"I was calculating how I'd manage, when I found two poor chaps close by who were worse off; so I braced up and did what I could for them. One had an arm blown away, and kept up a dreadful groaning. The other was shot bad, and bleeding to death for want of help, but never complained. He was nearest, and I liked his pluck, for he spoke cheerful and made me ashamed to growl. Such times make dreadful brutes of men if they haven't something to hold on to, and all three of us were most wild with pain and cold and hunger, for we'd fought all day fasting, when we heard a rumble in the road below, and saw lanterns bobbing 'round. That meant little to us, and we all tried to holler; two of us were pretty faint, but I managed a good yell, and they heard it.

"'Room for one more. Hard luck, old boys, but we are full and must save the worst wounded first. Take a drink, and hold on till we come back,' says one of them with the stretcher.

"'Here's the one to go,' I says, pointin' out my man, for I saw by the light that he was hard hit.

"'No, that one. He's got more chances than I, or this one; he's young and got a mother; I'll wait,' said the good feller, touchin' my arm, for he'd heard me mutterin' to myself about this dear old lady. We always want Mother when we are down, you know."

Saul's eyes turned to the beloved face with a glance of tenderest affection, and Aunt Plumy answered with a dismal groan at the recollection of his need that night and her absence.

"Well, to be short, the groaning chap was taken, and my man left. I was mad, but there was no time for talk; and the selfish one went off and left that poor feller to run his one chance. I had my rifle and guessed I could hobble up to use it, if need be. So we settled back to wait without much hope of help, everything being in a muddle. And wait we did, till morning; for that ambulance did not come back till next day when most of us were past needing it.

"I'll never forget that night. I dream it all over again as plain as if it was real. Snow, cold, darkness, hunger, thirst, pain, and all 'round us cries and cursing growing less and less, till at last only the wind went moaning over that meadow. It was awful! So lonesome, helpless, and seemingly godforsaken. Hour after hour we lay there side by side under one coat, waiting to be saved or die, for the wind grew strong and we grew weak."

Saul drew a long breath and held his hands to the fire as if he felt again the sharp suffering of that night.

"And the man?" asked Emily, softly, as if reluctant to break the silence.

"He *was* a man! In times like that men talk like brothers and show what they are. Lying there, slowly freezing, Joe Cummings told me about his wife and babies, his old folks waiting for him, all depending on him, yet all ready to give him up when he was needed. A plain man, but honest and true, and loving as a woman. I soon saw that as he went on talking, half to me and half to himself, for sometimes he wandered a little toward the end.

"I've read books, heard sermons, and seen good folks, but nothing ever came so close or did me so much good as seeing this man die. He had one chance and gave it cheerfully. He longed for those he loved, and let 'em go with a good-bye they couldn't hear. He suffered all the pains we most shrink from without a murmur and kept my heart warm while his own was growing cold. It's no use trying to tell that part of it; but I heard prayers that night that meant something, and I saw how faith could hold a soul up when everything was gone but God."

Saul stopped there with a sudden huskiness in his deep voice, and when he went on, it was in the tone of one who speaks of a dear friend.

"Joe grew still by and by, and I thought he was asleep; for I felt his breath when I tucked him up, and his hand held on to mine. The cold sort of numbed me, and I dropped off, too weak and stupid to think or feel. I never should have waked up if it hadn't been for Joe. When I came to, it was morning, and I thought I was dead, for all I could see was that great field of white mounds, like graves, and a splendid sky above. Then I looked at Joe, remembering. But he had put my coat back over me and lay stiff and still under the snow that covered him like a shroud, all except his face. A bit of my cape had blown over it, and when I took it off and the sun shone on his dead face, I declare to you it was so full of heavenly peace I felt as if that common man had been glorified by God's light, and rewarded by God's 'Well done.' That's all."

No one spoke for a moment, while the women wiped their eyes and Saul dropped his as if to hide something softer than tears.

"It was very noble, very touching. And you? How did you get off at last?" asked Randal, with real admiration and respect in his usually languid face.

"Crawled off," answered Saul, relapsing into his former brevity of speech.

"Why not before, and save yourself all that misery?"

"Couldn't leave Joe."

"Ah, I see. There were two heroes that night."

"Dozens, I've no doubt. Those were times that made heroes of men and women, too."

"Tell us more," begged Emily, looking up with an expression none of her admirers ever brought to her face by their softest compliments or wiliest gossip.

"I've done my part. It's Mr. Randal's turn now"; and Saul drew himself out of the ruddy circle of firelight, as if ashamed of the prominent part he was playing.

Sophie and her friend had often heard Randal talk, for he was an accomplished *raconteur*, but that night he exerted himself, and was unusually brilliant and entertaining, as if upon his mettle. The Bassets were charmed. They sat late and were very merry, for Aunt Plumy got up a little supper for them. Her cider was good and warmed them. When they parted for the night and Sophie kissed her aunt, Emily did the same, saying heartily:

"It seems as if I'd known you all my life, and this is certainly the most enchanting old place that ever was."

"Glad you like it, dear. But it isn't all fun, as you'll find out tomorrow when you go to work, for Sophie says you must," answered Mrs. Basset, as her guests trooped away, rashly promising to like everything.

They found it difficult to keep their word when they were called at half past six next morning. Their rooms were warm, however, and they managed to scramble down in time for breakfast, guided by the fragrance of coffee and Aunt Plumy's shrill voice singing the good old hymn:

"Lord, in the morning Thou shalt hear my voice ascending high."

An open fire blazed on the hearth; for the cooking was done in the lean-to, and the spacious, sunny kitchen was kept in all its old-fashioned perfection, with the wooden settle in a warm nook, the tall clock behind the door, copper and pewter utensils shining on the dresser, old china in the corner closet, and a little spinning wheel rescued from the garret by Sophie to adorn the deep window, full of scarlet geraniums, Christmas roses, and white chrysanthemums.

The young lady herself, in a checked apron and cap, greeted her friends with a dish of buckwheat pancakes in one hand and a pair of cheeks that proved she had been learning to fry these delectable cakes.

"You do 'keep it up' in earnest, upon my word; and very becoming it is, dear. But won't you ruin your complexion and roughen your hands if you do so much of this new fancywork?" asked Emily, much amazed at this novelty.

"I like it, and really believe I've found my proper sphere at last. Domestic life seems so pleasant to me that I feel as if I'd better keep it up for the rest of my life," answered Sophie, making a pretty picture of herself as she cut great slices of brown bread, with the early sunshine touching her happy face.

"The charming Miss Vaughan in the role of a farmer's wife. I find it difficult to imagine and shrink from the thought of the widespread dismay such a fate will produce among her adorers," added Randal, as he basked in the glow of the hospitable fire.

"She might do worse; but come to breakfast and do honor to my handiwork," said Sophie, thinking of her worn-out million-aire and rather nettled by the satiric smile on Randal's lips.

"What an appetite early rising gives one. I feel equal to almost anything, so let me help wash cups," said Emily, with unusual energy, when the hearty meal was over and Sophie began to pick up the dishes as if it was her usual work.

Ruth went to the window to water the flowers, and Randal followed to make himself agreeable, remembering her deference of him last night. He was used to admiration from feminine eyes and flattery from soft lips, but found something new and charming in the innocent delight, which showed itself at his approach, in blushes more eloquent than words and shy glances from eyes full of hero-worship.

"I hope you are going to spare me a posy for tomorrow night, since I can be fine in no other way to do honor to the dance Miss Sophie proposes for us," he said, leaning in the bay window to look down on the little girl, with the devoted air he usually wore for pretty women.

"Anything you like! I should be so glad to have you wear my flowers. There will be enough for all, and I've nothing else to give to people who have made me as happy as cousin Sophie and you," answered Ruth, half drowning her great calla as she spoke with grateful warmth.

"You must make her happy by accepting the invitation to go home with her, which I heard given last night. A peep at the world would do you good and be a pleasant change, I think."

"Oh, very pleasant! But would it do me good?" and Ruth looked up with sudden seriousness in her blue eyes, as a child questions an elder: eager, yet wistful.

"Why not?" asked Randal, wondering at the hesitation.

"I might grow discontented with things here if I saw splendid houses and fine people. I am very happy now, and it would break my heart to lose that happiness, or ever learn to be ashamed of home."

"But don't you long for more pleasure, new scenes and other friends than these?" asked the man, touched by the little creature's loyalty to the things she knew and loved.

"Very often, but mother says when I'm ready they will come, so I wait and try not to be impatient." But Ruth's eyes looked out over the green leaves as if the longing was very strong within her to see more of the unknown world lying beyond the mountains that hemmed her in.

"It is natural for a bird to hop out of the nest, so I shall expect to see you over there before long, and ask you how you enjoy your first flight," said Randal, in a paternal tone that had a curious effect on Ruth.

To his surprise, she laughed, then blushed like one of her own roses, and answered with a demure dignity that was very pretty to see.

"I intend to hop soon, but it won't be a very long flight or very far from mother. She can't spare me, and nobody in the world can fill her place to me."

Bless the child; does she think I'm in love with her? thought Randal, much amused but quite mistaken. Wiser women had thought so when he assumed the caressing air with which he beguiled them into the little revelations of character he liked to use, as the south wind makes flowers open their hearts to give up their odor, then leaves them to carry it elsewhere, the more welcome for the stolen sweetness.

"Perhaps you are right. The maternal wing is a safe shelter for confiding little souls like you, Miss Ruth. You will be as comfortable here as your flowers in this sunny window," he said, carelessly pinching geranium leaves, and ruffling the roses till the pink petals of the largest fluttered to the floor.

As if she instinctively felt and resented something in the man that his act symbolized, the girl answered quietly, as she went on with her work, "Yes, if the frost does not touch me, or careless people spoil me too soon."

Before Randal could reply, Aunt Plumy approached like a maternal hen who sees her chicken in danger.

"Saul is goin' to haul wood after he's done his chores. Mebbe you'd like to go along? The view is good, the roads well broke, and the day uncommon fine."

"Thanks; it will be delightful, I dare say," politely responded the lion, with a secret shudder at the idea of a rural promenade at 8 A.M. in the winter.

"Come on, then; we'll feed the stock, and then I'll show you how to yoke oxen," said Saul, with a twinkle in his eye as he led the way when his new aide had muffled himself up as if for a polar voyage.

"Now, that's too bad of Saul! He did it on purpose, just to please you, Sophie," cried Ruth presently, and the girls ran to the window to behold Randal bravely following his host with a pail of pigs' food in each hand, and an expression of resigned disgust upon his aristocratic face.

"To what base uses may we come," quoted Emily, as they all nodded and smiled upon the victim as he looked back from the barnyard where he was clamorously welcomed by his new charges.

"It is rather a shock at first, but it will do him good; and Saul won't be too hard upon him, I'm sure," said Sophie, going back to her work, while Ruth turned her best buds to the sun that they might be ready for a peace offering tomorrow.

There was a merry clatter in the big kitchen for an hour; then Aunt Plumy and her daughter shut themselves up in the pantry to perform certain culinary rites, and the young ladies went to inspect certain antique costumes laid forth in Sophie's room.

"You see, Emily, I thought it would be appropriate to the house and season to have an old-fashioned dance. Aunt has quantities of ancient finery stowed away, for great-grandfather Basset was a fine old gentleman and his family lived in state. Take your choice of the crimson, blue, or silver-gray damask.

Ruth is to wear the worked muslin and quilted white satin skirt with the coquettish hat."

"Being dark, I'll take the red and trim it up with this fine lace. You must wear the blue and primrose, with the distracting high-heeled shoes. Have you any suits for the men?" asked Emily, throwing herself at once in the all-absorbing matter of costume.

"A claret velvet coat and vest, silk stockings, cocked hat and snuffbox for Randal. Nothing large enough for Saul, so he must wear his uniform. Won't Aunt Plumy be superb in this plum-colored satin and immense cap?"

A delightful morning was spent in adapting the faded finery of the past to the blooming beauty of the present, and time and tongues flew till the toot of a horn called them down to dinner.

The girls were amazed to see Randal come whistling up the road with his trousers tucked into his boots, blue mittens on his hands, and an unusual amount of energy in his whole figure, as he drove the oxen, while Saul laughed at his vain attempts to guide the bewildered beasts.

"It's immense! The view from the hill is well worth seeing, for the snow glorifies the landscape and reminds one of Switzerland. I'm going to make a sketch of it this afternoon. Better come and enjoy the delicious freshness, young ladies."

Randal was eating with such an appetite that he did not see the glances the girls exchanged as they promised to go.

"Bring home some more wintergreen; I want things to be real nice, and we haven't enough for the kitchen," said Ruth, dimpling with girlish delight as she imagined herself dancing under the green garlands in her grandmother's wedding gown.

It was very lovely on the hill, for far as the eye could reach lay the wintry landscape sparkling with brief beauty of sunshine on virgin snow. Pines sighed overhead, hardy birds flitted to and

fro, and, in all the trodden spots rose the little spires of evergreen ready for its Christmas duty. Deeper in the woods sounded
the measured ring of axes, the crash of falling trees, while the red
shirts of the men added color to the scene and a fresh wind
brought the aromatic breath of newly cloven hemlock and pine.

"How beautiful it is! I never knew before what a winter
woods was like. Did you, Sophie?" asked Emily, sitting on a
stump to enjoy the novel pleasure at her ease.

"I've found out lately," answered Sophie, looking about
her with sparkling eyes, as if this was a kingdom where she
reigned supreme.

"Something is making a new creature of you; that is very
evident. I haven't yet discovered whether it is the air or some
magic herb among that green stuff you are gathering so dili-
gently," and Emily laughed to see the color deepen beautifully in
her friend's half-averted face.

"Scarlet is the only wear just now, I find. If we are lost like
babes in the woods, there are plenty of redbreasts to cover us
with leaves," and Randal joined Emily's laugh, with a glance at
Saul, who had just pulled his coat off.

"You wanted to see this tree go down, so stand from under,
and I'll show you how it's done," said the farmer, taking up his
axe, not unwilling to gratify his guests and display his manly
accomplishments at the same time.

It was a fine sight: the stalwart man swinging his axe with
magnificent skill, each blow sending a thrill through the stately
tree, till its heart was reached and it tottered to its fall. Never
pausing for breath, Saul shook his yellow mane out of his eyes
and hewed away, while the drops stood on his forehead and his
arm ached, as bent on distinguishing himself as if he had been a
knight against his rival for his lady's favor.

"I don't know which to admire most, the man or his muscle. One doesn't often see such vigor, size, and comeliness in these degenerate days," said Randal, mentally booking the fine figure in the red shirt.

"I think we have discovered a rough diamond. I only wonder if Sophie is going to try to polish it," answered Emily, glancing at her friend, who stood a little apart, watching the rise and fall of the axe intently as if her fate depended on it.

Down rushed the tree at last, and, leaving them to examine a crow's nest in its branches, Saul went off to his men, as if he found the praises of his prowess rather too much for him.

Randal fell to sketching, the girls to their garland-making, and for a little while, the sunny woodland nook was full of lively chat and pleasant laughter; for the air exhilarated them all like wine. Suddenly, a man came running from the woods, pale and anxious, saying, as he hastened by for help, "Blasted tree fell on him! Bleed to death before the doctor comes!"

"Who? Who?" cried the startled trio.

But the man ran on, with some breathless reply, in which only a name was audible—"Basset."

"The deuce it is!" and Randal dropped his pencil, while the girls sprang up in dismay. Then, with one impulse, they hastened to the distant group, half visible behind the fallen trees and corded wood.

Sophie was there first, and forcing her way through the little crowd of men, saw a red-shirted figure on the ground, crushed and bleeding, and threw herself down beside it with a cry that pierced the hearts of those who heard it. In the act, she saw it was not Saul and covered her bewildered face as if to hide its joy. A strong arm lifted her, and the familiar voice said cheeringly:

123

"I'm all right, dear. Poor Bruce is hurt, but we've sent for help. Better go right home and forget all about it."

"Yes, I will, if I can do nothing," and Sophie meekly returned to her friends, who stood outside the circle over which Saul's head towered, assuring them of his safety.

Hoping they had not seen her agitation, she led Emily away, leaving Randal to give what aid he could and bring them news of the poor woodchopper's condition.

Aunt Plumy produced the smelling salts the moment she saw Sophie's pale face and made her lie down. Then the brave old lady trudged briskly off with bandages and brandy to the scene of action. On her return she brought comforting news of the man, so the little flurry blew over and was forgotten by all but Sophie, who remained pale and quiet all the evening, tying evergreens with great concentration.

"A good night's sleep will set her up. She isn't used to such things, dear child, and needs comfortin'," said Aunt Plumy, purring over her until she was in her bed with a hot stone to warm her feet and a bowl of herb tea to quiet her nerves.

An hour later when Emily went up, she peeped in to see if Sophie was sleeping nicely and was surprised to find the invalid wrapped in a dressing gown writing busily.

"Last will and testament, or sudden inspiration, dear? How are you? Faint or feverish, delirious or in the dumps! Saul looks so anxious, and Mrs. Basset hushes us all up so, I came to bed, leaving Randal to entertain Ruth."

As she spoke Emily saw the papers disappear in a portfolio, and Sophie rose with a yawn.

"I was writing letters, but I'm sleepy now. Quite over my foolish fright, thank you. Go get your beauty sleep that you may dazzle the natives tomorrow."

"So glad; good night"; and Emily went away, saying to herself, "Something is going on, and I must find out what it is before I leave. Sophie can't blind *me*."

But Sophie did all the next day, being delightfully gay at the dinner and devoting herself to the young minister who was invited to meet the distinguished novelist, and evidently being afraid of him, gladly basked in the smiles of his charming neighbor. A dashing sleigh ride occupied the afternoon, and then great was the fun and excitement over the costumes.

Aunt Plumy laughed till the tears rolled down her cheeks as the girls compressed her into the plum-colored gown with its short waist, leg-of-mutton sleeves, and narrow skirt. But a fancy scarf hid all deficiencies, and the towering cap struck awe into the soul of the most frivolous observer.

"Keep an eye on me, girls, for I shall certainly split somewheres or lose my headpiece when I'm trottin' 'round. What would my blessed mother say if she could see me rigged out in her best things?" and with a smile and a sigh, the old lady departed to look after "the boys," and see that the supper was all right.

Three prettier damsels never tripped down the wide staircase than the brilliant brunette in crimson brocade, the pensive blonde in blue, or the rosy bride in old muslin and white satin.

A gallant court gentleman met them in the hall with a superb bow and escorted them to the parlor, where Grandma Basset's ghost was discovered dancing with a modern major in full uniform.

Mutual admiration and many compliments followed, till other ancient ladies and gentlemen arrived in all manner of queer costumes, and the old house seemed to wake from its humdrum quietude to sudden music and merriment, as if a past generation had returned to keep its Christmas there.

The village fiddler soon struck up the good old tunes, and then the strangers saw dancing that filled them with mingled mirth and envy—it was so droll, yet so hearty. The young men—unusually awkward in their grandfathers' knee breeches, flapping vests, and swallow-tail coats—footed it bravely with the buxom girls, who were the prettier for their quaintness and danced with such vigor that their high combs stood awry, their furbelows waved wildly, and their cheeks were as red as their hair knots, or hose.

It was impossible to stand still, and one after the other, the city folk yielded to the spell, Randal leading off with Ruth, Sophie swept away by Saul, and Emily being taken possession of by a young giant of eighteen, who spun her around with a boyish impetuosity that took her breath away. Even Aunt Plumy was discovered jigging it alone in the pantry, as if the music was too much for her, and the plates and glasses jingled gaily on the shelves in time to "Money Musk" and "Fishers' Hornpipe."

A pause came at last, however, and fans fluttered, heated brows were wiped, jokes were made, lovers exchanged confidences, and every nook and corner held a man and maid carrying on the sweet game that is never out of fashion. There was a glitter of gold lace in the back entry, and a train of blue and primrose shone in the dim light. There was a richer crimson than that of the geraniums in the deep window, and a dainty shoe tapped the bare floor impatiently as the brilliant black eyes looked everywhere for the court gentleman, while their owner listened to the gruff prattle of an enamored boy. But in the upper hall walked a little white ghost as if waiting for some shadowy companion, and when a dark form appeared, ran to take its arm, saying, in a tone of soft satisfaction:

"I was so afraid you wouldn't come!"

"Why did you leave me, Ruth?" answered a manly voice in a tone of surprise, though the small hand slipping from the velvet coat sleeve was replaced as if it was pleasant to feel it there.

A pause, and then the other voice answered demurely:

"Because I was afraid my head would be turned by the fine things you were saying."

"It is impossible to help saying what one feels to such an artless little creature as you are. It does me good to admire anything so fresh and sweet and won't harm you."

"It might if—"

"If what, my daisy?"

"I believed it," and a laugh seemed to finish the broken sentence better than the words.

"You may, Ruth, for I do sincerely admire the most genuine girl I have seen for a long time. And walking here with you in your bridal white I was just asking myself if I should not be a happier man with a home of my own and a little wife hanging on my arm than drifting about the world as I do now with only myself to care for."

"I know you would!" and Ruth spoke so earnestly that Randal was both touched and startled, fearing he had ventured too far in a mood of unwonted sentiment, born of the romance of the hour and the sweet frankness of his companion.

"Then you don't think it would be rash for some sweet woman to take me in hand and make me happy, since fame is a failure?"

"Oh, no; it would be easy work if she loved you. I know someone—if I only dared to tell her name."

"Upon my soul, this is cool," and Randal looked down, wondering if the audacious lady on his arm could be shy Ruth.

If he had seen the malicious merriment in her eyes, he would have been more humiliated still; but they were modestly averted, and the face under the little hat was full of a soft agitation rather dangerous even to a man of the world.

"She is a captivating little creature, but it is too soon for anything but a mild flirtation. I must delay further innocent revelations, or I shall do something rash." While making this excellent resolution, Randal had been pressing the hand upon his arm and gently pacing down the dimly lighted hall with the sound of music in his ears, Ruth's sweetest roses in his buttonhole, and a loving little girl beside him, as he thought.

"You shall tell me by and by when we are in town. I am sure you will come, and meanwhile don't forget me."

"I am going in the spring, but I shall not be with Sophie," answered Ruth, in a whisper.

"With whom then? I shall long to see you."

"With my husband. I am to be married in May."

"The deuce you are!" escaped Randal, as he stopped short to stare at his companion, sure she was not in earnest.

But she was, for as he looked the sound of steps coming up the back stairs made her whole face flush and brighten with the unmistakable glow of happy love, and she completed Randal's astonishment by running into the arms of the young minister, saying, with an irrepressible laugh, "Oh, John, why didn't you come before?"

The court gentleman was all right in a moment, and the coolest of the three as he offered his congratulations and gracefully retired, leaving the lovers to enjoy the tryst he had delayed. But as he went downstairs, his brows were knit, and he slapped the broad railing smartly with his cocked hat as if some irritation must find vent in a more energetic way than merely saying "Confound the little baggage!" under his breath.

Such an amazing supper came from Aunt Plumy's big pantry that the city guests could not eat for laughing at the queer dishes circulating through the rooms, being partaken of by the hearty young folks of the party.

Doughnuts and cheese, pie and pickles, cider and tea, baked beans and custards, cake and cold turkey, bread and butter, plum pudding and French bonbons, Sophie's contribution.

"May I offer you the native delicacies, and share your plate? Both are very good, but the china has run short, and after such vigorous exercise as you have had, you must need refreshment."

"I'm sure I do!" said Randal, bowing before Emily with a great blue platter laden with two doughnuts, two wedges of pumpkin pie and two spoons.

The smile with which she welcomed him, the alacrity with which she made room beside her and seemed to enjoy the supper he brought, was so soothing to his ruffled spirit that he soon began to feel that there is no friend like an old friend, that it would not be difficult to name a sweet woman who would take him in hand and would make him happy, if he cared to ask her. And he began to think he would by and by; it was so pleasant to sit in that green corner with waves of crimson brocade flowing over his feet and a fine face softening beautifully under his eyes.

The supper was not romantic, but the situation was, and Emily found the pie to be ambrosial food eaten with the man she loved, whose eyes talked more eloquently than the tongue just then busy with a doughnut. Ruth kept away but glanced at them as she served her company, and her own happy experience helped her to see that all was going well in another romantic quarter.

Saul and Sophie emerged from the back entry with shining countenances, but carefully avoided each other for the rest of the evening. No one observed this but Aunt Plumy from the recesses of her pantry, and she folded her hands as if well content, as she murmured fervently over a pan full of crullers, "Bless the dears! Now I can die happy."

Everyone thought Sophie's old-fashioned dress immensely becoming, and several of his former men said to Saul with blunt admiration, "Major, you look tonight as you used to after we'd gained a victory."

"I feel as if I had," answered the splendid major, with eyes much brighter than his buttons, and a heart under them infinitely prouder than when he was promoted on the field of honor. For his Waterloo was won.

There was more dancing, followed by games, in which Aunt Plumy shone preeminent now that the supper was off her mind and she could enjoy herself. There were shouts of merriment as the blithe old lady played the old-fashioned games like a girl of sixteen; her cap in a ruinous condition, and every seam of the purple dress straining like sails in a gale. It was great fun, but at midnight it came to an end. And the young folks, still bubbling over with innocent jollity, went jingling away along the snowy hills, unanimously pronouncing Mrs. Basset's party the best of the season.

"Never had such a good time in my life!" exclaimed Sophie, as the family stood together in the kitchen where the candles among the wreaths were going out, and the floor was strewn with wrecks of the night's joy.

"I'm proper glad, dear. Now you all go to bed and lay as late as you like tomorrow. I'm so kinder worked up I couldn't sleep, so Saul and me will put things to rights without a mite of noise to disturb you," and Aunt Plumy sent them off with a smile that was a benediction, Sophie thought.

"The dear old soul speaks as if midnight was an unheard-of hour for Christians to be up. What would she say if she knew how we seldom go to bed till dawn in the ball season? I'm so wide awake I've half a mind to pack a little. Randal must go at two, he says, and we shall want his escort," said Emily, as the girls laid away their brocades in the press in Sophie's room.

"I'm not going. Aunt can't spare me, and there is nothing to go for yet," answered Sophie, beginning to take the white chrysanthemums out of her pretty hair.

"My dear child, you will die of boredom up here. Very nice for a week or so, but frightful for a winter. We are going to be very jolly and cannot get on without you," cried Emily dismayed at the suggestion.

"You will have to, for I'm not coming. I am very happy here, and so tired of the frivolous life I lead in town that I have decided to try a better one," and Sophie's mirror reflected a face full of the sweetest content.

"Have you lost your mind? Experienced religion? Or any other dreadful thing? You always were odd, but this last mystery is the strangest of all. What will your guardian say, and the world?" added Emily in the awestricken tone of one who stood in fear of the unknown.

"My guardian will be glad to be rid of me, and I don't mind that for the world," cried Sophie, snapping her fingers with a joyful sort of recklessness that completed Emily's bewilderment.

"But Mr. Hammond? Are you going to throw away millions, lose your chance of making the best match in the city, and drive the girls of our set out of their wits with envy?"

Sophie laughed at her friend's despairing cry and turning around said quietly:

"I wrote to Mr. Hammond last night, and this evening received my reward for being an honest girl. Saul and I are to be married in the spring when Ruth is."

Emily fell prone upon the bed as if the announcement was too much for her, but was up again in an instant to declare with prophetic solemnity:

"I knew something was going on but hoped to get you away before you were lost. Sophie. You will repent. Be warned and forget this sad delusion."

"Too late for that. The pang I suffered yesterday when I thought Saul was dead showed me how well I loved him. Tonight he asked me to stay, and no power in the world can part us. Oh! Emily, it is all so sweet, so beautiful, that *everything* is possible, and I know I shall be happy in this dear old home, full of love and peace and honest hearts. I only hope you may find as true and tender a man to live for as my Saul."

Sophie's face was more eloquent than her fervent words, and Emily beautifully illustrated the inconsistency of her sex by suddenly embracing her friend, with the incoherent exclamation, "I think I have, dear! Your brave Saul is worth a dozen old Hammonds, and I do believe you are right."

It is unnecessary to tell how, as if drawn by the irresistible magic of sympathy, Ruth and her mother crept in one by one to join the midnight conference and add their smiles and tears, tender hopes, and proud delight to the joys of that memorable hour.

Peace fell upon the old house at last, and all slept as if some magic herb had touched their eyelids, bringing blissful dreams and a glad awakening.

"Can't we persuade you to come with us, Sophie?" asked Randal next day, as they made their adieux.

"I'm under orders now and dare not disobey my superior officer," answered Sophie, handing Saul his driving gloves, with a look which plainly showed that she had joined the great army of devoted women who enlist for life and ask no pay but love.

"I shall depend on being invited to your wedding, then, and yours, too, Miss Ruth," added Randal, shaking hands with "the little baggage," as if he had quite forgiven her mockery and forgotten his own brief lapse into sentiment.

Before Ruth could reply Aunt Plumy said, in a tone of calm conviction that made them all laugh and some of them look consideringly:

"Spring is a good time for weddin's, and I shouldn't wonder ef there was quite a number."

"Nor I," said Saul, while Sophie smiled at the way Randal carefully arranged Emily's wraps.

Then, with kisses, thanks, and all the good wishes that happy hearts could imagine, the guests drove away to remember long and gratefully that pleasant country Christmas.

Gwen's Adventure in the Snow

"Gwen, it looks so much like snow I think it would be wise to put off your sleighing party," said Mrs. Arnold, fretfully looking out at the heavy sky and streets still drifted by the last winter storm.

"Not before night, Mamma. We don't mind its being cloudy; we like it, because the sun makes the snow so dazzling when we get out of town. We can't give it up now, for here comes Patrick with the boys." And Gwen ran down to welcome the big sleigh, which just then drove up with four jolly lads skirmishing about inside.

"Come on!" called Mark, her brother, knocking his friends right and left to make room for the four girls who were to complete the party.

"What do you think of the weather, Patrick?" asked Mrs. Arnold from the window, still undecided about the wisdom of letting her flock go off alone, Papa having been called away after the plan had been made.

"Faith, Ma'am, it's an elegant day, if not fer the wind that's a trifle cold for the nose. I'll have me eye on the children, Ma'am, and there'll be no trouble at all, at all," replied the faithful coach-man, lifting a red muffler around his face and patting little Gus on the shoulder as he sat proudly on the high seat holding the whip.

"Be careful, dears, and come home early."

With which parting caution Mamma shut the window and watched the young folks drive gaily away, little dreaming what would happen before they got back.

The wind was more than a trifle cold, for when they got out of the city it blew across the open country in bitter blasts and made the bright little noses almost as red as the driver's whose face jutted cheerfully in the wind. The truth is, Patrick just loved driving at anytime, whether there was any danger or not.

When the lively crew had gotten out into the open country, the coachman stopped near a snowdrift. The lads enjoyed them-selves immensely snowballing one another, for the drifts were still fresh enough to furnish soft snow; and Mark, Bob, and Tony had many a friendly tussle in it as they went up hills or paused to rest the horses after a swift trot along a level bit of road.

Little Gus helped drive till his hands were benumbed in spite of the new red mittens, and he had to descend among the girls, who were cuddled cozily under the warm robes, telling secrets, eating candy, and laughing at the older boys' pranks.

Sixteen-year-old Gwendoline was matron of the party and kept excellent order among the girls, for Ruth and Alice were nearly her own age and Rita a most obedient younger sister.

"I say, Gwen, we are going to stop at the summerhouse on the way home and get some nuts for this evening. Papa said we might, and some of the big walnuts too. I've got baskets, and while we fellows fill them, you girls can look 'round the house," said Mark when the exhausted young gentlemen returned to their seats.

"That will be nice. I want to get some books, and Rita has been very anxious about one of her dolls, which she is sure was left in the nursery closet. If we are going to stop, we ought to be turning back, Pat, for it is beginning to snow and will be dark early," warned Gwen, suddenly realizing that great flakes were fast whitening the roads and the wind had risen to a gale.

"Sure, and I will, miss dear, as soon as I can. But it's 'round a good bit we must go, for I couldn't be turning the sleigh without upsettin' the whole of you; it's that drifted. Rest easy, and I'll fetch up at the old place in half an hour," said Pat, who had lost his way and wouldn't own it, being embarrassed at the turn of events.

On they went again, with the wind at their backs, caring little for the snow that now fell fast, or the gathering twilight, since they were going toward home, they thought. It was a very long half-hour before Pat brought them to the country house, which was shut up for the winter. With difficulty they ploughed their way up to the steps and scrambled on to the piazza, where they danced about to warm their feet till Mark unlocked the door and let them in, leaving Pat to enjoy a doze on his seat.

"Make haste, boys; it is cold and dark here, and we must get home. Mamma will be so anxious, and it really is going to be a bad storm," said Gwen, whose spirits were damped by the gloom of the old house, and who felt her responsibility, having promised to be home early.

Off went the boys to attic and cellar, being obliged to light the lantern left there for the use of whoever came now and then to inspect the premises. The girls, having found books and a doll, sat upon the rolled up carpets or peeped about at the once gay and hospitable rooms, now looking very empty and desolate with piled-up furniture, shuttered windows, and fireless hearths.

"If we were going to stay long, I'd have a fire in the library. Papa often does when he comes out to keep the books from moldering," began Gwen, but was interrupted by a shout from without, and—running to the door—saw Pat picking himself out of a drift while the horses went galloping down the avenue at full speed.

"Bejabbers, the horses gave a jump when that fallin' branch struck 'em, and out I went, being taken off guard by their fright. Don't worry now, dear! I'll fetch 'em back in a jiffy. Stop still till I come, and keep those boys busy."

With a blow to settle his hat, Patrick trotted gallantly away into the storm, and the girls went in to tell the exciting news to the lads, who came whooping back from their search with baskets of nuts and apples.

"Here's a go!" cried Mark. "Pat will run halfway to town before he catches the horses, and we are in for an hour or two at least."

"Then do make a fire, for we shall die of cold if we have to wait long," begged Gwen, rubbing Rita's cold hands and looking anxiously at little Gus, who was about making up his mind to cry.

"So we will, and be jolly till Patrick catches the horses. Camp down, girls, and you fellows, come and hold the lantern while I get wood and stuff. It is so confoundedly dark, I shall break my neck down the shed steps." And Mark led the way to the library where the carpet still remained and comfortable chairs and sofas invited the chilly visitors to rest.

"How can you light your fire when you get the wood?" asked Ruth, a practical damsel, who looked well after her own creature comforts and was longing for a warm supper.

"Papa hides the matches in a tin box, so the mice won't get at them. Here they are, and two or three bits of candle for the sticks on the chimney piece, if he forgets to have the lantern trimmed. Now we will light up and look cozy when the boys come back."

And producing the box from under a sofa cushion, Gwen cheered the hearts of all by lighting two candles, rolling up the chairs, and making ready to be comfortable. Thoughtful Alice went to see if Pat was returning and found a buffalo robe lying on the steps. Returning with this, she reported that there was no sign of the runaways and advised them to make ready for a long stay.

How Mamma will worry! thought Gwen, but made light of the affair, because she saw Rita looked timid, and Gus shivered till his teeth chattered.

"We will have a nice time and play we are shipwrecked people or Artic explorers. Here comes the captain and the sailors with supplies of food, so we can thaw our pemmican and warm our feet. Gus shall be the little Inuit boy, all dressed in fur, as he is in the picture we have at home," she said, wrapping the child

139

in the robe and putting her own sealskin cap on his head to divert his mind.

"Here we are! Now for a jolly blaze, boys; and if Pat doesn't come back, we can have our fun here instead of home," cried Mark, well pleased with the adventure as were his mates.

So they fell to work, and soon a bright fire was lighting up the room with its cheerful shine, and the children gathered about it, quite careless of the storm raging without and sure that Pat would come shortly.

"I'm hungry," complained Gus as soon as he was warm.

"So am I," added Rita from the rug where the two little ones sat basting themselves.

"Eat an apple," said Mark.

"They are so hard and cold I don't like them," began Gus.

"Roast some!" cried Ruth.

"And crack nuts," suggested Alice. "Pity we can't cook something in real camp style, it would be such fun," said Tony, who had spent weeks on Monadnock living upon the supplies he and his party tugged up the mountain on their backs.

"We shall not have time for anything but what we have. Put down your apples and crack away, or we shall be obliged to leave them," advised Gwen, coming back from an observation at the front door with an anxious line on her forehead; for the storm was rapidly increasing, and there was no sign of Pat or the horses.

The rest were in high glee, and an hour or two slipped quickly away as they enjoyed the impromptu feast and played games. Gus recalled them to the discomforts of their situation by saying with a yawn and a whimper: "I'm so sleepy! I want my own bed and Mamma."

"So do I!" echoed Rita, who had been nodding for some time and longed to lie down and sleep comfortably anywhere.

"Almost eight o'clock! By Jove, Pat sure is taking his time. I wonder if he has gotten into trouble? We can't do anything and may as well keep quiet here," said Mark, looking at his watch and beginning to understand that the joke was rather a serious one.

"Better make a night of it and all go to sleep. Pat can wake us up when he comes. The cold makes a fellow so drowsy." And Bob gave a stretch that nearly rent him asunder.

"I will let the children nap on the sofa. They are so tired of waiting and may as well amuse themselves in that way as in fretting. Come, Gus and Rita, each take a pillow, and I'll cover you up with my shawl."

Gwen made the little ones comfortable, and they were off in five minutes. The others kept up bravely till nine o'clock, then the bits of candles were burnt out, the stories all told, nuts and apples had lost their charm, and weariness and hunger caused spirits to fail perceptibly.

"I've eaten five walnuts, and yet I want more. Something filling and good. Can't we catch a rabbit and roast him?" proposed Bob, who was a hearty lad and was ravenous by this time.

"Isn't there anything in the house?" asked Ruth, who dared not eat nuts for fear of indigestion.

"Not a thing that I know of except a few pickles in the storeroom; we had so many Mamma left some here," answered Gwen, resolving to provision the house before she left it another autumn.

"Pickles alone are a rather sour feed. If we only had a biscuit now, they wouldn't be so bad for relish," said Tony, with the air of a man who had known what it was to live on burnt bean soup and rye flapjacks for a week.

"I saw a keg of soft soap in the shed. How would that go with the pickles?" suggested Bob, who felt equal to the biggest and acidest cucumber ever grown.

"Oh, ugh! Mamma knew an old lady who actually did eat soft soap and cream for her complexion," put in Alice, whose own fresh face looked as if she had tried the same distasteful remedy.

The boys laughed, and Mark, who felt that hospitality required him to do something for his guests, said briskly: "Let us go on a foraging expedition while the lamp holds out to burn, for the old lantern is almost gone and then we are done for. Come on, Bob. Your sharp nose will smell out food, if there is any."

"Don't set the house afire, and bring more wood when you come, for we must have light of some kind in this spooky place," called Gwen, with a sigh, wishing every one of them were safely at home and abed.

A great trampling of boots, slamming of doors, and shouting of voices followed the departure of the boys, as well as a crash, a howl, and then a roar of laughter, as Bob fell down the cellar stairs, having opened the door in search of food and poked his nose in too far. Presently, they came back, very dusty, cobwebby, and cold, but triumphantly bearing a droll collection of trophies. Mark had a piece of board and the lantern, Tony a big wooden box and a tin pail, and Bob fondly embraced a pickle jar and a tumbler of jelly which had been forgotten on a high shelf in the storeroom.

"Meal, pickles, jam, and boards. What a mess and what are we to do with it all?" cried the girls, much amused at the result of the expedition.

"Can any of you make a hoe cake?" demanded Mark.

"No, indeed! I can make caramels and coconut cakes," said Ruth proudly.

"I can make good toast and tea," added Alice.

"I can't cook anything," confessed Gwen, who was unusually accomplished in French, German, and music.

"That's not very promising," said Mark. "Take hold, Tony; you are the chap for me." And Mark disrespectfully turned his back on the young ladies, who could only sit and watch the lads work.

"He can't do anything without water," whispered Ruth.

"Or salt," answered Alice.

"Or a pan to bake in," added Gwen, and then the girls smiled at the dilemma they foresaw.

But Tony was equal to the occasion and calmly went on with his tasks, while Mark arranged the fire and Bob opened the pickles. First, the new cook filled the pail with snow till enough was melted to wet the meal brought in the wooden box. This mixture was stirred with a pine stick till thick enough, then spread on the board and set up before the bed of coals to brown.

"It never will bake in the world." "He can't turn it, so it won't be done on both sides." "Won't be fit to eat anyway!" And with these dark hints the girls consoled themselves for their want of skill.

143

But the bread did bake a nice brown; Tony did turn it neatly with his jackknife and the stick. And when it was done and cut into bits, smeared with jelly, and passed around on an old atlas, everyone said: "It really does taste good!"

Two more bakings were made and eaten with pickles for a change. Then all were satisfied, and after a vote of thanks to Tony, they began to think of sleep.

"Pat has gone home and told them we are all right, and Mamma knows we can manage here well enough for one night; so don't worry, Gwen, but take a nap and I'll lie on the rug and see to the fire."

Mark's happy-go-lucky way of taking things did not convince his sister; but, as she could do nothing, she submitted and made her friends as comfortable as she could.

All had plenty of wraps, so the girls nestled into the three large chairs, and Bob and Tony rolled themselves up in the robe, with their feet to the fire, and were soon snoring like weary hunters. Mark pillowed his head on a log and was sound asleep in ten minutes in spite of his promise to be sentinel.

Gwen's chair was the least easy of the three, and she could not forget herself like the rest, but sat wide awake, watching the blaze, counting the hours, and wondering why no one came to them.

The wind blew fiercely, the snow beat against the blinds, mice scuttled about inside the walls, and now and then a branch fell upon the roof with a crash. Weary, yet excited, the poor girl imagined all sorts of mishaps to Pat and the horses, recalled various ghost stories she had heard, and wondered if it was on such a night as this that a neighbor's house had been robbed. So nervous did she get at last that she covered up her face and resolutely began to count to a thousand, feeling that anything was better than having to wake Mark and own she was frightened.

Before she knew it, she fell into a drowse and dreamed that they were all cast away on an iceberg and a polar bear was coming up to devour Gus, who innocently called to the big white dog and waited to caress him.

"A bear! A bear! Oh, boys, save him!" murmured Gwen in her sleep, and the sound of her own distressed voice waked her.

The fire was nearly out, for she had slept longer than she knew. The room was full of shadows, and the storm seemed to have died away. In the silence which now reigned, unbroken even by a snore, Gwen heard a sound that made her start and tremble. Someone was coming softly up the back stairs. All the outer doors were locked, she was sure; all the boys lay in their places, for she could see and count the three long figures and little Gus in a bunch on the sofa. The girls had not stirred, and this was no mouse's scamper, but a slow and careful tread, stealing nearer and nearer to the study door, left ajar when the last load of wood was brought in.

Pat would knock or ring, and Papa would speak, so that we might not be scared. I want to scream, but I won't till I see that it really is someone, thought Gwen, while her heart beat fast, and her eyes were fixed on the door, straining to see through the gloom.

The steps drew nearer, paused on the threshold, and then a head appeared as the door noiselessly swung wider open. It was a man in a fur cap, but it was neither Papa nor Pat nor Uncle Ed. Poor Gwen would have called out then, but her voice was gone; and she could only lie back, looking mute and motionless.

A tiny spire of flame sprung up and flickered for a moment on the tall figure in the doorway, a big man with a beard, and in his hand something that glittered. *Is it a pistol or dagger or a dark lantern?* thought the girl, as the glimmer died away and the shadows returned to terrify her.

The man seemed to look about him keenly for a moment, then vanished, and the steps went down the hall to the front door, which was opened from within and someone admitted quietly. Whispers were heard, and then feet approached again, accompanied by a gleam of light.

Now I must scream! thought Gwen, and scream she did with all her might, as two men entered, one carrying a lantern, the other a bright tin can.

"Boys! Robbers! Fire! Tramps! Oh, do wake up!" cried Gwen, frantically pulling Mark by the hair and Bob and Tony by the legs, as the quickest way of rousing them.

Then there was a scene! The boys sprung up and rubbed their eyes, the girls hid theirs and began to shriek, while the burglars laughed aloud, and poor Gwen, quite worn out, fainted away on the rug. It was all over in a minute, however, for Mark had his wits about him, and his first glance at the man with the lantern allayed his fears.

"Hullo, Uncle Ed! We are all right. Got tired of waiting for you, so we went to sleep."

"Stop screaming, girls, and quiet those children! Poor little Gwen is badly frightened. Get some snow, Tom, while I pick her up," commanded the uncle, and order was soon established.

The boys were all right at once, and Ruth and Alice devoted themselves to the children, who were very cross and sleepy in spite of their fright. Gwen was herself in a moment and so ashamed of her scare that she was glad there was no more light to betray her pale cheeks.

"I should have known you, uncle, at once; but to see a strange man startled me, and he didn't speak, and I thought that can was a pistol," stammered Gwen, when she had collected her wits a little.

"Why, that's my old friend and captain, Tom May. Don't you remember him, child? He thought you were all asleep, so he crept out to tell me and let me in."

"How did he get in himself?" asked Gwen, glad to turn the conversation.

"Found the shed door open and surprised the camp by a flank movement. You wouldn't do for guard duty, boys," laughed Captain Tom, enjoying the dismay of the lads.

"Oh, thunder! I forgot to bolt it when we first went for the wood. Had to open it, the place was so dark," muttered Bob, much disgusted.

"Where's Pat?" asked Tony, with great presence of mind, feeling anxious to shift the blame to his broad shoulders.

Uncle Ed shook the snow from his hair and clothes, and, poking up the fire, leisurely sat down and took Gus on his knee: "The truth is, Pat got a terrible fright and nearly lost his wits. In the first place, after he found the horses, he found they were still a bit wild. Then he got on the sleigh and promptly lost his way again; it was snowing so hard. Then he hit a ditch and got tumbled overboard and let the horses go. He floundered after them for a mile or two; then lost his bearings in the storm again, tripped over a stump, and lay senseless until we found him, for we were out by then.

"The animals were stopped at a crossroads, and we got them and Pat back home. Then your mother remembered that you had mentioned stopping here, and we fitted out a new craft and set sail for a long voyage. Your father was away, so Tom volunteered, and here we are."

"A jolly lark! Now let us go home and go to bed," proposed Mark sensibly.

"Isn't it almost morning?" asked Tony, who had been sleeping like a dormouse.

"Just eleven. Now pack up and let us be off. The storm is over, the moon coming out, and we shall find a good supper waiting for the loved and lost. Bear a hand, Tom, and ship this little duffer, for he's off again."

Uncle Ed put Gus into the captain's arms, and, taking Rita himself, led the way to the sleigh which stood at the door. In they all bundled, and after making the house safe, off they went, feeling that they had had a pretty good time on the whole.

"I will learn cooking and courage, before I try camping out again," resolved Gwen. Really a brave girl, she was determined to learn from her adventure and add to her skills not only languages and music but also camping out!

THE EDITOR'S NOTES

Gwen's Adventure in the Snow—

This story is not so much about charity as it is about courage. Gwen, the main character, is already charitable and even responsible to a great degree. She is almost a little mother to her tribe of boys and girls out for a winter frolic. Yet her leadership is tested when the entire group must retreat to their summerhouse when things go awry and they are stranded in a sudden storm. Once in the house, the boys and their adventures seem to take over and become the focus of the story. The little men even find provisions and cook the evening meal while Gwen must calm the nervous smaller children.

But "Gwen's Adventure in the Snow" is not necessarily stereotypical or intended to be. Unlike other feminine reformers of her day, Louisa May Alcott had a great fondness for boys. She found them sometimes spirited and energetic in ways that girls were not. Louisa, as something of a tomboy herself, wanted to see girls adopt a more outgoing attitude, and Gwen's adventure certainly left its mark on the young heroine.

For Louisa May Alcott, the storyteller, there is always a lesson to be learned from every unexpected development.

A Christmas Dream, and How It Came True

Adapted by Stephen Hines

"I'm so tired of Christmas, I wish there never would be another one!" exclaimed a discontented-looking little girl, as she sat idly watching her mother arrange a pile of gifts two days before they were to be given.

"Why, Effie, what a dreadful thing to say! You are as bad as old Scrooge; and I'm afraid something will happen to you, as it did to him, if you don't care for Christmas," answered Mamma, almost dropping the silver horn she was filling with delicious candies.

"Who was Scrooge? What happened to him?" asked Effie, with a glimmer of interest in her listless face, as she picked out the sourest lemon drop she could find; for nothing sweet suited her just then.

"He was one of Dickens' best characters, and you can read the charming story about him someday. He hated Christmas until a strange dream showed him how dear and beautiful it was and made a better man of him."

"I shall read it; for I like dreams, and have a great many curious ones myself. But they don't keep me from being tired of Christmas," said Effie, poking discontentedly among the sweets for something worth eating.

"Why are you tired of what should be the happiest time of all the year?" asked Mamma, anxiously.

"Perhaps I shouldn't be if I had something new. But it is always the same, and there isn't any more surprise about it. I always find heaps of goodies in my stocking. Don't like some of them and soon get tired of those I do like. We always have a great dinner, and I eat too much, and feel ill next day. Then there is a Christmas tree somewhere, with a doll on top, or a stupid old Santa Claus, and children dancing and screaming over bonbons and toys that break, and shiny things that are of no use. Really, Mamma, I've had so many Christmases all alike that I don't think I *can* bear another one." And Effie laid herself flat on the sofa, as if the mere idea was too much for her.

Her mother laughed at her despair, but was sorry to see her little girl so discontented when she had everything to make her happy and had known but ten Christmas days.

"Suppose we don't give you *any* presents at all. How would that suit you?" asked Mamma, anxious to please her spoiled child.

"I should like one large and splendid one, and one dear little one, to remember some very nice person by," said Effie, who was a fanciful girl full of odd whims and notions, which her friends loved to gratify, regardless of time, trouble, or money; for she was the last of three little girls, and very dear to all the family.

"Well, my darling, I will see what I can do to please you and not say a word until all is ready. If I could only get a new idea to start with!" And Mamma went on tying up her pretty bundles with a thoughtful face while Effie strolled to the window to watch the rain that kept her indoors and made her dismal.

"Seems to me poor children have better times than rich ones. I can't go out, and there is a girl about my age splashing along, without any maid to fuss about rubbers and cloaks and umbrellas and colds. I wish I was a beggar girl."

"Would you like to be hungry, cold, and ragged, to beg all day and sleep on an ash heap at night?" asked Mamma, wondering what would come next.

"Cinderella did and had a nice time in the end. This girl out here has a basket of scraps on her arm, and a big old shawl all around her, and doesn't seem to care a bit, though the water runs out of the toes of her boots. She goes paddling along, laughing at the rain, and eating a cold potato as if it tasted nicer than the chicken and ice cream I had for dinner. Yes, I do think poor children are happier than rich ones."

"So do I, sometimes. At the orphanage today I saw two dozen merry little souls who have no parents, no home, and no hope of Christmas beyond a stick of candy or a cake. I wish you had been there to see how happy they were, playing with the old toys some richer children had sent them."

"You may give them all mine; I'm so tired of them I never want to see them again," said Effie, turning from the window to the pretty dollhouse full of everything a child's heart could desire.

"I will, and let you begin again with something you will not tire of, if I can only find it." And Mamma knit her brows trying to discover some grand surprise for this child who didn't care for Christmas.

Nothing more was said then; and wandering off to the library, Effie found "A Christmas Carol," and curling herself up in the sofa corner, read it all before tea. Some of it she did not understand, but she laughed and cried over many parts of the charming story and felt better without knowing why.

All the evening she thought of poor Tiny Tim, Mrs. Cratchit with the pudding, and the stout old gentleman who danced so gaily that "his legs twinkled in the air." Presently bedtime arrived.

"Come, now, and toast your feet," said Effie's nurse, "while I do your pretty hair and tell stories."

"I'll have a fairy tale tonight, a very interesting one," commanded Effie, as she put on her blue silk wrapper and little fur-lined slippers to sit before the fire and have her long curls brushed.

So Nursey told her best tales, and when at last the child lay down under her lace curtains, her head was full of a curious jumble of Christmas elves, poor children, snowstorms, sugarplums, and surprises. So it is no wonder that she dreamed all night, and this was the dream, which she never quite forgot.

She found herself sitting on a stone, in the middle of a great field, all alone. The snow was falling fast, a bitter wind whistled by, and night was coming on. She felt hungry, cold, and tired, and did not know where to go nor what to do.

I wanted to be a beggar girl, and now I am one; but I don't like it, and wish somebody would come and take care of me. I don't know who I am, and I think I must be lost, thought Effie, with the curious interest one takes in one's self in dreams.

But the more she thought about it, the more bewildered she felt. Faster fell the snow, colder blew the wind, darker grew the night; and poor Effie made up her mind that she was quite forgotten and left to freeze alone. The tears were chilled on her cheeks, her feet felt like icicles, and her heart died within her, so hungry, frightened, and forlorn was she. Laying her head on her knees, she gave herself up for lost, and sat there with the great flakes fast turning her to a little white mound, when suddenly the sound of music reached her, and starting up, she looked and listened with all her eyes and ears.

Far away a dim light shone and a voice was heard singing. She tried to run toward the welcome glimmer, but could not stir, and stood like a small statue of expectation while the light drew nearer, and the sweet words of the song grew clearer.

From Our Happy Home

Through the world we roam
One week in all the year,
Making winter spring
With the joy we bring,
For Christmastide is here.

Now the eastern star
Shines from afar
To light the poorest home;
Hearts warmer grow,
Gifts freely flow,
For Christmastide has come.

Now gay trees rise
Before young eyes,
Abloom with tempting cheer;
Blithe voices sing,
And blithe bells ring,
For Christmastide is here.

Oh, happy chime,
Oh, blessed time,

153

That draws us all so near!
"Welcome, dear day,"
All creatures say,
For Christmastide is here.

A child's voice sang; a child's hand carried the little candle; and in the circle of soft light it shed, Effie saw a pretty child coming to her through the night and snow. A rosy, smiling creature, he was wrapped in white fur, with a wreath of green and scarlet holly on his shining hair, the magic candle in one hand, and the other outstretched as if to shower gifts and warmly press all other hands.

Effie forgot to speak as this bright vision came nearer, leaving no trace of footsteps in the snow, only lighting the way with his little candle and filling the air with the music of his song.

"Dear child, you are lost, and I have come to find you," said the stranger, taking Effie's cold hands in his, with a smile like sunshine, while every holly berry glowed like a little fire.

"Do you know me?" asked Effie, feeling no fear, but a great gladness, at his coming.

"I know all children, and go to find them; for this is my holiday, and I gather them from all parts of the world to be merry with me once a year."

"Are you an angel?" asked Effie, looking for the wings.

"No; but I am a Christmas messenger, and live with my friends in a pleasant place, getting ready for our holiday, when we are let out to roam about the world, helping make this a happy time for all who will let us in. Will you come and see how we work?"

"I will go anywhere with you. Don't leave me again," cried Effie, gladly.

"First I will make you comfortable. That is what we love to do. You are cold, and you shall be warm; hungry, and I will feed you; sorrowful, and I will make you glad."

With a wave of his candle all three miracles were wrought instantly—for the snowflakes turned to a white fur cloak and hood on Effie's head and shoulders. A bowl of hot soup came sailing to her lips and vanished when she had eagerly drunk the last drop; and suddenly the dismal field changed to a new world so full of wonders that all her troubles were forgotten.

Bells were ringing so merrily that it was hard to keep from dancing. Green garlands hung on the walls, and every tree was a Christmas tree full of toys and blazing with candles that never went out.

In one place many little Christmas messengers sewed like mad on warm clothes, turning off work faster than any sewing machine ever invented; and great piles were made ready to be sent to poor people. Other busy creatures packed money into purses and wrote checks which they sent flying away on the wind—a lovely kind of snowstorm to fall into a world below full of poverty.

Older and graver Christmas messengers were looking over piles of little books, in which the records of the past year were kept, telling how different people had spent it, and what sort of gifts they had gotten. It was an amazing list. Some got peace, some disappointment, some remorse and sorrow, some great joy and hope. The rich had generous thoughts sent them; the poor, gratitude and contentment. Children had more love and duty to parents; and parents renewed patience, wisdom, and satisfaction for and in their children. No one was forgotten.

"Please tell me what splendid place this is," asked Effie, as soon as she could collect her wits after the first look at all these astonishing things.

155

"This is the Christmas world; and here we work all year round, never tired of getting ready for the happy day. See, these are the messengers just setting off; for some have far to go, and the children must not be disappointed."

As he spoke, the Christmas messenger pointed to four gates, out of which four great sleighs were just driving, laden with toys, while a jolly old Santa Claus (There were several!) sat in the middle of each, drawing on his mittens and tucking up his wraps for a long, cold drive.

"Why, I thought there was only one Santa Claus, and even he was a humbug," cried Effie, astonished at the sight.

"Never give up your faith in the old fairy tales, because they may be, after all, a pleasant shadow of a lovely truth."

Just then the sleighs went off with a great jingling of bells and pattering of reindeer hoofs, while all the messengers gave a cheer that was heard on earth, where people said, "Hear the stars sing."

"I never will say there isn't any Santa Claus again, then, when you put it that way. Now, show me more."

"You will like to see this place, I think, and may learn something here perhaps."

The messenger smiled as he led the way to a little door through which Effie peeped into a world of dolls. Dollhouses were in full blast, with dolls of all sorts going on like live people. Waxen ladies sat in their parlors elegantly dressed; others cooked in the kitchens; nurses walked out with the younger dolls; and the streets were full of tin soldiers marching, wooden horses prancing, express wagons rumbling, and little men hurrying to and fro. Shops were there, and tiny people buying legs of mutton, pounds of tea, mites of clothes, and everything dolls use or wear or want.

But presently she saw that in some ways the dolls improved upon the manners and customs of human beings, and she watched eagerly to learn why they did these things. A fine Paris doll driving in her carriage took up a servant doll who was hobbling along with a basket of clean clothes, and carried her to her journey's end, as if it were the proper thing to do. Another interesting china lady took off her comfortable red cloak and put it round a poor wooden creature done up in a paper shift, and so badly painted that its face would have sent some babies into fits.

"Seems to me I once knew a rich girl who didn't give her things to poor girls. I wish I could remember who she was, and tell her to be as kind as that china doll," said Effie, much touched at the sweet way the pretty creature wrapped up the poor doll, and then ran off in her little gray gown to buy a shiny fowl stuck on a wooden platter for her invalid mother's dinner.

"We recall these things to people's minds by dreams. I think the girl you speak of won't forget this one." And the messenger smiled, as if he enjoyed some joke which she did not see.

A little bell rang as she looked, and away scampered the children into the red and green schoolhouse with the roof that lifted up, so one could see how nicely they sat at their desks with small books, or drew on the inch-square blackboards with crumbs of chalk.

"They know their lessons very well and are as still as mice. We make a great racket at our school and get bad marks every day. I shall tell the girls they had better mind what they do, or their dolls will be better scholars than they are," said Effie, much impressed, as she peeped in and saw no rod in the hand of the little mistress, who looked up and shook her head at the intruder, as if begging her to go away before the order of the school was disturbed.

157

Effie retired at once, but could not resist one look in at the window of a fine mansion, where the family was at dinner. The children behaved so well at table and never grumbled a bit when their mamma said they could not have any more fruit.

"Now, show me something else," she said, as they came again to the low door that led out of Doll Land.

"You have seen how we prepare for Christmas; let me show you where we love best to send our good and happy gifts," answered the messenger, giving her his hand again.

"I know. I've seen ever so many," began Effie, thinking of her own Christmases.

"No, you have never seen what I will show you. Come away, and remember what you see tonight."

Like a flash, that bright world vanished, and Effie found herself in a part of the city she had never seen before. It was far away from the nicer places, where every store was brilliant with lights and full of pretty things, and every house wore a festival air, while people hurried to and fro with merry greetings. It was down among the dingy streets where the poor lived, and where there was no making ready for Christmas.

Hungry women looked in at the shabby shops, longing to buy meat and bread, but empty pockets forbade. Tipsy men drank up their wages in the barrooms; and in many cold, dark chambers little children huddled under thin blankets, trying to forget their misery in sleep.

No nice dinners filled the air with savory smells; no gay trees dropped toys and bonbons into eager hands; no little stockings hung in rows beside the chimneypiece ready to be filled; no happy sounds of music, gay voices, and dancing feet were heard; and there were no signs of Christmas anywhere.

"Don't they have any in this place?" asked Effie, shivering, as she held fast the messenger's hand, following where he led her.

"We come to bring it. Let me show you our best workers." And he pointed to some sweet-faced men and women who came stealing into the poor houses, working such beautiful miracles that Effie could only stand and watch.

Some slipped money into the empty pockets and sent the happy mothers to buy all the comforts they needed; others led the drunken men out of temptation and took them home to find safer pleasures there. Fires were kindled on cold hearths, tables spread as if by magic, and warm clothes wrapped round shivering limbs. Flowers suddenly bloomed in the chambers of the sick; old people found themselves remembered; sad hearts were consoled by a tender word; and wicked ones softened by the story of Christ, who forgave all sin.

But the sweetest work was for the children; and Effie held her breath to watch these human fairies hang up and fill the little stockings without which a child's Christmas is not perfect, putting in things that once she would have thought very humble presents, but which now seemed beautiful and precious because these poor babies had nothing.

"That is so beautiful! I wish I could make merry Christmases as these good people do, and be loved and thanked as they are," said Effie, softly, as she watched the busy men and women do their work and steal away without thinking of the reward but their own satisfaction.

"You can if you will. I have shown you the way. Try it, and see how happy your own holiday will be hereafter."

As he spoke, the messenger seemed to put his arms about her and vanished with a kiss.

"Oh, stay and show me more!" cried Effie, trying to hold him fast.

"Darling, wake up, and tell me why you are smiling in your sleep," said a voice in her ear; and opening her eyes, there was Mamma bending over her, and morning sunshine streaming into the room.

"Are they all gone? Did you hear the bells? Wasn't it splendid?" she asked, rubbing her eyes, and looking about her for the pretty child messenger who was so real and sweet.

"You have been dreaming at a great rate—talking in your sleep, laughing, and clapping your hands as if you were cheering someone. Tell me what was so splendid," said Mamma, smoothing the tumbled hair and lifting up the sleepy head.

Then, while she was being dressed, Effie told her dream, and Nursey thought it very wonderful; but Mamma smiled to hear that the curious things the child had thought, read, heard, and seen through the day were really mixed up in her sleep of the night.

"The child said I could work lovely miracles if I tried; but I don't know how to begin, for I have no magic candle to make feasts appear and light up groves of Christmas trees, as he did," said Effie, sorrowfully.

"Yes, you have. We will do it! We will do it!" And clapping her hands, Mamma suddenly began to dance all over the room as if she had lost her wits.

"How? how? You must tell me, Mamma," cried Effie, dancing after her and ready to believe anything possible when she remembered the adventures of the past night.

"I've got it! I've got it!—the new idea. A splendid one, if I can only carry it out!" And Mamma waltzed the little girl 'round till her curls flew wildly in the air, while Nursey laughed as if she would die.

"Tell me! tell me!" shrieked Effie.

"No, no; it is a surprise—a grand surprise for Christmas Day!" sung Mamma, evidently charmed with her happy thought. "Now, come to breakfast; for we must work like bees if we want to play spirits tomorrow. You and Nursey will go out shopping and get heaps of things while I arrange matters behind the scenes."

They were running downstairs as Mamma spoke, and Effie called out breathlessly:

"It won't be a surprise; for I know you are going to ask some poor children here and have a tree or something. It won't be like my dream; for they had ever so many trees, and more children than we can find anywhere."

"There will be no tree, no party, no dinner, in this house at all, and no presents for you. Won't that be a surprise?" And Mamma laughed at Effie's bewildered face.

"Do it. I shall like it, I think; and I won't ask any questions, so it will all burst upon me when the time comes," she said; and she ate her breakfast thoughtfully, for this really would be a new sort of Christmas.

All that morning Effie trotted after Nursey in and out of shops, buying dozens of barking dogs, woolly lambs, and squeaking birds; tiny tea sets, lively picture books, mittens and hoods, dolls and candy. Parcel after parcel was sent home; but when Effie returned she saw no trace of them, though she peeped everywhere. Nursey chuckled, but wouldn't give a hint, and went out again in the afternoon with a long list of more things to buy. Effie wandered forlornly about the house, missing the usual merry stir that went before the Christmas dinner and the evening fun.

As for Mamma, she was quite invisible all day and came in at night so tired that she could only lie on the sofa to rest, smiling as if some very pleasant thought made her happy in spite of weariness.

"Is the surprise going on all right?" asked Effie, anxiously; for it seemed an immense time to wait till another evening came.

"Beautifully! Better than I expected; for several of my good friends are helping, or I couldn't have done it as I wish. I know you will like it, dear, and long remember this new way of making Christmas merry."

Mamma gave her a very tender kiss, and Effie went to bed.

The next day was a very strange one; for when she woke there was no stocking to examine, no pile of gifts under her napkin, no one said "Merry Christmas!" to her, and the dinner was just as usual to her. Mamma vanished again, and Nursey kept wiping her eyes and saying: "The dear things! It's the prettiest idea I ever heard of. No one but your blessed Ma could have done it."

"Do stop, Nursey, or I shall go crazy because I don't know the secret!" cried Effie, more than once; and she kept her eye on the clock, for at seven in the evening the surprise was to come off.

The longed for hour arrived at last, and the child was too excited to ask questions when Nurse put on her cloak and hood, led her to the carriage, and they drove away, leaving their house the one dark and silent one in the row.

"I feel like the girls in the fairy tales who are led off to strange places and see fine things," said Effie, in a whisper, as they jingled through the gay streets.

"Ah, my deary, it *is* like a fairy tale I do assure you, and you *will* see finer things than most children will tonight. Steady, now, and do just as I tell you and don't say one word whatever you see," answered Nursey, quite quivering with excitement as she patted a large box in her lap and nodded and laughed with twinkling eyes.

They drove into a dark yard, and Effie was led through a back door to a little room, where Nurse coolly proceeded to take off not only her cloak and hood, but her dress and shoes also. Effie stared and bit her lips, but kept still until out of the box came a little white fur coat and boots, a wreath of holly leaves and berries, and a candle with a frill of gold paper round it. A long "Oh!" escaped her then; and when she was dressed and saw herself in the glass, she started back, exclaiming, "Why, Nursey, I look like the child in my dream!"

"So you do, and that's the part you are to play, my pretty! Now wait while I blind your eyes and put you in your place."

"Shall I be afraid?" whispered Effie, full of wonder; for as they went out she heard the sound of many voices, the tramp of many feet, and, in spite of the bandage, was sure a great light shone upon her when she stopped.

"You needn't be; I shall stand close by, and your ma will be there."

After the handkerchief was tied about her eyes, Nurse led Effie up some steps and placed her on a high platform, where something like leaves touched her head, and the soft snap of lamps seemed to fill the air.

Music began as soon as Nurse clapped her hands, the voices outside sounded nearer, and the tramp of steps was evidently coming up the stairs.

"Now, my precious, look and see how you and your dear ma have made a merry Christmas for them that needed it!"

Off went the bandage; and for a minute Effie really did think she was asleep again, for she actually stood in "a grove of Christmas trees," all gay and shining as in her vision. Twelve on a side, in two rows down the room, stood the little pines, each on its low table; and behind Effie a taller one rose to the roof, hung with wreaths of popcorn, apples, oranges, horns of candy, and cakes of all sorts, from sugary hearts to gingerbread Jumbos.

On the smaller trees she saw many of her own discarded toys and those Nursey bought, as well as heaps that seemed to have rained down straight from that delightful Christmas country where she felt as if she was again.

"How splendid! Who is it for? What is that noise? Where is Mamma?" cried Effie, pale with pleasure and surprise, as she stood looking down the brilliant little street from her high place.

Before Nurse could answer, the doors at the lower end flew open, and in marched twenty-four little blue-gowned orphan girls, singing sweetly, until amazement changed the song to cries of joy and wonder as the shining spectacle appeared. While they stood staring with round eyes at the wilderness of pretty things about them, Mamma stepped up beside Effie, and holding her hand fast to give her courage, told the story of the dream in a few simple words, ending in this way:

"So my little girl wanted to be a Christmas messenger, too, and make this a happy day for those who had not as many pleasures and comforts as she has. She likes surprises, and we planned this for you all. She shall play the good fairy, and give each of you something from this tree, after which everyone will find her own name on a small tree, and can go to enjoy it in her own way. March by, my dears, and let us fill your hands."

Nobody told them to do it, but all the hands were clapped heartily before a single child stirred; then one by one they came to look up wonderingly at the pretty giver of the feast as she leaned down to offer them great yellow oranges, red apples, bunches of grapes, bonbons, and cakes, till all were gone, and a double row of smiling faces turned toward her as the children filed back to their places in the orderly way they had been taught.

Then each was led to her own tree by the good ladies who had helped Mamma with all their hearts; and the happy hubbub that arose would have gratified even the most tiresome Scrooge himself—shrieks of joy, dances of delight, laughter, and tears (for some tender little things could not bear so much pleasure at once, and sobbed with mouths full of candy and hands full of toys). How they ran to show one another their new treasures! How they peeped and tasted, pulled and pinched, until the air was full of queer noises, the floor covered with papers, and the little trees left bare of all but candles!

"I wonder if heaven is like this," sighed one small girl, as she looked about her in a blissful gaze, holding her full apron with one hand, while she luxuriously carried sugarplums to her mouth with the other.

"Is that a truly angel up there?" asked another, fascinated by the little white figure with the wreath on its shining hair, who in some mysterious way had been the cause of all this merrymaking.

"I wish I dared to go and kiss her for this splendid party," said a lame child, leaning on her crutch, as she stood near the steps, wondering how it seemed to sit in a mother's lap, as Effie was doing, while she watched the happy scene before her.

Effie heard her, and remembering Tiny Tim, ran down and put her arms about the pale child, kissing the wistful face, as she said sweetly, "You may; but Mamma deserves the thanks. She did it all; I only dreamed about it."

Lame Katy felt as if "a truly angel" was embracing her and could only stammer out her thanks, while the other children ran to see the pretty spirit, and touch her soft dress, until she stood in a crowd of blue gowns laughing as they held up their gifts for her to see and admire.

Mamma leaned down and whispered one word to the older girls; and suddenly they all took hands to dance round Effie, singing as they skipped.

It was a pretty sight, and the ladies found it hard to break up the happy revel; but it was late for small people, and too much fun is a mistake. So the girls fell into line and marched before Effie and Mamma again to say good night with such grateful little faces that the eyes of those who looked grew dim with tears. Mamma kissed every one; and many a hungry childish heart felt as if the touch of those tender lips was their best gift. Effie shook so many small hands that her own tingled; and when Katy came she pressed a small doll into Effie's hand, whispering: "You didn't have a single present, and we had lots. Do keep that; it's the prettiest thing I got."

"I will," answered Effie, and held it fast until the last smiling face was gone, the surprise all over, and she safe in her own bed, too tired and happy for anything but sleep.

"Mamma, it *was* a beautiful surprise, and I thank you so much! I don't see how you did it, but I like it best of all the Christmases I ever had, and mean to make one every year. I had my splendid big present, and here is the dear little one to keep for love of poor Katy; so even that part of my wish came true."

And Effie fell asleep with a happy smile on her lips, her one humble gift still in her hand, and a new love for Christmas in her heart that never changed through a long life spent in doing good.

A Song

For a Christmas Tree
Cold and wintry is the sky,
Bitter winds go whistling by,
Orchard boughs are bare and dry,
Yet here stands a fruitful tree.
Household fairies kind and dear,
With loving magic none need fear,
Bade it rise and blossom here,
Little friends, for you and me.

Come and gather as they fall,
Shining gifts for great and small;
Santa Claus remembers all
When he comes with goodies piled.
Corn and candy, apples red,
Sugar horses, gingerbread,
Babies who are never fed,
Are hanging here for every child.

Shake the boughs and down they come,
Better fruit than peach or plum,
'Tis our little harvest home;
For though frosts the flowers kill,
Though birds depart and squirrels sleep,
Though snows may gather cold and deep,

Little folk their sunshine keep,
And mother love makes summer still.

Gathered in a smiling ring,
Lightly dance and gayly sing,
Still at heart remembering
The sweet story all should know,
Of the little child whose birth
Has made this day throughout the earth
A festival for childish mirth,
Since that first Christmas long ago.

A Merry Christmas

(From the immortal *Little Women*.

No Christmas collection of Miss Alcott's

would be complete without this story.)

o was the first to wake in the gray dawn of Christmas morning. No stockings hung at the fireplace, and for a moment she felt as much disappointment as she did long ago, when her little sock fell down because it was so crammed with goodies. Then she remembered her mother's promise, and slipping her hand under her pillow, drew out a little crimson-covered book. She knew it very well, for it was that beautiful old story of the best life ever lived, and Jo felt that it was a true guidebook for any pilgrim going the long journey. She woke Meg with a "Merry Christmas" and bade her see what was under her pillow. A green-covered book appeared, with the same picture inside, and a few words written by their mother, which made their one present very precious in their eyes. Presently Beth and Amy woke, to rummage and find their little books also—one dove-colored, the other blue; and all sat looking at and talking about them, while the East grew rosy with the coming day.

In spite of her small vanities, Margaret had a sweet and pious nature, which unconsciously influenced her sisters, especially Jo, who loved her very tenderly, and obeyed her because her advice was so gently given.

"Girls," said Meg, seriously, looking from the tumbled head beside her to the two little nightcapped ones in the room beyond, "Mother wants us to read and love and mind these books, and we must begin at once. We used to be faithful about it; but since father went away, and all this war trouble unsettled us, we have neglected many things. You can do as you please; but I shall keep my book on the table here, and read a little every morning as soon as I wake, for I know it will do me good, and help me through the day."

Then she opened her new book and began to read. Jo put her arm around her, and, leaning cheek to cheek, read also, with the quiet expression so seldom seen on her restless face.

"How good Meg is! Come, Amy, let's do as they do. I'll help you with the hard words, and they'll explain things if we don't understand," whispered Beth, very much impressed by the pretty books and her sisters' example.

"I'm glad mine is blue," said Amy; and then the rooms were very still while the pages were softly turned, and the winter sunshine crept in to touch the bright heads and serious faces with a Christmas greeting.

"Where is Mother?" asked Meg, as she and Jo ran down to thank her for their gifts, half an hour later.

"Goodness only knows. Some poor creeter come a-beggin', and your ma went straight off to see what was needed. There never *was* such a woman for givin' away vittles and drink, clothes and firin'," replied Hannah, who had lived with the family since Meg was born, and was considered by them all more as a friend than a servant.

"She will be back soon, I guess; so do your cakes, and have everything ready," said Meg, looking over the presents which were collected in a basket and kept under the sofa, ready to be produced at the proper time. "Why, where is Amy's bottle of cologne?" she added, as the little flask did not appear.

"She took it out a minute ago, and went off with it to put a ribbon on it, or some such notion," replied Jo, dancing about the room to take the first stiffness off the new army slippers.

"How nice my handkerchiefs look, don't they? Hannah washed and ironed them for me, and I marked them all myself," said Beth, looking proudly at the somewhat uneven letters which had cost her such labor.

171

"Bless the child; she's gone and put 'Mother' on them instead of M. March; how funny!" cried Jo, taking up one.

"Isn't it right? I thought it was better to do it so, because Meg's initials are 'M.M.,' and I don't want anyone to use these but Marmee," said Beth, looking troubled.

"It's all right, dear, and a very pretty idea; quite sensible, too, for no one can ever mistake now. It will please her very much, I know," said Meg, with a frown for Jo and a smile for Beth.

"There's mother; hide the basket, quick!" cried Jo, as a door slammed and steps sounded in the hall.

Amy came in hastily and looked rather abashed when she saw her sisters all waiting for her.

"Where have you been, and what are you hiding behind you?" asked Meg, surprised to see, by her hood and cloak, that lazy Amy had been out so early.

"Don't laugh at me, Jo; I didn't mean anyone should know till the time came. I only meant to change the little bottle for a big one, and I gave *all* my money to get it, and I'm truly trying not to be selfish anymore."

As she spoke, Amy showed the handsome flask which replaced the cheap one; and looked so earnest and humble in her little effort to forget herself that Meg hugged her on the spot and Jo pronounced her "a trump," while Beth ran to the window and picked her finest rose to ornament the stately bottle.

"You see I felt ashamed of my present, after reading and talking about being good this morning, so I ran 'round the corner and changed it the minute I was up; and I'm *so* glad, for mine is the handsomest now."

172

Another bang of the street door sent the basket under the sofa and the girls to the table eager for breakfast.

"Merry Christmas, Marmee! Lots of them! Thank you for our books; we read some, and mean to every day," they cried in chorus.

"Merry Christmas, little daughters! I'm glad you began at once and hope you will keep on. But I want to say one word before we sit down. Not far away from here lies a poor woman with a little newborn baby. Six children are huddled into one bed to keep from freezing, for they have no fire. There is nothing to eat over there; and the oldest boy came to tell me they were suffering hunger and cold. My girls, will you give them your breakfast as a Christmas present?"

They were all unusually hungry, having waited nearly an hour, and for a minute no one spoke; only a minute, for Jo exclaimed impetuously:

"I'm so glad you came before we began!"

"May I go and help carry the things to the poor little children?" asked Beth, eagerly.

"I shall take the cream and the muffins," added Amy, heroically giving up the articles she most liked.

Meg was already covering the buckwheats and piling the bread into one big plate.

"I thought you'd do it," said Mrs. March, smiling as if satisfied. "You shall all go and help me, and when we come back, we will have bread and milk for breakfast and make it up at dinner time."

They were soon ready, and the procession set out. Fortunately, it was early, and they went through back streets, so few people saw them, and no one laughed at the funny party.

A poor, bare, miserable room it was, with broken windows, no fire, ragged bedclothes, a sick mother, wailing baby, and a group of pale, hungry children cuddled under one old quilt, trying to keep warm. How the big eyes stared and the blue lips smiled, as the girls went in!

"Ach, mein Gott! It is good angels come to us!" cried the poor woman, crying for joy.

"Funny angels in hoods and mittens," said Jo, and set them laughing.

In a few minutes it really did seem as if kind spirits had been at work there. Hannah, who had carried wood, made a fire, and stopped up the broken panes with old hats and her own shawl. Mrs. March gave the mother tea and gruel, and comforted her with promises of help, while she dressed the little baby as tenderly as if it had been her own. The girls, meantime, spread the table, set the children round the fire, and fed them like so many hungry birds; laughing, talking, and trying to understand the funny broken English.

"Das ist gute!" "Der angel-kinder!" cried the poor things, as they ate and warmed their purple hands at the comfortable blaze. The girls had never been called angel children before, and thought it very agreeable, especially Jo, who had been considered "a Sancho" ever since she was born. That was a very happy breakfast, though they didn't get any of it; and when they went away, leaving comfort behind, I think there were not in all the city four merrier people than the hungry little girls who gave away their breakfasts, and contented themselves with bread and milk on Christmas morning.

"That's loving our neighbor better than ourselves, and I like it," said Meg, as they set out their presents, while their mother was upstairs collecting clothes for the poor Hummels.

Not a very splendid show, but there was a great deal of love done up in the few little bundles; and the tall vase of red roses, white chrysanthemums, and trailing vines, which stood in the middle, gave quite an elegant air to the table.

"She's coming! Strike up, Beth, open the door, Amy. Three cheers for Marmee!" cried Jo, prancing about, while Meg went to conduct mother to the seat of honor.

Beth played her gayest march, Amy threw open the door, and Meg enacted escort with great dignity. Mrs. March was both surprised and touched, and smiled with her eyes full as she examined her presents and read the little notes which accompanied them. The slippers went on at once; a new handkerchief was slipped into her pocket, well scented with Amy's cologne; the rose was fastened in her bosom; and the nice gloves were pronounced "a perfect fit."

There was a good deal of laughing and kissing and explaining, in the simple loving fashion which makes these home festivals so pleasant at the time, so sweet to remember long afterward, and then all fell to work.

The morning charities and ceremonies took so much time that the rest of the day was devoted to preparations for the evening festivities. Being still too young to go often to the theatre, and not rich enough to afford any great outlay for private performances, the girls put their wits to work, and, necessity being the mother of invention, made whatever they needed. Very clever were some of their productions; pasteboard guitars, antique lamps made of old-fashioned butter-boats covered with silver paper, gorgeous robes of old cotton glittering with tin spangles from a pickle factory, and armour covered with the same useful diamond-shaped bits left in sheets when the lids of tin preserve pots were cut out. The furniture was used to being turned into topsy-turvy, and the big chamber was the scene of many innocent revels.

No gentlemen were admitted; so Jo played male parts to her heart's content and took immense satisfaction in a pair of russet-leather boots given her by a friend who knew a lady who knew an actor. These boots, an old foil, and a slashed doublet once used by an artist for some picture, were Jo's chief treasures, and appeared on all occasions. The smallness of the company made it necessary for the two principal actors to take several parts apiece; and they certainly deserved some credit for the hard work they did in learning three or four different parts, whisking in and out of various costumes, and managing the stage besides. It was excellent drill for their memories, a harmless amusement, and employed many hours which otherwise would have been idle, lonely, or spent in less profitable society.

On Christmas night, a dozen girls piled on to the bed, which was the dress circle, and sat before the blue and yellow chintz curtains, in a most flattering state of expectancy. There was a good deal of rustling and whispering behind the curtain, a trifle of lamp smoke, and an occasional giggle from Amy, who was apt to get hysterical in the excitement of the moment. Presently a bell sounded, the curtains flew apart, and the Operatic Tragedy began.

"A gloomy wood," according to the one playbill, was represented by a few shrubs in pots, a green baize on the floor, and a cave in the distance. This cave was made with a clotheshorse for a roof, bureaus for walls; and in it was a small furnace in full blast, with a black pot on it, and an old witch bending over it. The stage was dark, and the glow of the furnace had a fine effect, especially as real steam issued from the kettle when the witch took off the cover. A moment was allowed for the first thrill to subside; then Hugo, the villain, stalked in with a clanking sword at his side, a slouched hat, black beard, mysterious cloak, and the boots. After pacing to and fro in much agitation, he struck his forehead, and burst out in a wild strain, singing of his hatred to Roderigo, his love for Zara, and his pleasing resolution to kill the one and win the other. The gruff tones of Hugo's voice, with an occasional shout when his feelings overcame him, were very impressive, and the audience applauded the moment he paused for breath. Bowing with the air of one accustomed to public praise, he stole to the cavern and ordered Hagar to come forth with a commanding, "What ho! Minion! I need thee!"

Out came Meg, with gray horsehair hanging about her face, a red and black robe, a staff, and cabalistic signs upon her cloak. Hugo demanded a potion to make Zara adore him, and one to destroy Roderigo. Hagar, in a fine dramatic melody promised both, and proceeded to call up the spirit who would bring the love philter:

"Hither, hither, from thy home,
Airy sprite, I bid thee come!
Born of roses, fed on dew,
Charms and potions canst thou brew?
Bring me here, with elfin speed,
The fragrant philter which I need;
Make it sweet, and swift and strong;
Spirit, answer now my song!"

A soft strain of music sounded, and then at the back of the cave appeared a little figure in cloudy white, with glittering wings, golden hair, and a garland of roses on its head. Waving a wand, it sung:

"Hither I come,
From my airy home,
Afar in the silver moon;
Take the magic spell,
Oh, use it well!
Or its power will vanish soon!"

And dropping a small gilded bottle at the witch's feet, the spirit vanished. Another chant from Hagar produced another apparition—not a lovely one, for, with a bang, an ugly, black imp appeared, and having croaked a reply, tossed a dark bottle at Hugo, and disappeared with a mocking laugh. Having warbled his thanks and put the potions in his boots, Hugo departed; and Hagar informed the audience that, as he had killed a few of her friends in times past, she has cursed him, and intends to thwart his plans and be revenged on him. Then the curtain fell, and the audience reposed and ate candy while discussing the merits of the play.

A good deal of hammering went on before the curtain rose again; but when it became evident what a masterpiece of stage-carpentering had been got up, no one murmured at the delay. It was truly superb! A tower rose to the ceiling; halfway up appeared a window with a lamp burning at it, and behind the white curtain appeared Zara in a lovely blue and silver dress, waiting for Roderigo. He came, in gorgeous array, with plumed cap, red cloak, chestnut lovelocks, a guitar, and the boots, of course. Kneeling at the foot of the tower, he sung a serenade in melting tones. Zara replied, and after a musical dialogue, consented to fly. Then came the grand effect of the play. Roderigo produced a ropeladder with five steps to it, threw up one end, and invited Zara to descend. Timidly she crept from her lattice, put her hand on Roderigo's shoulder and was about to leap gracefully down, when, "alas, alas for Zara!" she forgot her train—it caught in the window; the tower tottered, leaned forward, fell with a crash, and buried the unhappy lovers in the ruins!

A universal shriek arose as the russet boots waved wildly from the wreck, and a golden head emerged, exclaiming, "I told you so! I told you so!" With wonderful presence of mind Don Pedro, the cruel sire, rushed in, dragged out his daughter with a hasty aside—

"Don't laugh, act as if it was all right!" and ordering Roderigo up, banished him from the kingdom with wrath and scorn. Though decidedly shaken by the fall of the tower upon him, Roderigo defied the old gentleman, and refused to stir. This dauntless example fired Zara; she also defied her sire, and he ordered them both to the deepest dungeons of the castle. A stout little retainer came in with chains, and led them away, looking very much frightened, and evidently forgetting the speech he ought to have made.

Act third was the castle hall; and here Hagar appeared, having come to free the lovers and finish Hugo. She hears him coming and hides; sees him put the potions into two cups of wine, and bid the timid little servant, "Bear them to the captives in their cells, and tell them I shall come anon." The servant takes Hugo aside to tell him something, and Hagar changes the cups for two others which are harmless. Ferdinando, the "minion," carries them away, and Hagar puts back the cup which holds the poison meant for Roderigo. Hugo, getting thirsty after a long warble, drinks it, loses his wits, and after a good deal of clutching and stamping, falls flat and dies while Hagar informs him what she has done in a song of exquisite power and melody.

This was a truly thrilling scene; though some persons might have thought that the sudden tumbling down of a quantity of long hair rather marred the effect of the villain's death. He was called before the curtain, and with great propriety appeared leading Hagar, whose singing was considered more wonderful than all the rest of the performance put together.

Act fourth displayed the despairing Roderigo on the point of stabbing himself, because he has been told that Zara has deserted him. Just as the dagger is at his heart, a lovely song is sung under his window, informing him that Zara is true, but in danger, and he can save her if he will. A key is thrown in which unlocks the door, and in a spasm of rapture he tears off his chains and rushes away to find and rescue his ladylove.

Act fifth opened with a stormy scene between Zara and Don Pedro. He wishes her to go into a convent, but she won't hear of it; and, after a touching appeal, is about to faint, when Roderigo dashes in and demands her hand. Don Pedro refuses because he is not rich. They shout and gesticulate tremendously, but cannot agree, and Roderigo is about to bear away the exhausted Zara, when the timid servant enters with a letter and a bag from

Hagar, who has mysteriously disappeared. The letter informs the party that she bequeaths untold wealth to the young pair and an awful doom to Don Pedro if he doesn't make them happy. The bag is opened, and several quarts of tin money shower down upon the stage, till it is quite glorified with the glitter. This entirely softens the "stern sire"; he consents without a murmur, all join in a joyful chorus, and the curtain falls upon the lovers kneeling to receive Don Pedro's blessing, in attitudes of the most romantic grace.

Tumultuous applause followed, but received an unexpected check; for the cot-bed on which the "dress circle" was built, suddenly shut up and extinguished the enthusiastic audience. Roderigo and Don Pedro flew to the rescue, and all were taken out unhurt, though many were speechless with laughter. The excitement had hardly subsided when Hannah appeared, with "Mrs. March's compliments, and would the ladies walk down to supper?"

This was a surprise, even to the actors; and when they saw the table they looked at one another in rapturous amazement. It was like "Marmee" to get up a little treat for them, but anything so fine as this was unheard of since the departed days of plenty. There was ice cream—actually two dishes of it, pink and white— and cake and fruit and distracting French bonbons, and in the middle of the table four great bouquets of hothouse flowers!

It quite took their breath away; and they stared first at the table and then at their mother, who looked as if she enjoyed it immensely.

"Is it fairies?" asked Amy.

"It's Santa Claus," said Beth.

"Mother did it," and Meg smiled her sweetest, in spite of her gray beard and white eyebrows.

"Aunt March had a good fit, and sent the supper," cried Jo, with a sudden inspiration.

"All wrong; old Mr. Laurence sent it," replied Mrs. March.

"The Laurence boy's grandfather! What in the world put such a thing into his head? We don't know him," exclaimed Meg.

"Hannah told one of his servants about your breakfast party; he is an odd old gentleman, but that pleased him. He knew my father, years ago, and he sent me a polite note this afternoon, saying he hoped I would allow him to express his friendly feeling toward my children by sending them a few trifles in honor of the day. I could not refuse, and so you have a little feast at night to make up for the bread and milk breakfast."

"That boy put it into his head; I know he did!" He's a capital fellow, and I wish we could get acquainted. He looks as if he'd like to know us, but he's bashful, and Meg is so prim she won't let me speak to him when we pass," said Jo, as the plates went round, and the ice began to melt out of sight, with ohs! and ahs! of satisfaction.

"You mean the people who live in the big house next door, don't you?" asked one of the girls. "My mother knows old Mr. Laurence, but says he's very proud and doesn't like to mix with his neighbors. He keeps his grandson shut up when he isn't riding or walking with his tutor, and makes him study dreadful hard. We invited him to our party, but he didn't come. Mother says he's very nice, though he never speaks to us girls."

"Our cat ran away once, and he brought her back, and we talked over the fence and were getting on capitally, all about cricket, and so on, when he saw Meg coming and walked off. I mean to know him some day, for he needs fun, I'm sure he does," said Jo decidedly.

"I like his manners, and he looks like a little gentleman, so I've no objection to your knowing him if a proper opportunity comes. He brought the flowers himself, and I should have asked him in if I had been sure what was going on upstairs. He looked so wistful as he went away, hearing the frolic, and evidently having none of his own."

"It's a mercy you didn't, Mother," laughed Jo, looking at her boots. "But we'll have another play sometime, that he *can* see. Maybe he'll help act; wouldn't that be jolly?"

"I never had a bouquet before; how pretty it is," and Meg examined her flowers with great interest.

"They *are* lovely, but Beth's roses are sweeter to me," said Mrs. March, sniffing at the half-dead posy in her belt.

Beth nestled up to her and whispered softly, "I wish I could send my bunch to Father. I'm afraid he isn't having such a merry Christmas as we are."

What Love Can Do

The small room had nothing in it but a bed, two chairs, and a big chest. A few little gowns hung on the wall, and the only picture was the wintry sky, sparkling with stars, framed by the uncurtained window. But the moon, pausing to peep, saw something touching and heard something pleasant. Two heads in little, round nightcaps lay on one pillow, two pairs of wide-awake blue eyes stared up at the light, and two tongues were going like bell clappers.

"I'm so glad we finished our shirts in time! It seemed as though we never should, and I don't think six cents is half enough for a great, red flannel shirt with four buttonholes, do you?" said one voice rather wearily.

"No, but then we each made four, and fifty cents is a good deal of money. Are you sorry we didn't keep our quarters for ourselves?" asked the other voice with an undertone of regret.

"Yes, I am, till I think how pleased the children will be with our tree, for they don't expect anything at all and will be so surprised. I wish we had more toys to put on it, for it looks so small and mean with only three or four things hanging from it."

"Oh, it won't hold anymore, so I wouldn't worry about it. The toys are very red and yellow, and I guess the babies won't know how cheap they are but like them as much as if they cost heaps of money."

With that brave, cheery reply, the four blue eyes turned toward the chest under the window, and the kind moon did her best to light up the tiny tree standing there. A very pitiful little tree it was—only a branch of hemlock in an old flowerpot propped up with bits of coal and hung with a few penny toys earned by the patient fingers of the elder sisters that the younger ones should not be disappointed.

But in spite of the magical moonlight, the broken branch, with its scanty supply of fruit, looked pathetically poor, and one pair of eyes filled slowly with tears, while the other pair lost their happy look as if a cloud had covered the moonbeams.

"Are you crying, Dolly?"

"Not much, Grace."

"What makes you sad, dear?"

"I didn't know how poor we were till I saw the tree, and then I couldn't help it," sobbed the elder sister, for at twelve she already knew something of the cares of poverty and missed the happiness that seemed to vanish out of all their lives when Father died.

"It's dreadful! I never thought we'd have to earn our tree and only be able to get a broken branch, after all, with nothing on it but three sticks of candy, two squeaking dogs, a red cow, and an ugly bird with one feather in its tail." Overcome by a sudden sense of destitution, Grace sobbed even more despairingly than Dolly.

"Hush, dear. We must cry softly, or Mother will hear and come up; and then we shall have to tell. You know we said we wouldn't mind not having any Christmas, she seemed so sorry about it."

"I *must* cry, but I'll be quiet about it."

So the two heads went under the pillow for a few minutes and not a sound betrayed them as the sisters cried softly in one another's arms, lest Mother should discover that they were no longer careless children, but brave young creatures trying to bear their share of poverty cheerfully.

When the shower was over, the faces came out shining like roses after rain, and the voices went on again as before.

"Don't you wish there really was a Santa Claus who knew what we wanted and would come and put two silver half dollars in our stockings, so we could go to see Puss 'n' Boots at the theatre tomorrow afternoon?"

"Yes, indeed; but we didn't hang up any stockings anyway, you know, because Mother had nothing to put in them. It does seem as if rich people might think of the poor now and then. Such small considerations would help us feel remembered, and it couldn't be much trouble to take two small girls to the play."

"*I* shall remember to do something when I'm rich, like Mr. Chrome and Miss Kent. I shall go 'round every Christmas with a big basket of goodies and give all the poor children some."

"Perhaps if we sew ever so many flannel shirts we may be rich by-and-by. I should give Mother a new bonnet first of all, for I heard Miss Kent say no lady would wear such a shabby one. Mrs. Smith said fine bonnets didn't make real ladies, though. I like her best, but I do want a locket like Miss Kent's."

"I should give Mother some new rain shoes, and then I should buy a white apron with frills like Miss Kent's and bring home nice bunches of grapes and good things to eat, as Mr. Chrome does. I often smell them, but he never gives me any. He only says, 'Hullo, little chick,' and I'd rather have oranges anytime."

"It will take us a long while to get rich, I'm afraid. It makes me tired to think of it. I guess we'd better go to sleep now, dear."

"Good night, Dolly."

"Good night, Grace."

They kissed each other softly, a nestling sound followed, and presently the little sisters lay fast asleep cheek against cheek on the pillow wet with their tears, never dreaming of what was going to happen to them tomorrow.

Now Miss Kent's room was next to theirs, and as she sat sewing she could hear the children's talk, for they had soon forgotten to whisper. At first she smiled, then she looked sober, and when the prattle ceased, she said to herself, as she glanced about her pleasant chamber: "Poor little things! They think I'm rich and envy me when I'm only a ladies' hatmaker earning my living. I ought to have taken more notice of them, for their mother does have a hard time, I fancy, but never complains.

"I'm sorry they heard what I said, and if I knew how to do it without offending her, I'd trim a nice bonnet for a Christmas gift, for their mother is a dear lady in spite of her poor clothes. Perhaps I can give the children something they want anyhow— and I will! The idea of those mites making a fortune out of shirts at six cents apiece!"

Miss Kent laughed at the innocent delusion but sympathized with her little neighbors, for she knew all about hard times. She had good wages now but spent them on herself and liked to be considered fine rather than neat. Still, she was a good-hearted young woman and what she had overheard set her to thinking soberly about what she might do.

"If I hadn't spent all my money on my dress for the party tomorrow night, I'd give each of them a half dollar. As I cannot, I'll hunt up the other things they wanted, for it's a shame they shouldn't have a bit of Christmas when they have tried so hard to please other little ones."

As she spoke, she stirred about her room and soon had a white apron, an old carnelian heart on a fresh blue ribbon, and two papers of bonbons ready. As no stockings were hung up, she laid a clean towel on the floor before the door and spread forth the small gifts to look their best.

Miss Kent was so busy that she did not hear a step come quietly upstairs, and Mr. Chrome, the artist, peeped at her through the balusters, wondering what she was about. He soon saw and watched her with pleasure, thinking that she never looked prettier than now.

Presently, she caught him at it and hastened to explain, telling what she had heard and how she was trying to atone for her past neglect of these young neighbors. Then she said good night and both went into their rooms—she to sleep happily, and he to meditate thoughtfully.

His eye kept turning to some bundles that lay on his table as if the story he had heard suggested how he might follow Miss Kent's example. I rather think he would not have disturbed himself if he had not heard the story told in such a soft voice, with a pair of bright eyes full of pity looking into his; for little girls were not particularly interesting to him, and he was usually too tired to notice the industrious creatures who toiled up and down stairs on various errands. He was busy himself, after all.

Now that he knew something of their small troubles, he felt as if it would please Miss Kent and be a good joke to do his share of the pretty work she had begun.

So presently he jumped up, and, opening his parcels, took out two oranges and two bunches of grapes; then he looked up two silver half dollars, and, stealing into the hall, laid the fruit upon the towel and the money atop the oranges. This addition improved the display very much, and Mr. Chrome was stealing back, well pleased, when his eye fell on Miss Kent's door, and he said to himself: "She too shall have a little surprise, for she is a dear, kindhearted soul."

In his room was a prettily painted plate, and this he filled with green and purple grapes, tucked a sentimental note underneath, and, leaving it on her threshold, crept away as stealthily as a burglar.

The house was very quiet when Mrs. Smith, the landlady, came to turn off the gas. "Well, upon my word, here's fine doings, to be sure!" she said when she saw the state of the upper hall. "Now I wouldn't have thought it of Miss Kent, she is such a giddy girl, nor of Mr. Chrome, he is so busy with his own affairs. I meant to give those children each a cake tomorrow; they are such good little things. I'll run down and get them now, as my contribution to this fine display."

Away trotted Mrs. Smith to her pantry and picked out a couple of tempting cakes, shaped like hearts and full of plums. There was a goodly array of pies on the shelves, and she took two of them, saying, as she climbed the stairs again, "They remembered the children, so I'll remember them and have my share of the fun."

So up went the pies, for Mrs. Smith had not much to give, and her spirit was generous, though her pastry was not of the best. It looked very droll to see pies sitting about on the thresholds of closed doors, but the cakes were quite elegant and filled up the corners of the towel handsomely, for the apron lay in the middle, with oranges right and left, like two sentinels in orange uniform.

It was very late when the flicker of a candle came upstairs and a pale lady, with a sweet, sad face, appeared, bringing a pair of red and a pair of blue mittens for her Dolly and Grace. Poor Mrs. Blake did have a hard time, for she stood all day in a great store that she might earn bread for the poor children who stayed at home and took care of one another.

Her heart was heavy that night, because it was the first Christmas she had ever known without gifts and festivity of some sort. But Petkin, the youngest child, had been ill, times were hard, the little mouths gaped for food like the bills of hungry birds, and there was no tender mate to help fill them.

The angels hovering about the dingy hall just then must have seen the mother's tired face brighten beautifully when she discovered the gifts, and found that her little helpers had been so kindly remembered. Something more brilliant than the mock diamonds in Miss Kent's best earrings fell and glittered on the dusty floor as Mrs. Blake added the mittens to the other things and went to her lonely room again, smiling as she thought how she could thank all the contributors in a pleasant and simple way.

Her windows were full of flowers, for the delicate tastes of the poor lady found great comfort in their beauty. "I have nothing else to give, and these will show how grateful I am," she said as she rejoiced that the scarlet geraniums were so full of gay clusters, the white chrysanthemum stars were all out, and the pink roses at their loveliest.

The flowers slept now, dreaming of a sunny morrow as they sat safely sheltered from the bitter cold. But that night was their last, for a gentle hand cut them all, and soon three pretty nosegays stood in a glass, waiting for dawn, to be laid at three doors, with a few grateful words which would surprise and delight the receivers, for flowers were rare in those hardworking lives, and kind deeds often come back to the givers in fairer shapes than they go.

Now one would think that there had been gifts enough, and no more could possibly arrive, since all had added his or her mite except Betsey, the maid, who was off on a holiday, and the babies fast asleep in their trundle bed with nothing to give but love and kisses. Nobody dreamed that the old cat would take it into her head that her kittens were in danger, because Mrs. Smith had said she thought they were nearly old enough to be given away. But the cat must have understood, for when all was dark and still, the anxious mother went patting upstairs to the children's door, meaning to hide her babies under their bed, sure they would be saved destruction. Mrs. Blake had shut the door, however, so poor Puss was disappointed; but finding a soft, clean spot among a variety of curious articles, she laid her kits there and kept them warm all night, with her head pillowed on the blue mittens.

In the cold morning Dolly and Grace got up and scrambled into their clothes, not with joyful haste to see what their stockings held, for they had none, but because they had the little ones to dress while Mother got the breakfast.

Dolly opened the door and started back with a cry of astonishment at the lovely spectacle before her. The other people had taken in their gifts, so nothing destroyed the magnificent effect of the treasures so curiously collected in the night. Puss had left her kits asleep and gone down to get her own breakfast; and there, in the middle of the ruffled apron, as if in a dainty cradle, lay the two Maltese darlings, with white bibs and boots on, and white tips to the tiny tails curled round their little noses.

Grace and Dolly could only clasp their hands and look in rapturous silence for a minute; then they went down on their knees and reveled in the unexpected richness before them.

"I do believe angels must have heard us, for here is everything we wanted," said Dolly, holding the carnelian heart in one hand and the plumy one in the other.

"How can we ever explain this, for we didn't mention kittens, but we wanted one, and here are two darlings," cried Grace, almost purring with delight as the downy bunches unrolled and gaped till their bits of pink tongues were visible.

"Mrs. Smith must have been one angel, I guess, and Miss Kent was another, for that is her apron. I shouldn't wonder if Mr. Chrome gave us the oranges and the money; men always have lots, and his name is on this bit of paper," said Dolly.

"Oh, I'm so glad! Now we shall have a Christmas like other people, and I'll never say again that rich folks don't remember poor folks. Come and show all our treasures to Mother and the babies; they must have some," answered Grace, feeling that the world was all right and life not half as hard as she thought it last night.

Shrieks of delight greeted the sisters, and all that morning there was joy and feasting in Mrs. Blake's room; and in the afternoon Dolly and Grace went to the theatre and actually saw *Puss 'n' Boots*, for their mother insisted on their going, having discovered how the hard-earned quarters had been spent. This was such unhoped for bliss they could hardly believe it and kept smiling at one another so brightly that people wondered who the happy girls in the shabby cloaks could be who clapped their new mittens so heartily and laughed till it was better than music to hear them.

This was a remarkable Christmas Day, and they long remembered it; for while they were absorbed in the fortunes of the Marquis of Carabas and the funny cat, who tucked his tail in his belt, washed his face so awkwardly, and didn't know how to purr, strange things were happening at home, and more surprises were in store for Dolly and Grace.

You see, when people once begin to do kindnesses, it is so easy and pleasant, they find it hard to leave off; and sometimes it beautifies them so that they find they love one another very much—as Mr. Chrome and Miss Kent discovered that wondrous day.

They were very jolly at dinner and talked a good deal about the Blakes, who ate in their own rooms. Miss Kent told what the children said, and it touched the soft spot in all their hearts to hear about the red shirts, though they laughed at Grace's lament over the bird with only one feather in its tail.

"I'd give them a better tree if I had any place to put it and knew how to trim it up," said Mr. Chrome, with a sudden burst of generosity, which so pleased Miss Kent that her eyes shone like Christmas candles.

"Put it in the back parlor. All the Browns are away for a week, and we'll help you trim it—won't we, my dear?" cried Mrs. Smith warmly; for she saw that he was in a sociable mood and thought it a pity the Blakes should not profit by it.

"Yes, indeed, I should like it of all things, and it needn't cost much, for I have some skill in trimming, as you know." And Miss Kent looked so gay and pretty as she spoke that Mr. Chrome made up his mind that millinery must be a delightful occupation.

"Come on then, ladies, and we'll have a little fun. I'm a lonely old bachelor with nowhere to go today, and I'd like to be in good company and have a good time."

They had it, I assure you, for they all fell to work as busy as bees, flying and buzzing about with much laughter as they worked their pleasant miracle. Mr. Chrome acted more like a father of a large family than a crusty bachelor. Miss Kent's skillful fingers flew as they never did before, and Mrs. Smith trotted up and down as briskly as if she were sixteen instead of being a stout, elderly woman of seventy.

The children were so full of the play and telling about it that they forgot their tree till after supper, but when they went to look for it, they found it gone and in its place a great paper hand with one finger pointing downstairs, and on it these mysterious words in red: "Look in the Browns' back parlor!"

At the door of that interesting apartment they found their mother with Will and Petkin, for another hand had suddenly appeared to them pointing up. The door flew open quite as if it were a fairy play, and they went in to find a pretty tree planted in a red box on the center table, lighted with candles, hung with gilded nuts, red apples, gay bonbons, and a gift for each child.

Mr. Chrome was hidden behind one folding door, and stout Mrs. Smith squeezed behind the other, and they both thought it a great improvement upon an old-fashioned Santa Claus to have Miss Kent, in her new white dress, with Mrs. Blake's roses in her hair, step forward as the children gazed in silent rapture, and with a few sweet words welcome them to surprises their friends had made.

There were many Christmas trees in the city that night, but none that gave such hearty pleasures as the one which so magically took the place of the broken branch and its few poor toys. They were all there, however, and Dolly and Grace were immensely pleased to see that, of all their gifts, Petkin chose the forlorn bird to carry to bed with her, the one yellow feather being just to her taste.

Mrs. Blake put on her neat bonnet and was so gratified that Miss Kent thought it the most successful one she ever trimmed. She was well paid for it by the thanks of one neighbor and the admiration of another; for when she went to her party, Mr. Chrome went with her and said something on the way which made her heart dance more lightly than her feet that night.

Good Mrs. Smith felt that her house had covered itself with glory by this event, and Dolly and Grace declared that it was the most perfect and delightful surprise party ever seen.

It was all over by nine o'clock and with good night kisses for everyone, the little girls climbed up to bed laden with treasures and too happy for many words. But as they tied their round caps

Dolly said, thoughtfully: "On the whole, I think it's rather nice to be poor when people are kind to you."

"Well, I'd rather be rich, but if I can't be, it is very good fun to have Christmas trees like this one," answered Grace truthfully, never guessing that they had planted the seed from which the little pine tree grew so quickly and beautifully.

When the moon came to look in at the window on her nightly round, two smiling faces lay on the pillow, which was no longer wet with tears, but rather knobby with the mine of riches hidden underneath—firstfruits of the neighborly friendship which flourished in that house until another and a merrier Christmas came.

THE EDITOR'S NOTES

What Love Can Do—

Louisa May Alcott was never able to entirely leave behind the effects of her childhood's poverty. Bronson Alcott was such a spiritual man, he once refused to work as a carpenter, though he was a good one, because to do so would have been to debase the purity of his soul. In fact Mr. Alcott barely approved of commerce at all.

Fortunately, the Alcotts had a beloved benefactor, who didn't mind working, named Ralph Waldo Emerson. Emerson contributed of his wealth to what the Alcotts called their "sinking fund." The funds were always sinking, it seemed. Emerson's generosity was so great that Louisa felt he literally kept their family from starving.

Thus, it is no surprise that the virtue of charity plays a large part in many of Alcott's stories. However difficult the struggle against poverty might be, kindness can make life bearable, even hopeful. In "What Love Can Do" the givers also receive a gift in that friendship dispels the isolation of a lonely set of boarders who instead are destined to grow in love and good feeling—and in humanity.

Tessa's Surprises

Adapted by Stephen W. Hines

*T*essa sat alone by the fire waiting for her father to come home from work. The children were fast asleep, all three in the big bed behind the curtain; the wind blew hard outside, and the snow beat on the windowpanes; the room was large, and the fire so small and feeble that it didn't half warm the little bare toes peeping out of the old shoes on the hearth.

Tessa's father was an Italian plaster worker, very poor but kind and honest. The mother had died not long ago and left twelve-year-old Tessa to take care of the children. She tried to be wise and motherly and worked for them like any little woman, but it was so hard to keep the small bodies warm and fed and the small souls good and happy that poor Tessa was often at her wit's end. She always waited for her father, no matter how tired she was, so that he might find his supper warm, and a bit of fire and a loving little face to welcome him.

Tessa thought over her troubles at these quiet times and made her plans, because her father left things to her a good deal; and she had no friends but Tommo, the harp boy upstairs, and the lively cricket who lived in the chimney. Tonight her face was very sober and her pretty brown eyes very thoughtful as she stared at the fire and knit her brows as if perplexed. She was not thinking of her old shoes or the empty closet or the boys' ragged clothes just then. No, she had a fine plan in her good little head and was trying to imagine how she could carry it out.

You see, Christmas was coming in a week, and she had set her heart on putting something in the children's stockings, as Mother used to do; for while she had lived things had been comfortable. Now Tessa had not a penny in the world and didn't know how to get one. All the father's earnings had to go for food, fire, and rent.

"I must earn the money; there is no one to give it to me, and I cannot beg. But what can I do, so small and stupid and shy as I am?" Tessa said to herself. "I *must* find some way to give the little ones a nice Christmas. I *must!* I *must!*" And Tessa pulled her long hair as if that would help her think.

But it didn't; and her heart grew heavier and heavier, for it did seem hard that in a great city full of fine things there should be none for poor Nono, Sep, and little Speranza. Just as Tessa's tears began to tumble off her eyelashes onto her brown cheeks, the cricket began to chirp. Of course, he didn't say a word, but before he had piped a dozen shrill notes, an idea popped into Tessa's head—such a truly splendid idea that she clapped her hands and burst out laughing. "I'll do it! I'll do it! If Father will let me," she said to herself, smiling and nodding at the fire.

"Tommo will like to have me go with him and sing while he plays his harp in the streets. I know many songs and may get money if I am not frightened. People throw pennies to other little girls who only play the tambourine. I will sing, yes, I will try; and then, if I do well, the little ones will have a merry Christmas."

So full of her plan was Tessa that she ran upstairs at once and asked Tommo if he would take her with him on the morrow. Her friend was delighted, for he thought Tessa's songs very sweet and was sure she would get money if she tried.

"But see, then, it is cold in the streets; the wind bites, and the snow freezes one's fingers. The day is very long, people are cross, and at night one is ready to die with weariness. Thou art so small, Tessa, I am afraid it will go badly with thee," said Tommo, who was a merry, black-eyed boy of fourteen, with the kindest heart in the world under his old jacket.

"I do not mind cold and wet and cross people, if I can get the pennies," answered Tessa, feeling very brave with such a friend to help her. She thanked Tommo and ran away to get ready, for she felt sure her father would not refuse her anything. She sewed up the holes in her shoes as well as she could, for she had much of that sort of cobbling to do. She mended her only gown and laid ready the old hood and shawl that had been her mother's. Then she washed out little Ranza's frock and put it to dry, because she would not be able to do it the next day. She set the table and got things ready for breakfast, for Tommo went out early and must not be kept waiting for her.

199

Tessa longed to make the beds and dress the children over-night, she was in such a hurry to have it all in order; but as that could not be, she sat down again and tried over all the songs she knew. She chose six pretty ones; and she sung away with all her heart in a fresh little voice and so sweetly that the children smiled in their sleep and her father's tired face brightened as he entered, for Tessa was his cheery cricket on the hearth. When she had told her plan, Peter Benari shook his head and thought it would never do, but Tessa begged so hard, he consented at last that she should try it for one week and sent her to bed the happiest little girl in New York.

Next morning the sun shone, but the cold wind blew and the snow lay thick in the streets. As soon as her father was gone, Tessa flew about and put everything in order, telling the children she was going out for the day and they were to mind Tommo's mother, who would see about the fire and the dinner. The good woman loved Tessa and entered into her plans with all her heart. Nono and Guiseppe, or Sep, as they called him, wondered what she was going away for, and little Ranza cried at being left, but Tessa told them they would know all about it in a week and have a fine time if they were good. So they kissed her all 'round and let her go.

Poor Tessa's heart beat fast as she trudged away with Tommo, who slung his harp over his shoulder and gave her his hand. It was a rather grimy hand, but so kind that Tessa clung to it and kept looking up at the friendly brown face for encouragement.

"We go first to the *café* where many French and Italians eat breakfast. They like my music and often give me sips of hot coffee, which I like so much. You too shall have the sips, and perhaps the pennies, for these people are greatly kind," said Tommo, leading her into a large, smoky place, where many people sat at little tables, eating and drinking. "See, now, have no fear. Give them 'Bella Monica'; that is merry and will make them laugh," whispered Tommo, tuning his harp.

For a moment Tessa felt so frightened that she wanted to run away; but she remembered the empty stockings at home and the fine plan, and she resolved *not* to give it up. One fat old Frenchman nodded to her, and it seemed to help her very much; for she began to sing before she thought. Her voice trembled, and her cheeks grew redder and redder as she went on; but she kept her eyes fixed on her old shoes and so got through without breaking down. The people laughed, for the song *was* merry, and the fat man smiled and nodded again. This gave her courage to try another, and she sang better and better each time; for Tommo played his best and kept whispering to her, "Yes, we go well; this is fine. They will give the money and coffee."

So they did; for when the little concert was over, several men put pennies in the cap Tessa offered, and the fat man took her on his knee and ordered a mug of coffee and some bread and butter for them both. This quite won her heart, and when they left the *café*, she kissed her hand to the old Frenchman and said to her friend, "How kind they are! I like this very much, and now it is not hard."

But Tommo shook his curly head and answered, soberly: "Yes, I took you there first, for they love music and are of our country, but up among the great houses we shall not always do well. The people there are busy or hard or idle and care nothing for harps and songs. Do not skip and laugh too soon, for the day is long, and we have but twelve pennies yet."

Tessa walked more quietly and rubbed her cold hands, feeling that the world was a very big place and wondering how the children got on at home without their little mother. Till noon they did not earn much, for everyone seemed in a hurry, and the noise of many sleigh bells drowned the music. Slowly they made their way up to the great squares where the big houses were, with fine ladies and pretty children at the windows. Here Tessa sung all her best songs, and Tommo played as fast as his fingers could fly; but it was too cold to have the windows open, so the pretty children could not listen long, and the ladies tossed out a little money and soon went back to their own affairs.

All the afternoon the two friends wandered about, singing and playing and gathering up their small harvest. At dusk they went home—Tessa so hoarse she could hardly speak and so tired she fell asleep over her supper. But she had made half a dollar, for Tommo divided the money fairly, and she felt rich with her share. Other days were very much like this. Sometimes they made more, sometimes less, but Tommo always "went halves"; and Tessa kept on, in spite of cold and weariness. Her plans grew as her earnings increased, and now she hoped to get useful things instead of candy and toys alone.

On the day before Christmas, she made herself as tidy as she could, for she hoped to earn a good deal. She tied a bright scarlet handkerchief over the old hood, and the brilliant color set off her brown cheeks and bright eyes, as well as the pretty black braids of her hair. Tommo's mother lent her a pair of boots so big that they turned up at the toes; but there were no holes in them, and Tessa felt quite elegant in whole boots. Her hands were covered with chilblains, for she had no mittens; but she put them under her shawl and scuffled merrily away in her big boots, feeling so glad that the week was over and nearly three dollars safe in her pocket. How gay the streets were that day! How brisk everyone was, and how bright the faces looked as people trotted about with big baskets, holly wreaths, and young evergreens going to blossom into splendid Christmas trees!

"If I could have a tree for the children, I'd never want anything again. But I can't, so I'll fill the socks all full and be happy," said Tessa, as she looked wistfully into the gay stores and saw the heavy baskets go by.

"Who knows what may happen if we do well?" returned Tommo, nodding wisely, for he had a plan as well as Tessa and kept chuckling over it as he trudged through the mud. They did *not* do well, somehow, for everyone seemed so full of their own affairs they could not stop to listen, even to "Bella Monica," but bustled away to spend their money in turkeys, toys, and trees. In the afternoon it began to rain and poor Tessa's heart to fail her.

The big boots tired her feet; the cold wind made her hands ache; and the rain spoiled the fine red handkerchief. Even Tommo looked sober and didn't whistle as he walked, for he also was disappointed; and his plan looked rather doubtful, the pennies came in so slowly.

"We'll try one more street, and then go home, thou art so tired, little one. Come, let me wipe thy face and give me thy hand here in my jacket pocket. There it will be as warm as any kitten." Then kind Tommo brushed away the drops that were not *all* rain from Tessa's cheeks, tucked the poor hand into his ragged pocket, and led her carefully along the slippery streets, for the boots nearly tripped her.

II

At the first house, a cross old gentleman flapped his newspaper at them; at the second, a young gentleman and lady were so busy talking that they never turned their heads; and at the third, a servant came out and told them to go away, because someone was sick. At the fourth, some people let them sing all their songs and gave nothing. The next three houses were empty, and the last of all showed not a single face, as they looked up anxiously. It was so cold, so dark and discouraging that Tessa couldn't help one sob. As he glanced down at the little red nose and wet figure beside him, Tommo gave his harp an angry thump and said something very fierce in Italian. They were just going to turn away; but they didn't because that angry thump happened to be the best thing they could have done. All of a sudden a little head appeared at the window, as if the sound had brought it; then another and another, till there were five, of all heights and colors, and five eager faces peeped out, smiling and nodding to the two below.

"Sing, Tessa, sing! Quick! Quick!" cried Tommo, twanging away with all his might, as he smiled back at the gentlefolk.

How Tessa did tune up at that! She chirped away like a bird, forgetting all about the tears on her cheeks, the ache in her hands, and the heaviness at her heart. The children laughed and clapped their hands, and cried, "More! More! Sing another, little girl! Please, do!" And away they went again, piping and playing, till Tessa's breath was gone and Tommo's stout fingers tingled.

"Mamma says, come to the door. It's too muddy to throw money in the street!" cried out a kindly child's voice, as Tessa held up the old cap with beseeching eyes.

Up the wide stone steps went the street musicians, and the whole flock came running down to give a handful of silver and ask all sorts of questions. Tessa felt so grateful that, without waiting for Tommo, she sang her sweetest little song all alone. It was about a lost lamb, and her heart was in the song; therefore, she sang it well, so well that a pretty young lady came down to listen and stood watching the bright-eyed child, who looked about her as she sang, evidently enjoying the light and warmth of the fine hall and the sight of the lovely children with their gay dresses, shining hair, and dainty little shoes.

"You have a charming voice, child. Who taught you to sing?" asked the young lady kindly.

"My mother. She is dead now, but I do not forget," answered Tessa in her pretty, broken English.

"I wish she could sing at our tree, since Bella is ill," cried one of the children, peeping through the banisters.

"She is not fair enough for the angel and too large to go up in the tree. But she sings sweetly and looks as if she would like to see a tree," said the young lady.

"Oh, so much!" exclaimed Tessa, adding eagerly, "My sister Ranza is small and pretty as a baby angel. She could sit up in the fine tree, and I could sing for her from under the table."

"Sit down and warm yourself, and tell me about Ranza," said the kind elder sister, who liked the confiding little girl in spite of her shabby clothes.

So Tessa sat down and dried her big boots over the furnace and told her story, while Tommo stood modestly in the background and the children listened with faces full of interest.

"O Rose! Let us see the little girl, and if she will do, let us have her; and Tessa can learn our song, and it will be splendid!" cried the biggest boy, who sat astride a chair and stared at the harp with round eyes.

"I'll ask Mamma," said Rose, and away she went into the dining room close by. As the door opened, Tessa saw what looked to her like a grand feast—all silver mugs and flowery plates and oranges and nuts and punch in tall glass pitchers and smoking dishes that smelt so deliciously she could not restrain a little sniff of satisfaction.

"Are you hungry?" asked the boy in a grand tone.

"Yes, sir," meekly answered Tessa.

"I say, Mamma, she wants something to eat. Can I give her an orange?" called the boy, prancing away into the splendid room quite like a prince, Tessa thought.

A plump, motherly lady came out and looked at Tessa, asked a few questions, and then told her to come tomorrow with Ranza, and they would see what could be done. Tessa clapped her hands for joy—she didn't mind the chilblains now—and Tommo played a lively march, he was so pleased.

"Will you come, too, and bring your harp? You shall be paid and shall have something from the tree, likewise," said the lady, who admired what Tessa gratefully told about his kindness.

"Ah, yes; I shall come with much gladness, and play as never in my life before," cried Tommo with a flourish of his old cap.

"Give these to your brothers," said the prince of the household, stuffing nuts and oranges into Tessa's hands.

"And these to the little girl," added one of the young princesses, flying out of the dining room with cakes and rosy apples for Ranza.

Tessa didn't know what to say; but her eyes were full, and she took the mother's white hand in both her little grimy ones and kissed it many times in her pretty Italian fashion. The lady understood her and stroked her cheek softly, saying to her elder daughter, "We must take care of this good little creature. Freddy, bring me your mittens; these poor hands must be covered. Alice, get your play hood; this handkerchief is all wet. And Maud, bring the old chinchilla tippet."

The children ran, and in a minute there were lovely blue mittens on the red hands, a warm hood over the black braids, and a soft fur 'round the sore throat.

"Ah! So kind, so very kind! I have no way to say thank you; but Ranza shall be for you a heavenly angel, and I will sing my heart out for your tree!" cried Tessa, folding the mittens as if she would say a prayer of thankfulness.

Then they went away, and the pretty children called after them, "Come again, Tessa! Come again, Tommo!" Now the rain didn't seem dismal, the wind cold, or the way long, as they shopped for gifts and hurried home.

The spirit of Christmas, who flies about on Christmas Eve to help the loving fillers of little stockings, smiled very kindly on Tessa as she brooded joyfully over the small store of presents that seemed so magnificent to her. All the goodies were divided evenly into three parts and stowed away in Father's three big socks, which hung against the curtain. With her three dollars, she had bought a pair of white stockings for Ranza. To her she also gave the new hood; to Nono the mittens; and to Sep the tippet.

"Now the dear boys can go out, and my Ranza will be ready for the lady to see in her nice new things," said Tessa, quite sighing with pleasure to see how well the gifts looked pinned up beside the bulging socks, which wouldn't hold them all. The little mother kept nothing for herself but the pleasure of giving everything away, yet, I think, she was both richer and happier than if she had kept them all. Her father laughed as he had not done since the mother died when he saw how comically the old curtain had broken out into boots and hoods, stockings and tippets.

"I wish I had a gold gown and a silver hat for thee, my Tessa, thou art so good. May God bless and keep thee always!" said Peter Benari tenderly, as he held his little daughter close and gave her a good-night kiss.

Tessa felt very rich as she crept under the faded counterpane, feeling as if she had received a lovely gift, and fell happily asleep with chubby Ranza in her arms and the two rough black heads peeping out at the foot of the bed. She dreamed wonderful dreams that night and woke in the morning to find real wonders before her eyes. She got up early, to see if the socks were all right, and there she found the most astonishing sight. Four socks, instead of three, and by the fourth, pinned out quite elegantly, was a little dress, evidently meant for her—a warm, woolen dress, all made and with bright buttons on it. It nearly took her breath away—so did the new boots on the floor and the funny long stocking like a gray sausage, with a wooden doll staring out at the top, as if she said, politely, "A Merry Christmas, Ma'am!"

Tessa screamed and danced in her delight, and up tumbled all the children to scream and dance with her, making a regular carnival on a small scale. Everybody hugged and kissed everybody else, offered sucks of orange, bites of cake, and exchanges of candy. Everyone tried on the new things and pranced about in them like a flock of peacocks. Ranza skipped to and fro airily, dressed in her white socks and the red hood; the boys promenaded in their little shirts, one with his creaking new shoes and mittens, the other in his cap and fine tippet; and Tessa put her dress straight on, feeling that her father's "gold gown" was not all a joke. In her long stocking she found all sorts of treasures, for Tommo had stuffed it full of unusual things; and his mother had made gingerbread into every imaginable shape from fat pigs to full omnibuses.

What happy little souls they were that morning; and when they were quiet again, how like a fairy tale did Tessa's story sound to them! Ranza was quite ready to be an angel, and the boys promised to be marvellously good if they were only allowed to see the tree at the "palace," as they called the great house.

Little Ranza was accepted with delight by the kind lady and her children, and Tessa learned the song quite easily. The boys *were* asked to play a part; and after a happy day, the young Italians all returned to be part of the fine Christmas party. Mamma and Miss Rose drilled them all; and when the folding doors flew open, one rapturous "Oh!" arose from the crowd of children gathered at the festival. It was splendid. The great tree glittered with lights and gifts; and on her invisible perch, up among the green boughs, sat the little golden-haired angel, all in white, with downy wings, a shining crown on her head, and the most serene satisfaction in her blue eyes as she stretched her chubby arms to those below and smiled her baby smile at them.

Before anyone could speak, a voice, as fresh and sweet as a lark's, sang a Christmas carol so blithely that everyone stood still to hear and then clapped till the little angel shook on her perch and cried out, "Be 'till, or me'll fall!" How they laughed at that, and what fun they had talking to Ranza, while Miss Rose stripped the tree; for the angel could not resist temptation and amused herself by eating all the bonbons she could reach till she was taken down to dance about like a fairy in a white frock and red shoes. Tessa and her friends had many presents; the boys were perfect lambs; Tommo played for the little folks to dance; and every one said something friendly to the strangers, so that they did not feel shy in spite of shabby clothes. It was a happy night, and all their lives they remembered it as something too beautiful and bright to be quite true.

209

Before they went home, the kind mamma told Tessa she would be her friend and gave her a motherly kiss, which warmed the child's heart and seemed to set a seal upon that promise. It was faithfully kept, because the rich lady had been touched by Tessa's patient struggles and sacrifices. And for many years, thanks to her benevolence, there was no end to Tessa's Surprises.

A Christmas Turkey

Adapted by Stephen W. Hines

"I know we can't do it."

"I say we can if we all helped."

"Well, how can we?"

"I've planned lots of ways. Only you mustn't laugh at them, and you mustn't say a word to Mother. I want it all to be a surprise."

"She'll find us out."

"No, she won't if we tell her we won't get into mischief."

"Fire away, then, and let's hear your fine plans."

"We must talk softly, or we shall wake Father. He's got a headache."

A curious change came over the faces of the two boys as their sister lowered her voice with a nod toward a half-opened door. They looked sad and ashamed, and Kitty sighed as she spoke, because all knew that Father's headaches always began by his coming home sluggish or cross, with only a part of his wages. And mother frequently cried when she thought they did not see her, and after the long sleep, Father looked as if he didn't like to meet their eyes but went off early.

They knew what it meant, but never spoke of it—only pondered over it and mourned with Mother at the change that was slowly altering their kind, industrious father into a moody man and Mother into an anxious, overworked woman.

Kitty was thirteen, and a very capable girl, who helped with the housekeeping, took care of the two little ones, and went to school. Tommy and Sammy looked up to her and thought her a remarkably good sister. Now, as they sat 'round the stove having "a go-to-bed talk," the three heads were close together; and the boys listened eagerly to Kitty's plans, while the rattle of the sewing machine in another room went on as tirelessly as it had done all day. Mother's work was more and more needed every month.

"Well!" began Kitty in an impressive tone, "we all know that there won't be a bit of Christmas in this family if we don't make it. Mother's too busy, and Father doesn't care, so we must see what *we* can do. It would be awful to go to school and say we hadn't had any turkey or plum pudding. Don't expect presents, but we *must* have some kind of a decent dinner."

"So I say; I'm tired of fish and potatoes," said Sammy, the youngest.

"But where's the dinner coming from?" asked Tommy, who had already taken some of the cares of life on his young shoulders and knew that Christmas dinners did not walk into people's houses without money.

"We'll earn it." And Kitty looked like a small Napoleon planning the passage of the Alps. "You, Tom, must go early tomorrow to Mr. Brisket and offer to carry baskets. He will be dreadfully busy, and want you, I know; and you are so strong you can lug as much as some of the big fellows. He pays well, and if he won't give much money, you can take your wages in things to eat."

"What shall I do?" cried Sammy, while Tom sat turning this plan over in his mind.

"Take the old shovel and clear sidewalks. The snow came on purpose to help you."

"It's awful hard work, and the shovel's half gone," began Sammy, who preferred to spend his holiday coasting on an old food tray.

"Don't growl, or you won't get any dinner," said Tom, making up his mind to lug baskets for the good of the family like the manly lad he was.

"I," continued Kitty, "have taken the hardest part of all, because after my work is done and the babies safely settled, I'm going to beg for the leavings of the holly and pine swept out of the church down below, and make some wreaths and sell them."

"If you can," put in Tommy, who had tried to sell pencils and failed to make a fortune.

"Not in the street?" cried Sam, looking alarmed.

"Yes, at the corner of the Park. I'm bound to make some money and don't see any other way. I shall put on an old hood and shawl, and no one will know me. Don't care if they do." And Kitty tried to mean what she said, but in her heart she felt that it would be a trial to her pride if any of her schoolmates should happen to recognize her.

"Don't believe you'll do it."

"See if I don't. I *will* have a good dinner one day in the year!"

"Well, it doesn't seem right for us to do it. Father ought to take care of us, and we only buy some presents with the little bit we earn. He never gives us anything now." And Tommy scowled at the bedroom door with a strong sense of injury struggling with the natural sense of affection he felt in his boyish heart.

"Hush!" cried Kitty. "Don't blame him. Mother says we never must forget he's our father. I try not to, but when she cries, it's hard to feel as I ought." And a sob made the little girl stop short as she poked the fire to hide the trouble in the face that should have been all smiles.

For a moment the room was very still, as the snow beat on the window and the firelight flickered over the six shabby little boots put up on the stove hearth to dry.

Tommy's cheerful voice broke the silence, saying stoutly, "Well, if I've got to work all day, I guess I'll go to bed early. Don't fret, Kit. We'll help all we can and have a good time. See if we don't."

"I'll go out real early and shovel like fury. Maybe I'll get a dollar. Would that buy a turkey?" asked Sammy with the air of a millionnaire.

"No, dear, one big enough for us would cost two dollars, I'm afraid. Perhaps we'll have one sent us. We belong to the church, though folks don't know how poor we are now, and we can't beg." And Kitty bustled about, clearing up, rather exercised in her mind about going and asking for the much desired fowl.

Soon all three were fast asleep, and nothing but the whir of the machine broke the quiet that fell upon the house. Then from the inner room, a man came and sat over the fire with his head in his hands and his eyes fixed on the ragged little boots left to dry. He had heard the children's talk, and his heart was very heavy as he looked about the shabby room that used to be so neat and pleasant. What he thought, no one knows; what he did we shall see by-and-by. But the sorrow and shame and tender silence of his children worked a miracle that night more lasting and lovely than the white beauty which the snow wrought upon the sleeping city.

Bright and early the boys were away to their work, while Kitty sang as she dressed her little sisters, put the house in order, and made her mother smile at the mysterious hints she gave of something splendid that was going to happen. Father was gone, and though all rather dreaded evening, nothing was said, but each worked with a will, feeling that Christmas should be merry in spite of poverty and care.

All day Tommy lugged fat turkeys, roasts of beef, and every sort of vegetable for other people's good dinners on the morrow, wondering meanwhile where his own was coming from. Mr. Brisket had an army of boys trudging here and there and was too busy to notice any particular lad till the hurry was over and only a few belated buyers remained to be served. It was late, but the stores kept open. Although so tired he could hardly stand, brave Tommy held on when the other boys left hoping to earn a trifle more by extra work. He sat down on a barrel to rest during a leisure moment, and presently his weary head nodded sideways into a basket of cranberries, where he slept quietly till the sound of gruff voices roused him.

It was Mr. Brisket scolding because one dinner had been forgotten.

"I told that rascal Beals to be sure to carry it, for the old gentleman will be in a rage if it doesn't come and take away his business. Every boy gone, and I can't leave the store, nor you either, Pat, with all the clearing up to do."

"Here's a boy, sir, sleeping amongst the cranberries. Bad luck to him!" answered Pat, with a shake that set poor Tom on his legs wide awake at once.

"*Good* luck to him, you mean. Here, what's-your-name. You take this basket to that number, and I'll make it worth your while," said Mr. Brisket, much relieved by this unexpected help.

"All right, sir," said Tommy, and off he trudged as briskly as his tired legs would let him, cheering the long cold walk with visions of a turkey with which his employer might reward him. There were still piles of them, and Pat wanted to have one for his family.

His brilliant dreams were disappointed, however. Since Mr. Brisket naturally supposed Tom's father would attend to that part of the dinner, he generously heaped a basket with vegetables, rosy apples, and a quart of cranberries.

"There, if you ain't too tired, you can take one more load to that number, and a merry Christmas to you!" said the stout man, handing over his gift with the promised dollar.

"Thank you, sir, good night," answered Tom, shouldering his last load with a grateful smile and trying not to look longingly at the poultry. He had set his heart on at least a skinny bird as a surprise to Kitty.

Sammy's adventures that day had been more varied and his efforts more successful than Tom's; for Sammy was a most engaging little fellow, and no one could look into his blue eyes without wanting to pat his curly, yellow head with one hand while the other gave him something. The cares of life had not lessened his confidence in people; and only the most abandoned ruffians had the heart to deceive or disappoint him. His very tribulations usually led to something pleasant, and whatever happened, sunshiny Sam came right side up, lucky and laughing.

Undaunted by the drifts or the cold wind, he marched off with the remains of the old shovel to seek his fortune and found it at the third house he called. The first two sidewalks were easy jobs, and he pocketed his dimes with a growing conviction that this was his chosen work. The third sidewalk was a fine, long one, since the house stood on the corner and two pavements must be cleared.

"It ought to be fifty cents, but perhaps they won't give me so much; I'm such a young one. I'll show 'em I can work, though, like a man." And Sammy rang the bell with the energy of a telegraph boy.

But before the bell could be answered, a big boy rushed up, exclaiming roughly, "Get out of this! I'm going to have the job. You can't do it. Start, now, or I'll chuck you into a snow bank."

"I won't!" answered Sammy, indignant at the brutal tone and unjust claim. "I got here first, and it's my job. You let me alone. I ain't afraid of you or your snow banks either."

The big boy wasted no time in words, for steps were heard inside, but after a brief scuffle, hauled Sammy, fighting bravely all the way, down the steps, and tumbled him into a deep drift. Then he ran up the steps and respectfully asked for the job when a neat maid opened the door. He would have got it if Sam had not roared out, as he floundered in the drift, "I came first. He knocked me down 'cause I'm the smallest. Please let me do it. Please!"

Before another word could be said, a little old lady appeared in the hall, trying to look stern and failing entirely, because she was the picture of a dear, fat, cozy grandma.

"Send that *bad*, big boy away, Maria, and call in the poor little fellow. I saw the whole thing, and *he* shall have the job if he can do it."

The bully slunk away, and Sammy came panting up the steps, white with snow, a great bruise on his forehead, and a beaming smile on his face, looking so like a jolly little Santa Claus who had taken a "header" out of his sleigh that the maid laughed. The old lady exclaimed, "Bless the boy! He's dreadfully

217

hurt and doesn't know it. Come in and be brushed and get your breath, child, and tell me how that scamp came to treat you so."

Not loathing to be comforted, Sammy told his tale while Maria dusted him off on the mat, and the old lady hovered in the doorway of the dining room where a nice breakfast smoked and smelled so deliciously that the boy sniffed the odor of coffee and buckwheats like a hungry hound.

"He'll catch his death if he goes to work before he's dried a bit. Put him over the heat register, Maria, and I'll give him a hot drink. It's bitter cold, poor dear!"

Away trotted the kind old lady and in a minute came back with coffee and cakes, on which Sammy feasted as he warmed his toes and told of Kitty's plans for Christmas, led on by the old lady's questions and quite unconscious that he was letting all sorts of cats out of the bag.

Mrs. Bryant understood the little story and made her plans also, because the rosy-faced boy was very like a certain little grandson who had died only last year. Her sad old heart was very tender to all other small boys. So when she found out where Sammy lived, she nodded and smiled at him most cheerily as he shoveled stoutly away at the snow on the long pavements till all was done and the little workman came for his wages.

A bright silver dollar and a pocketful of gingerbread sent him off a rich and happy boy to shovel the sidewalks till noon, when he proudly showed his earnings at home and feasted the babies on the carefully hoarded gingerbread; for Dilly and Dot were the idols of the household.

"Now, Sammy dear, I want you to take my place here this afternoon, because Mother will have to take her work home by and by, and I must sell my wreaths. I only got enough green for six, and two bunches of holly; but if I can sell them for ten or twelve cents apiece, I shall be glad. Girls never *can* earn as much money as boys somehow," sighed Kitty, surveying the thin wreaths tied up with carpet ravellings and vainly puzzling her young wits over a sad problem.

"I'll give you some of my money if you don't get a dollar; then we'll be even. Men always take care of women, you know, and ought to," cried Sammy, setting a fine example to his father if he had only been there to profit by it.

With thanks, Kitty left him to rest on the old sofa, while the happy babies swarmed over him. After putting on a shabby hood and shawl, she slipped away to stand at the Park gate, modestly offering her little wares to the passersby. A nice old gentleman bought two, and his wife scolded him for getting such bad ones; but the money gave more happiness than any other he spent that day. A child took a ten-cent bunch of holly with its red berries, and there Kitty's market ended. It was very cold; people were in a hurry; bolder hucksters pressed before the timid little girl; and the balloon man told her to "clear out."

Hoping for better luck, she tried several other places; but the short afternoon was soon over, the streets began to thin, and the keen wind chilled her to the bone. Her heart was very heavy to think that in all the rich, merry city, where Christmas gifts passed her in every hand, there were none for the dear babies and boys at home, and the Christmas dinner was a failure.

"I must go and get supper anyway, and I'll hang these up in our own rooms, as I can't sell them," said Kitty, wiping a very big tear from her cold cheek and turning to go away.

A smaller, shabbier girl than herself stood near, looking at the bunch of holly with wistful eyes. And glad to do to others as she wished someone would do to her, Kitty offered the only thing she had to give, saying kindly, "You may have it; merry

Christmas!" and ran away before the delighted child could thank her.

I am very sure that one of the angels who fly about at this season of the year saw the little act, made a note of it, and in about fifteen minutes rewarded Kitty for her sweet remembrance of the golden rule.

As she went sadly homeward, Kitty looked up at some of the big houses where every window shone with the festivities of Christmas Eve, and more than one tear fell, for the little girl found life pretty hard just then.

"There don't seem to be any wreaths at these windows. Perhaps they'd buy mine. I can't bear to go home with so little for my share," she said, stopping before one of the biggest and brightest of these homes, where the sound of music was heard and many little heads peeped from behind the curtains as if watching for someone.

Kitty was just going up the steps to make another trial when two small boys came racing 'round the corner, slipped on the icy pavement, and both went down with a crash that would have broken older bones. One was up in a minute, laughing; the other lay squirming and howling, "Oh, my knee! My knee!" till Kitty ran and picked him up with the motherly consolations she had learned to give.

"It's broken; I know it is," wailed the small sufferer as Kitty carried him up the steps while his friend wildly rang the doorbell.

It was like going into something out of a dream, for the house was all astir with a children's Christmas party. Servants flew about with smiling faces; open doors gave ravishing glimpses of a feast in one room and a splendid tree in another; while a crowd of little faces peered over the balusters in the hall above, eager to come down and enjoy the glories prepared for them.

A pretty, young girl came to meet Kitty and listened to her story of the accident, which proved to be less severe than it at first appeared. Bertie, the injured party, forgot his anguish at sight of the tree and hopped upstairs so nimbly that everyone laughed.

"He said his leg was broken, but I guess he's all right," said Kitty, reluctantly turning from this happy scene to go out into the night again.

"Would you like to see our tree before the children come down?" asked the pretty girl, seeing the wistful look in the child's eyes and the shine of half-dried tears on her cheek.

"Oh, yes, I never saw anything so lovely. I'd like to tell the babies all about it," and Kitty's face beamed at the prospect.

"How many babies are there?" asked the girl as she led the way into the brilliant room. Kitty told her, adding several other facts, since the friendly atmosphere seemed to make them friends at once.

"I will buy your wreaths, for we haven't any," said the girl in silk, as Kitty told how she was just coming to offer them when the boys fell.

It was pleasant to see how carefully the little hostess laid away the shabby garlands and slipped a half-dollar into Kitty's hand; prettier still, to watch the sly way in which she tucked some bonbons, a red ball, a blue whip, two china dolls, two pairs of little mittens, and some gilded nuts into an empty box for "the babies"; and prettiest of all, to see the smiles and tears make daylight in Kitty's face as she tried to tell her thanks for this beautiful surprise.

The world was all right when she got into the street again and ran home with the precious box hugged close, feeling that at last she had something to make a merry Christmas of.

Shrieks of joy greeted her, for Sammy's nice old lady had sent a basketful of pies, nuts and raisins, oranges and cake, and—oh, happy Sammy!—a sled, all for love of the blue eyes that twinkled so merrily when he told her about the food tray for sliding. Piled upon his red car of triumph, Dilly and Dot were being dragged about while the other treasures were set forth on the table.

"I must show mine," cried Kitty. "We'll look at them tonight and have them tomorrow." And amid more cries of rapture *her* box was unpacked; *her* money added to the pile in the middle of the table where Sammy had laid his handsome contribution toward the turkey.

"I'm afraid I ought to keep my money for shoes. I've walked the soles off these today and can't go to school barefooted," he said, bravely trying to put the temptation of skates behind him.

"We've got a good dinner without a turkey, and perhaps we'd better not get it," added Kitty with a sigh as she surveyed the table and remembered the blue knit hood marked seventy-five cents that she saw in a shop window.

"Oh, we *must* have a turkey! We worked so hard for it, and it's so Christmasy," cried Sam, who always felt that pleasant things ought to happen.

"Must have turty," echoed the babies as they eyed the dolls tenderly.

"You *shall* have a turkey, and there he is," said an unexpected voice, as a noble bird was placed upon the table and lay there sticking up his legs as if enjoying the surprise immensely.

It was Father's voice, and there stood Father, neither cross nor depressed, but looking as he used to look, kind and happy. Beside him stood Mother, smiling as they had not seen her smile for months. It was not because the work was well paid for, and more promised, but because she had received a gift that made the world bright, a home happy again—Father's promise to drink no more!

"I've been working today as well as you, and you may keep your money for yourselves. There are shoes for all; and never again, please God, shall my children be ashamed of me or want a dinner for Christmas Day."

As Father said this with a choke in his voice, and Mother's head went down on his shoulder to hide the happy tears that wet her cheeks, the children didn't know whether to laugh or cry, till Kitty, with the instinct of a loving heart, settled the question by saying, as she held out her hands, "We haven't any tree, so let's dance around our goodies and be merry."

Then the tired feet in the old shoes forgot their weariness, and five happy little souls skipped gaily around the table, where, in the midst of all the treasures earned and given, Father's Christmas turkey proudly lay in state.

Becky's Christmas Dream

Adapted by Stephen W. Hines

*L*ittle Becky sat all alone by the kitchen fire, for everyone else had gone away to keep Christmas and left her to take care of the house. Nobody had thought to give her any presents or to take her to any merrymaking. Nor had they remembered that Christmas should be made a happy time to every child, whether poor or rich. She was only twelve years old—this little girl from the poorhouse, who was bound to work for the farmer's wife till she was eighteen. She had no father or mother, no friends or home but this, and, as she sat alone by the fire, her heart ached for someone to love and cherish her.

Becky was a shy, quiet child, with a thin face and wistful eyes that always seemed trying to find something she wanted very much. She worked away, day after day, so patiently and silently that no one ever guessed what curious thoughts filled the little cropped head, or what a tender child's heart was hidden under the blue-checked pinafore.

Tonight she was wishing that there were fairies in the world who would whisk down the chimney and give her quantities of pretty things, as they did in delightful fairy tales.

"I'm sure I am as poor and lonely as Cinderella and need a kind godmother to help me as much as ever she did," said Becky to herself, as she sat on her little stool staring at the fire. She felt too much out of sorts to care whether things looked cheerful, and the fire did not burn brightly at all.

There is an old belief that all dumb things can speak for one hour on Christmas Eve. Now Becky knew nothing of this story, and no one can say whether what happened was true or whether she fell asleep and dreamed it. This I do believe: all sorts of kindly spirits seem to fly about at Christmastime, putting good thoughts, merry words, and generous wishes into people's hearts. Maybe this accounts for some of the surprising and delightful things that happen then, making Christmas the happiest time of all the year.

When Becky compared herself to Cinderella, she was amazed to hear a small voice reply:

"Well, my dear, if you want advice, I shall be very glad to give you some, for I've had much experience in this trying world."

Becky stared about her, but all she saw was the old gray cat, blinking at the fire as she sat purring comfortably with her tail neatly folded round her paws.

"Did you speak, Tabby?" said the child.

"Of course I did. If you wish a godmother, here I am;" and Mrs. Tabby drew herself up with a wise and dignified air.

Becky laughed at the idea; but Puss, with her silver-gray suit, white handkerchief crossed on her bosom, kind, motherly old face, and cozy purr, did make a very good little godmother after all.

"Please, Ma'am, I'm ready to listen," said Becky, respectfully, for somehow the old cat's manner was impressive.

"Well, my child, what do you want most?" asked the god-mother, quite in the fairy book style.

"To be loved by everybody," answered Becky, telling what really was the first wish of her solitary heart.

"Good!" said the cat. "I'm pleased with that answer. It's sensible, and I'll tell you how to get your wish. Learn to make people love you by loving them."

"I don't know how," sighed Becky, somehow disturbed by the simplicity of the answer.

"No more did I, in the beginning," returned Puss. "When I first came here, a shy young kitten, I thought only of keeping out of everybody's way, for I had been cruelly treated at my last place, and I was afraid of everyone. I hid under the barn and only came out when no one was near. I stole my food slyly. I never would let the children touch me, and no coaxing could win my confidence. I wasn't happy, for I wanted to be petted but didn't know how to begin and had no faith in the gentle voices that called me.

"One day I heard Aunt Sally say to the master, 'James, that wild kitten ain't no use at all; you'd better give her away and get a nice tame one to amuse the children and clear the house of mice.'

" 'The poor thing has been abused, I guess; so we'll give her another trial, and maybe she'll come to trust us after a while,' said the good master.

"I thought over these things as I lay under the barn and resolved to do my best, for I didn't wish to be cast away again. It was hard at first, but I began by coming out when little Jane called me; and I let her play with me. Then I ventured into the house, and, finding a welcome at my first visit, I went again and took a mouse with me to show that I wasn't idle. To my surprise, everyone was charmed with my confiding ways; no one hurt or

227

frightened me, and soon I was the household pet. For several years I have led a happy life—doing my work, beloved by everybody, and always anxious to show my affection by letting the little ones play with me, though I don't enjoy it much myself. And I purr my best when I sit here among the family, feeling quite one of them, though once I was only a poor, forlorn stranger-kitten."

Becky listened intently, and when Puss ended, she said, timidly:

"Do you think if I try not to be afraid, and show that I want to be affectionate, the people will let me and will like it?"

"Very sure. I heard the mistress say you were a good, handy worker. Aunt Sally thought you were sly because quiet children sometimes are; but the master said of you as he did of me, 'Give the poor child a fair trial. She has had a hard time of it and hasn't learned to trust us yet.' Do as I did, my dear, and you will find that there is plenty of love in the world."

"I will. Thank you, dear old Puss, for your advice. You were my first friend here, and I've always loved you, because you came and got into my lap that first day when I was so frightened. It was so kind of you I wanted to cry, but I didn't dare."

"I couldn't talk then, but I tried to show my sympathy. Do your best, my child, and remember that Tabby is always your friend."

As she spoke, Puss came to rub her soft cheek against Becky's hand, and then settled herself in a cozy hunch in Becky's lap, purring away like a kind old grandma humming a lullaby. Becky stroked the soft, gray head and gave Mrs. Tabby a grateful kiss as the big, yellow eyes blinked kindly at her.

Before Becky could say another word, a queer, monotonous voice said high above her:

"Tick, tick; wish again, little Becky, and I'll tell you how to find your wish."

It was the old, moon-faced clock behind the door, which had struck twelve just before Tabby first spoke.

"Dear me," said Becky, "how queerly things do act tonight!" She thought a moment, then said, soberly, "I wish I liked my work better, but washing dishes, picking chips, and hemming towels is such tiresome work, I don't see how I *can* go on doing it for six more years."

"Just what I used to feel," said the clock. "I couldn't bear to think that I had to stand here and do nothing but tick year after year. I flatly said I wouldn't, and I stopped a dozen times a day. Bless me, what a fuss I made! Never right, always too fast or too slow, weights out of order, hands pointing wrong, and no end of worry with my works inside. At last my constitution was nearly ruined by these pranks; everyone was out of patience with me, and I was put in this corner to stand idle for several months.

"At first I rejoiced; then I got tired of doing nothing and began to reflect that, as I was born a clock, it would be wiser to do my duty and get some satisfaction out of it if I could.

"So one day, to the amazement of everyone, I struck twelve times and began to go. It produced a great sensation in the family, and from that day to this, I have kept excellent time. That was fifty years ago, when the master was a boy. But he remembers it, and we laugh over it sometimes. We have grown old together, and, as he says, 'keep one another going steadily.' He never forgets to wind me up; I never forget to strike regularly, and, though my work is tedious, I do it faithfully, teaching punctuality and the worth of time to all who know and love me."

"Teach me to be as faithful and to love my duty as you do," cried Becky.

"I will," and the old clock grandly struck the half hour with a smile on its round face as it steadily ticked on.

Here the fire blazed up, and the teakettle, hanging on the crane, began to sing.

"How cheerful that is!" said Becky, as the whole kitchen brightened with the ruddy glow. "If I could have a third wish, I'd wish to be as cheerful as the fire."

"Have your wish if you choose, but you must work for it as I do," cried the fire, as its flames embraced the old kettle till it gurgled with pleasure. "Don't get smothered under the ashes or discouraged by green sticks; burn away as brightly as you can, no matter if you have only a wood chip to feed you. Brighten up the dark places, and warm the cold ones. Dance and crackle till the room where you are is as pleasant as this kitchen, and shine on everyone with a genial glow that will touch even the sternest, as I have won the cross old kettle to sing a little song."

Here the kettle not only sung, but its lid began to dance a jig, and Becky thought she heard a queer voice humming these words:

> "I'm an old black kettle,
>   With a very crooked nose,
> But I can't help being gay
>   When the jolly fire glows.
>
> "I'm everybody's servant,
>   There's no end to my toil,
> And all my days are spent
>   In an everlasting boil.
>
> "In my smoky corner here
>   No holidays I see,
> Yet all Christmas feasts
>   Were spoiled without me.

"So contentedly I work,
And hope yet to be told
I'm a good and faithful kettle,
Though ugly, black, and old."

As the song ended, a silvery cloud of steam gushed from the kettle and floated in the red firelight, as if to show how much beauty could come from a happy heart, no matter how homely or how humble. Becky felt this, but said not a word; for the cloud, instead of melting away, seemed to lift like a curtain, showing a picture of herself years later. Not a splendid picture, but one that she was glad to see; for in the brisk, bright-faced old woman who was surrounded by a flock of children, all clinging lovingly to "our Becky," she saw herself. Only a servant still, but trusted, respected, and beloved for years of faithful, cheerful work that had won a place for her in the hearts of all.

"A good and faithful servant—yes, I'll try to be that with all my heart, and the pretty picture may come true at last," said Becky, as the mist floated away and the old kettle boiled over as if it could contain itself no longer.

"I shouldn't wonder a mite if that little hussy has been up to mischief tonight, rummaged all over the house, ate herself sick, and stole something to run away with," croaked Aunt Sally, as the family went jingling home from the Christmas party in the big sleigh at one o'clock.

"Tut, tut, Aunty, I wouldn't think evil of the poor thing. If I'd had my way, she'd have gone with us and had a good time. She don't look as if she'd seen many, and I've a notion it's what she needs," said the farmer kindly.

"The thought of her alone at home has worried me all the evening; but she didn't seem to mind, and I haven't had time to get a decent dress ready for her; so I let it go," added the farmer's wife, as she cuddled little Jane under the cloaks and shawls with a regretful memory of Becky knocking at her heart.

"I've got some popcorn and a bouncing big apple for her," said Billy, the red-faced lad perched up by his father playing drive.

"And I'll give her one of my dolls. She said she never had one—wasn't that dreadful?" put in little Jane, popping out her head like a bird from its nest.

"Better see what she has been about first," advised Aunt Sally. "If she hasn't done no mischief, and has remembered to have the kettle boiling so I can have a warm cup of tea after my ride, and if she's kept the fire up, and warmed my slippers, I don't know but I'll give her the red mittens I knit for Betsey's boy. I didn't give them to him today, for I caught him laughing at me, and I've got them in my pocket now. Mercy sakes! I do believe the house is afire," added the old lady, as they drove into the yard and saw a bright light shining out from the kitchen windows.

"Only a good fire," said the farmer.

"I do believe the child has run away, just as I said," croaked Aunt Sally when no one opened the door or heard the bells as the horses stopped.

"Most likely, she's fast asleep, poor dear," said the mother, hurrying in.

The rest followed, and there was poor Becky lying on the bare floor, her head pillowed on the stool, and old Tabby in her arms, with a corner of the blue pinafore spread over her. The fire was burning splendidly, the kettle simmering, and in a row upon the hearth stood, not only Aunt Sally's old slippers, but those of master and mistress also; and over a chair hung two little night-gowns warming also for the children.

"Well, now, if that don't beat all for thoughtfulness and sense! *Becky* shall have them mittens, and I'll knit her a couple of pair of stockings as sure as she's living" said Aunt Sally, completely won over by this unusual proof of enterprise in a servant.

I don't know how it was, but I fancy that some of the kindly spirits, of whom I spoke, had come in with the family, and now took possession of the hearts full of Christmas goodwill; for, as they looked down on their little handmaid, something in the quiet figure spoke to them louder than any words and made the task Becky had set herself much easier than she expected.

Aunt Sally laid the gay mittens close to the little, rough hand that worked so busily all day. Billy set his big, red apple and bag of popcorn just where she would see them when she woke. Jane laid the doll in Becky's arms, and Tabby smelt of it approvingly to the children's delight. The farmer had no present ready, but he stroked the little, cropped head with a fatherly touch that made Becky smile in her sleep, as he said within himself, "I'll do by this forlorn child as I'd wish anyone to do by my Janey if she was left alone." But the mother gave the best gift of all, for she stooped down and kissed Becky as only mothers can kiss; for the good woman's heart reproached her for neglect of the child who had no mother.

That unusual touch awakened Becky at once, and, looking about her with astonished eyes, she saw such a wonderful change in all the faces that her own lost its pathetic sadness as she clapped her hands and cried with a child's happy laugh:

"My dream's come true! Oh, my dream's come true!"

And so it had, thanks to the spirit of Christmas; for when Becky, leaning confidently on the mother's knee, told what a very humble little dream hers had been, the good farmer nodded thoughtfully at the fire, and said:

233

"Yes, a life spent in cheerfully serving others *is* the best life after all, my little Becky, and we'll all help to make yours a happy one."

Kate's Choice

"Well, what do you think of her?"

"I think she's a perfect dear and not a bit stuck up with all her money."

"A real little lady and ever so pretty."

"She kissed me lots, and she doesn't tell me to run away, so I love her."

The group of brothers and sisters standing round the fire laughed as little May finished the chorus of praise with these crowning virtues.

Tall Kent had asked the question and seemed satisfied with the general approval of the new cousin who had just arrived from England to live with them.

They had often heard of Kate and rather prided themselves on the fact that she lived in a fine house, was very rich, and sent them charming presents. Now pity was added to the pride, for Kate was an orphan, and all her money could not buy back the parents she had lost.

They had watched impatiently for her arrival, had welcomed her cordially, and after a day spent in trying to make her feel at home, they were comparing notes in the twilight, while Kate was having a quiet talk with Mamma.

"I hope she will choose to live with us. You know she can go to any of the uncles she likes best," said Kent.

"We are nearer her age than any of the other cousins, and Papa is the oldest uncle, so I guess she will," added Milly, the fourteen-year-old daughter of the house.

"She said she liked America," said quiet Frank.

"Wonder if she will give us a lot of her money?" put in practical Fred, who was always in debt.

"Stop that!" commanded Kent. "Mind now, if you ever ask her for a penny, I'll shake you out of your jacket."

"Hush! She's coming," cried Milly, and a dead silence followed the lively chatter.

A fresh-faced, bright-eyed girl of fifteen came in quietly, glanced at the group on the rug, and paused as if uncertain whether she was wanted.

"Come on!" said Fred, encouragingly.

"Would I be in the way?" she asked.

"Oh, dear, no! We were only talking," answered Milly, drawing her cousin nearer with an arm about her waist.

"It sounded like something pleasant," said Kate, not exactly knowing what to say.

"We were talking about you," began Little May. A poke from Frank made her stop to ask, "What's that for? We *were* talking about Kate, and we all said we liked her, so it's no matter if I tell."

"You are very kind," said Kate looking so pleased that the children forgave May's awkward frankness.

"Yes, and we hoped you'd like us and stay with us," added Kent, in the lofty and polite manner that he thought became a young man of his stature.

"I am going to live with all the uncles in turn, and then decide," Kate answered. "Papa wished it." The words made her lips tremble slightly, for her father was the only parent she could remember and had been unusually dear to her for that reason.

"Can you play billiards?" asked Fred, who had a horror of seeing girls cry.

"Yes, and I will be glad to teach you."

"You had a pony carriage at your house, didn't you?" added Frank, eager to hear more.

"At Grandma's—I had no other home, you know," answered Kate.

"What will you buy first with your money?" asked May, who seemed determined to ask improper questions.

"I'd buy a grandma if I could," and Kate both smiled and sighed.

"How funny!" said May. "We have a grandma who lives ever so far away in the country. We don't think of her much."

"You do?" said Kate, who turned quickly, looking full of interest.

"Yes! Papa's mother is very old," added Milly. "Papa writes to her sometimes, and Mamma sends her things every Christmas. We don't know much about her, for we've only seen her once, a great long time ago. But we do care for her."

"Perhaps I shall go and see her," said Kate with a smile. "I can't get on without a grandmother. Tell me all you know about her. Is she a dear lady?"

"We only know this. She is lame and lives in the old house where Papa grew up. She has a maid named Dolly, and—that's all I can tell you about her," said Molly looking a little vexed that she could say no more of the subject that seemed to interest her cousin so much.

Kate looked surprised, but said nothing and stood looking at the fire as if turning the matter over in her mind and trying to answer the question she was too polite to ask—how could they have a grandmother and know so little about her?

At that moment, the tea bell rang, and the flock ran laughing downstairs. Kate said no more to her cousins, but she remembered the conversation and laid a plan in her resolute little mind.

According to her father's wish, Kate was to live for a while with the families of each of her four uncles before she decided with which she would make her home. All were anxious to have her, one because of her money, another because her great-grandfather had been a lord, a third hoped to secure her hand for the son of a close friend, while the fourth and best family loved her for herself alone.

They were worthy people, as the world goes—busy, ambitious, and prosperous; and every one, old and young, was fond of bright, pretty, generous Kate. Each family was anxious to keep her, a little jealous of the rest, and very eager to know which she would choose.

But Kate surprised them all by saying decidedly when the time came, "I would like to meet my grandma before I choose. Perhaps I should have visited her first, as she is the oldest. I believe Papa would have wished it so. At any rate, I feel I must pay her tribute before I settle anywhere."

Some of the young cousins laughed at the idea and her old-fashioned, respectful way of putting it. It was a strong contrast to their free and easy American speech. The uncles were also surprised, but they agreed to humor her whim.

Uncle George, the eldest said softly, "I should have remembered that poor Anna was mother's only daughter. Naturally, she would love to see the girl. But dear, I must warn you, it will be desperately dull. Just two old women and a quiet, country town. No fun, no company. You won't want to stay long, I can assure you."

"I shall not mind the dullness for the chance to meet my grandmother," Kate replied. "Perhaps the sight of me will please her, for many say I look like my mamma."

Something in the earnest, young face reminded Uncle George of the sister he had almost forgotten and recalled his own youth so pleasantly that he said, with a caress of the curly head beside him, "I believe it would. In fact, I'm sure of it. Now that you say it, I have a mind to go with you and 'pay tribute' to my mother as you have so sweetly put it."

"Oh my, but I would like to surprise her and have her all to myself for a little while. Would you mind if I went quite alone? All of you could come later if it pleases you," answered Kate.

"Of course, it will be managed exactly as you like," answered Uncle George. "I know you will bring sunshine to our old mother's life, just as you have to ours. I haven't seen her for a year, but I know she is well and comfortable, and Dolly guards her like a dragon. Give her my love, sweet Kate, and tell her we have sent her something she will value a hundred times more than the very best tea, the finest cap, or the most handsome tabby cat who ever purred."

So, in spite of the protestations of her cousins, Kate went happily off to find the grandmother whom no one else seemed to value as she did.

Grandpa had been a farmer and lived contentedly on the old place until he died, but his four sons wanted to be something better, so they went away one after the other to make their way in the world. All worked hard, earned a good living, and forgot, as far as possible, the dull lives they had led in the old place from which they had come.

They were all good sons in their own way and had each offered his mother a home with him if she cared to come. But Grandma clung to the old home, the simple ways, and the quiet life. She thanked them gratefully, but chose to remain in the big farmhouse, empty, lonely, and plain though it was compared to the fine homes in which her sons lived.

Little by little the busy men seemed to forget their quiet, uncomplaining old mother, who spent her years thinking of them, longing to see and know their children, and hoping that one day they would remember how much she loved them.

Now and then one of her sons would pay her a hasty visit, and all sent gifts of far less value to her than one loving look, one hour of dutiful, affectionate companionship.

"If you ever want me, send and I'll come. Or if you ever need a home, remember the old place is always open, and you are always welcome here," the good old lady had told them. But they never seemed to need her and so seldom came that she concluded the old place evidently held no charming memories for them.

It was hard. But the sweet old woman bore it patiently and lived her lonely life quietly and usefully, with her faithful maid Dolly, who served and loved and supported her.

Anna, her only daughter, had married young, gone to England, and, dying early, had left her only child to her husband and his family. Among them, little Kate had grown up, knowing scarcely anything about her American relatives.

She had been the pet of her English grandmother, and, finding all her aunts to be busy, fashionable women, had longed for the tender fostering she had known and now felt as if only grandmothers could give.

With a flutter of hope and expectation, she approached the old house after the long journey was over. Leaving the luggage at the inn and accompanied only by her nurse, Bessie, Kate went up the village street and, pausing at the gate, looked with interest at the home where her mother had been born.

It was a large, old-fashioned farmhouse, with a hospitable porch and tall trees in front. Her uncles had told her that the house also had a lovely orchard in back and a hill, which grew over with luscious wild blackberries in summer and provided the perfect place for sledding in winter.

Kate noticed that all the upper windows were curtained, making the house look as if it were half asleep. At one of the lower windows, she spotted a portly puss, blinking in the sun. Just to the side and behind, she was certain she could see a cap, a regular grandmotherly old cap, with a little black bow on the back.

Something about the lonely look of the house and the pensive droop of that cap made Kate hurry on up the walk and eagerly tap the front door with the antique knocker. A brisk little old woman peered out, as if startled at the sound. Kate asked, smiling. "Does Madam Coverley live here?"

"She surely does, my dear," said the maid, "Come right in." Then throwing wide the door, she led the way down the long, wide hall and announced in a low tone to her mistress, "A lovely young girl is here to see you, mum."

"I would love to see a young face, Dolly. Who is it?" she asked in a gentle voice.

Before Dolly could answer that she didn't know the identity of their visitor, Kate stepped straight up to the old lady with both hands out. "Grandma, can't you guess?" she asked. The first sight of her grandmother's dear face had won her heart.

Lifting her spectacles, Grandma examined her for a moment, then opened her arms without a word. In the long embrace that followed, Kate felt assured that she was welcome in the home she wanted.

"So like my Anna! And this is her little girl? God bless you, my darling! You are so good to come and see me!" said Grandma when the emotion had passed and she was able to speak again.

"Why Grandma, as soon as I knew where to find you, I was in a tizzy to come. Already I know that I will want to stay here with you as long as you will have me," Kate said, caressing her grandmother's hand affectionately.

"Then you shall never leave, for I will always want you, my darling," Grandma assured her. "Now tell me everything. It is like an angel coming to see me quite unannounced. Sit close, and let me feel sure it isn't one of the dreams I create to cheer myself when I'm feeling lonely."

Kate sat on a little stool at her grandmother's feet and, leaning on her knee, told all her little story. All the while, the old lady fed her hungry eyes with the sight of the fresh, young face, listened to the music of the child's loving voice, and felt the happy certainty that God had sent her a wonderful gift.

Kate spent the long, happy day talking and listening, looking at her new home and, to her delight, being fawned over by the two old women. Her eyes quickly read the truth of Grandma's lonely life, and her warm heart was soon flooded with tender pity for her. Kate resolved to devote herself to making her grandmother happy in her few remaining years, for at eighty, everyone should have the blessing of loving children.

To Dolly and Madam, it really did seem as if an angel had come, a singing, smiling, chattering sprite, who danced all over the old house, making blithe echoes in the silent house and brightening every room she entered. They also soon grew fond of Bessie, who welcomed their help caring for her charge.

Kate opened all the shutters and let in the sun, saying she must see which room she liked best before she settled in. She played on the old piano, which wheezed and jangled, all out of tune. But no one minded, for the girlish voice was as sweet as a lark's. She invaded Dolly's sacred kitchen and messed to her heart's content, delighting the old soul by praising her skill and begging to be taught all she knew.

She took possession of Grandma's little parlor and made it so cozy that the old lady felt as if she might have stumbled into someone else's front room. Cushioned armchairs, fur footstools, soft rugs, and delicate warm shawls appeared like magic.

Kate planted flowers in the deep, sunny window seats and hung pictures of lovely places on the oaken walls. She found a dainty workbasket for herself and placed it near Grandma's quaint one. And, best of all, she spent plenty of time in the little chair next to Grandma's rocker.

The first thing in the morning, Kate awakened her grandmother with a kiss and a cheery, "Good morning!" And all day, she hovered about her with willing hands and quick feet. Kate's loving heart returned her grandmother's love and pledged her the tender reverence, which is the beautiful tribute the young should pay the old. In the twilight, the bright head could always be found at the old woman's knee, listening to the stories of the past or making lively plans for the future. Together, they whiled away the time that had once been filled with sadness.

Kate never found it lonely, seldom wished for other society, and grew every day more certain that, in this home, she would find the cherishing she needed and do the good she hoped to do for others.

Dolly and Bessie were on capital terms; each trying to see which could sing "Little Kate's" praises loudest and spoil her quickest by unquestioning obedience to her every whim. They were a happy family, indeed! And the dull November days went by so fast that Christmas was at hand before they knew it.

All the uncles had written to ask Kate to pass the holidays with them, feeling sure that by then she would be longing for a change. But she had refused them all, thanking them for their gracious invitations. "I wish to stay with Grandma," she told them, "for she cannot go to join other people's merrymaking."

Her uncles urged, her aunts advised, and her cousins teased, but Kate denied them all, yet offended no one, for she was inspired by a grand idea and carried it out with help from Dolly and Bessie. Her grandma never suspected a thing.

"We are going to have a little Christmas fun up here among ourselves, and you mustn't know about it until we are ready. So just sit all cozy in your chair, and let me riot about as I like. I know you won't mind, and I think you'll say it is splendid when I've carried out my plan," said Kate, when the old lady wondered what she was thinking about so deeply, with her brows knit and her lips smiling.

"Very well, dear, do anything you like, and I shall enjoy it, only please don't tire yourself out by trying to do too much," said Grandma. And with that she became deaf and blind to the mysteries that went on about her.

Because her Grandma was lame and seldom left her few favorite rooms, Kate, with the help of her devoted helpers, was able to turn the house topsy-turvy. Together, the three trimmed the hall and parlor and great dining room with shining holly and evergreen, lay fires ready for kindling on the hearths that had been cold for years, and made beds fit for sleeping all over the house.

What went on in the kitchen, only Dolly could tell. But such delicious odors as stole out made Grandma sniff the air and think of merry Christmas revels long ago.

Up in her room, Kate wrote lots of letters and sent so many orders to the city that Bessie was soon throwing up her hands. More letters came in reply, and Kate studied each one carefully with a look of pure happiness on her face.

Big bundles were left by the express man, who came so often that the gates were left open and the lawn was full of sleigh tracks. The shops in the village were ravaged by Mistress Kate, who laid in stores of bright ribbon, toys, nuts, and all manner of delightful things.

"I really think the sweet young thing has lost her mind," said the postmaster as she flew out of the office one day with a handful of letters.

If Grandma had thought the girl out of her wits, no one could have blamed her, for on Christmas day she really did behave in the most puzzling manner.

"You are going to church with me this morning, Grandma. It's all arranged. A closed sleigh is coming for us; the sleighing is lovely, the church all trimmed out for the holidays, and I must have you see it. I shall wrap you in fur, and we will go and say our prayers together, like good girls, won't we?" said Kate, who was in an unusual flutter, her eyes shining bright, her lips full of smiles, and her feet dancing in spite of her.

"Anywhere you like, my darling," Grandma answered. "I'd start for Australia tomorrow, if you wanted me to go with you."

So they went to church, and Grandma did enjoy it, for she had many blessings to thank God for, chief among them the treasure of a dutiful, loving child. Kate tried to keep herself quiet, but the odd little flutter would not subside and seemed to get worse and worse as time went on. It increased rapidly as they drove home, and when Grandma was safe in her little parlor again, Kate's hands trembled so she could hardly tie the strings of the old lady's fancy cap.

"We must take a look in the big parlor. It is all trimmed out, and I have my presents in there. Is it ready, Dolly?" Kate asked, as the dear, old servant appeared, looking greatly excited.

"We have been quiet so long, poor Dolly doesn't know what to make of a little gayety," Grandma said, smiling at her beloved companion.

"Lord, bless us, my dear mum! It's all so beautiful and kind of surprising. I feel as if miracles are coming to pass again," answered Dolly, actually wiping away a tear with her best apron.

"Come, Grandma," urged Kate offering her arm. "You look so sweet and dear," she added, smoothing the soft, silken shawl about the old lady's shoulders and kissing the placid, old face that beamed at her from under the festive, new cap.

"I always said Madam was the finest and dearest of women," Dolly went on. "But, do hurry, Miss Kate. That parlor door could burst open at any moment and spoil the surprise," with which mysterious remark Dolly vanished, giggling.

Across the hall they went, but at the door Kate paused, and said with a look Grandma never forgot, "I hope I have done right. I hope you will like my present and not find it too much for you. At any rate, remember that I meant to please you and give you the thing you need and long for most, my dear, sweet grandmother."

"My good child, don't be afraid. I shall like anything you do and thank you for your thoughtfulness," Grandma answered. "But, oh my! What a curious noise."

Without another word, Kate threw open the door and led Grandma in. Only a step or two—for the lady stopped short and stared about her, as if she didn't know her own best parlor. No wonder she didn't, for it was full of people, and such people! All her sons, their wives, and children rose as she came in, and turned to greet her with smiling faces. Uncle George went up and kissed her, saying, with a choke in his voice, "A merry Christmas, Mother!" and everybody echoed the words in a chorus of goodwill that went straight to the heart.

Poor Grandma could not bear it and sat down in her big chair, trembling and sobbing like a little child. Kate hung over her, fearing the surprise had been too much; but joy seldom kills, and presently, the old lady was calm enough to look up and welcome them all by stretching out her feeble hands and saying, brokenly yet heartily, "God bless you, my children!

This is a merry Christmas, indeed! Now tell me all about what you've been doing. And give me names, for I don't know half the little ones."

Then Uncle George explained that it was Kate's plan, and told how she had made everyone agree to it, pleading so eloquently for Grandma that all the other plans were given up. They had arrived while she was at church and had been, with difficulty, kept from bursting out before the time.

"Do you like your present?" whispered Kate, quite calm and happy now that the grand surprise was safely over.

Grandma answered with a silent kiss that said more than the warmest words, and then Kate put everyone at ease by leading up the children, one by one, and introducing each with some lively speech. Everyone enjoyed this and became acquainted quickly, for Grandma thought the children the most remarkable she had ever seen. The little people soon made up their minds that an old lady who had such a very nice, big house and such a dinner waiting for them (of course, they had peeped everywhere) was a most desirable and charming grandma.

By the time the first raptures were over, Dolly and Bessie had dinner on the table, and the procession, headed by Madam proudly escorted by her eldest son, filed into the dining room where such a party had not met for years.

The dinner itself was most spectacular. Everyone partook copiously of everything, and they laughed and talked, told stories, and sang songs. The cheer they gave Grandma was almost too much for her to bear.

After that, the elders sat with Grandma in the parlor, while the younger part of the flock trooped after Kate all over the house. Fires burned everywhere, and the long unused toys that had belonged to their fathers were brought out for their amusement. The big nursery was full of games, and here Bessie collected the little ones when the older boys and girls were invited by Kate to go outside for sledding. The evening ended with a cozy tea and a dance in the long hall.

The going to bed that night was the best joke of all, for though Kate's arrangements were a bit odd, everyone loved them quite well. There were many rooms, but not enough for all to have one apiece. So the uncles and aunts had the four big chambers, all the boys were ordered into the great playroom, where beds were made on the floor and a great fire was blazing. The nursery was devoted to the girls, and the little ones were sprinkled 'round wherever a snug corner was found.

How the riotous flock were ever packed away into their beds no one knows. The lads caroused until long past midnight, and no knocking on the walls of paternal boots or whispered entreaties of maternal voices through the keyholes had any effect, for it was impossible to resist the present advantages for a grand Christmas rampage.

The older girls giggled and told secrets, while the little ones tumbled into bed and went to sleep at once, quite exhausted by the festivities of this remarkable day.

Grandma, down in her own cozy room, sat listening to the blithe noises with a smile on her face, for the past seemed to have come back again. It was as if her own boys and girls were once again frolicking in the rooms above her head, as they had done forty years before.

"It's all so beautiful. I can't go to bed, Dolly, and lose any of it. They'll go away tomorrow, and I may never see them again," she said, as Dolly tied on her nightcap and brought her slippers.

"Yes, you will, Mum. That dear child has made it so pleasant that they won't be able to stay away. You'll see plenty of them, if they carry out half the plans they had made. Mrs. George wants to come up and pass the summer here; Mr. Tom says he shall send his boys to school here; and every girl among them has promised Kate to make her a long visit. You'll never be lonely again, Mum."

"Thank God for that!" Grandma said bowing her head to acknowledge that she had received a great blessing. "Dolly, I want to go and look at those children. It seems so like a dream to have them here, I must be sure of it," said Grandma, folding her wrapper about her, and getting up with great decision.

"Oh my, Mum," Dolly protested. "You haven't been up those stairs in months. The dears are just fine, sleeping warm as toast."

But Grandma would go, so Dolly gave her an arm, and together the two dear friends hobbled up the wide stairs and peeped in at the precious children. The lads looked like a camp of weary warriors reposing after a victory, and Grandma went laughing away when she had taken a proud survey of this promising portion of the younger generation.

The nursery was like a little convent full of rosy nuns sleeping peacefully, while a picture of Saint Agnes, with her lamb, smiled on them from the wall. The firelight flickered over the white figures and sweet faces, as if the sight were too fair to be lost in darkness. The little ones lay about, looking like little Cupids with sugar hearts and faded roses still clutched in their chubby hands.

"My darlings!" whispered Grandma, lingering fondly over them to cover a pair of rosy feet, put back a pile of tumbled curls, or kiss a little mouth still smiling in its sleep.

But when she came to the coldest corner of the room, where Kate lay on the hardest mattress, under the thinnest quilt, the old lady's eyes were full of tender tears. Forgetting the stiff joints that bent so painfully, she knelt slowly down and, putting her arms about the girl, blessed her in silence for the happiness she had given one old heart.

Kate woke at once and started up, exclaiming with a smile, "Why Grandma, I was dreaming about an angel, and you look like one with your white gown and silvery hair!"

"No, dear, you are the angel in this house. How can I ever give you up?" answered Madam, holding fast the treasure that came to her so late.

"You never need to, Grandma, for I have made my choice."

Kate's Choice—

Louisa May Alcott never wrote her autobiography, but she did use her personal experiences to give authenticity to her stories. When she traveled to England in 1870, she found she was treated as something of a celebrity. It was her predisposition to like the English, and she set some of her stories in London.

In "Kate's Choice" she uses her experience to draw the character of Kate, who is someone intensely aware of family connections, English, and eager to do the right thing. Though Kate is new to this country and happens to be well off, her relationship with her American relatives is always utmost in her mind and of far more importance than money and social standing.

When Kate decides to live with her grandmother over other more exciting choices, she shows a nobility of character that Alcott thought she saw in the English people, who demonstrated great consideration for family and familial connections. Kate takes charge of bringing her new family together in much the same way that Alcott took charge of her own family and kept them together.

Gentle May Alcott took drawing lessons in Europe because sister Louisa paid for them and accompanied her on a European tour. When May married and later died while giving birth to a child, Louisa took over the raising of May's daughter Lulu. Louisa's mother, Abba, was able to retire from her job because Louisa paid the family bills and, no doubt, financed some of her father's philosophical projects. Certainly, Bronson Alcott had no money of his own. Louisa and Kate were in some ways almost the same person: independent, domestic women determined to make a home.

Bertie's Box

Adapted by Stephen W. Hines

"Here's a letter for you, Mamma, and, please, I want the red picture that is on it," said little Bertie, as he came trotting into the room where his mother and aunt sat busily putting the last touches to their generous store of Christmas gifts.

"Do read it, Jane; my hands are too sticky," said Mrs. Field, who was filling pretty horns and boxes with bonbons.

"Whom do you know in Iowa?" asked Aunt Jane, looking at the postmark.

"No one. It is probably a begging letter. As secretary of our great charitable society, I often get them. Let us see what it is." And Mrs. Field popped a broken barley-sugar dog into Bertie's mouth to cheer him during the long process of picking off the stamp.

"Well, I never! What will folks ask for next? Just hear this!" exclaimed Aunt Jane, after running her eye over the neatly written page:

"Mrs. Field:

"Dear Madame, knowing your kind heart, I venture to hope that you may be willing to help me from your abundant stores. I will state my request as briefly as possible. I am so poor that I have nothing for my two little boys on Christmas. I have seen better days, but my husband is dead, my money is gone. I am sick, alone, and in need of everything. But I only ask for some small presents for the children, that they may not feel forgotten at this season of universal pleasure and plenty. Your mother's heart will feel how hard it will be for me to see their disappointment when, for the first time in their lives, Santa Claus brings nothing.

"Hopefully yours, Ellen Adams."

"Isn't that queer?" said Aunt Jane.

"It is pathetic," answered Mrs. Field, looking from the loaded table before her to the curly head at her knee.

"It's only a new and sentimental way of begging. She says she needs everything, and, of course, expects you will send money. I hope you won't be foolish, Anna."

"I shall not send money; but surely out of all this plenty we can spare something for the poor babies and let them keep their faith in charity. It won't take long to make up a little bundle and will be no great loss if this woman has deceived us. My blessed mother used to say it was better to be deceived now and then than to turn away one honest and needy person. I only hope I may not forget all about it in my hurry." And having finished her job, Mrs. Field went away to wash her hands before beginning another.

As they talked, neither of the ladies observed that a pair of large, blue eyes were fixed upon their faces, while a pair of sharp little ears took in the story, and a busy little mind thought about it after both had put the subject aside.

Bertie sat thinking for several minutes, while Aunt Jane forgot him in her anxiety over the new cap she was making. At last he got up and walked slowly into the nursery, saying to himself, with a thoughtful face:

'Mamma won't remember, and aunty don't care, and those poor little boys won't have any Twismuss if I don't 'tend to it. I've got lots of nice things, and going to have more, so I guess I'll give 'em some of the bestest ones."

Full of goodwill, but uncertain how to begin, Bertie stood with his hands behind his back, looking about the pleasant room, strewn with all manner of half-used-up and broken play-things. A good-sized wooden box in which a little horse had come still stood where he had left it, with two chairs harnessed to it, and whip and reins lying near.

"That will do," said Bertie; and fell to work so busily that Aunt Jane heard nothing of him until a loud bang made her jump and call out sharply, "What are you doing, child?"

"Playing Santy Claus, Aunty, and packing my sleigh. Don't you hear the bells wing?" answered Bertie, shaking the reins and cracking the whip, with a sly twinkle in his eye; for he didn't want to be disturbed yet.

"Well, don't get into mischief." And Aunt Jane went on with her cap, just ready for the pink bows.

More bangs followed, and nails were evidently being driven; but Bertie often played carpenter, so no notice was taken, and soon he was busy pasting bits of paper on the box with his own particular glue pot.

"Now it's all ready, and Mamma will be so pleased, 'cause I saved her lots of trouble," he said to himself, surveying the bedaubed box with great satisfaction. "I guess I better put it under the bed till I come back. Aunty might see it and say it was clutter," he added and tugged and shoved until it was safely hidden.

Then he went out for his walk and forgot all about his work until the next day.

"Where *is* Bertie's best hat? I want to put a new elastic on it and cannot find it anywhere. Whatever does the child do with his things?" said Mary, the nurse, fussing about to get her odd jobs done that she might get off early to her Christmas shopping. There was a great hunt, but no hat appeared until Mary spied a bit of the feather sticking out of a crack in the badly fastened cover of the box under the bed.

"My patience! What a fine mess it will be in, crammed up in that way," scolded Mary, pulling it out and looking 'round for the hammer.

Aunt Jane was sewing at the window, and Mrs. Field had just come in with a parcel in her hand. Both looked on with interest while the lid came off the queer box, stuck full of nails and gay with red and blue labels that would have puzzled the wisest express man.

Out came the hat crushed flat, Bertie's best coat, several of his most costly books, a collection of toys, pictures, and sticky rolls of candy, while on the top of all appeared the piece of gingerbread given for lunch the day before.

"What has the dear child been at, I wonder?"

"He said he was playing Santa Claus yesterday when I heard him pounding those nails," answered Aunt Jane, adding severely, "he ought to be whipped for spoiling good things in that way."

"Here he comes. We'll see what his idea was before we scold him," said Mamma, as the familiar little trot was heard coming through the hall.

The moment Bertie's eye fell upon the box the music stopped, and he looked distressed.

"Why, that's mine! What made you spoil it, Mary?"

"Tell me about it, dear." And Mamma turned the troubled face up to her own.

"It's for the poor little boys you read about. I was afraid you'd forget them, so I packed it all myself and thought you'd be so pleased," cried the boy, eagerly.

"So I am. But why put in your nice things, dear, and not ask me about it?"

"You told me always to give the best pieces away, and I thought they ought to be my very bestest, 'cause the little boys were so poor. Can't it go, Mamma?"

Mrs. Field stood silent for a moment, looking from the small parcel in her hand to the overflowing box, then she kissed her son, saying, with like tears in her eyes:

"My blessed little Christian, you rebuke your mother and show her what she ought to do—give generously and gladly, and trust her fellow creatures as you do. See the difference between our boxes! Mine so small and mean, his full of all his dearest treasures, even the bread out of his mouth. Bertie, I'll fill *your* box with treats and send it in your name. You shall play Santa Claus in earnest and have all the thanks."

Why Mamma hugged him and Aunt Jane sniffed without another word of blame, Bertie did not know or care; but hopping gaily 'round his box, he cried with a beaming face:

"Yes, fill it cram-full and let me help. Mamma, have lots to eat in it. I know the boys will like that best."

"We will! Get your little wagon, and we will go round picking up all sorts of things for this remarkable box," said Mamma, as she led the way to the great closet where her charity stores were kept.

It was a pretty sight, the packing of that box, for Mamma kept finding something more to put in, and Bertie played express man to his heart's content as he dragged the creaking yellow cart to and fro full of hand-me-down clothes, toys he was tired of, and things to eat, all for "the poor little boys who hadn't any Twismuss."

"Now a few odds and ends to fill the corners, and it will be ready for Papa to nail up when he comes in to dinner," said Mamma as the last pair of little hose and her own warm wrapper went in.

"I'll send my purple shawl. It makes me look like a granny, and it will be comfortable for the woman if she really does need clothing," said Aunt Jane, who had watched the packing and melted in spite of herself.

"Another bit of Christmas work, my little Santa Claus. Warm the cold hearts, open the closed hands, and make us all love and help one another," whispered Mrs. Field, as old aunty went away to get the shawl.

"I like this play," cried Bertie, patting down the bundles and rejoicing over the goodies he had seen put in.

"It is better to give than to receive, so play away, dear, and fill a bigger box each year," answered Mamma with a hand on the yellow head as if she blessed it. Here Papa came in, and having read the letter and had a good laugh over Bertie's first box, he was very ready to nail up the second and send it off. He also pulled out his full pocketbook, and, after hesitating a moment over a five and a ten dollar bill, hastily slipped the latter into an envelope and hid it in the pocket of the wrapper that lay on the top.

"Foolish, I dare say, but I must follow my boy's good example and hope it is all right," he said and then went to look up the hammer.

The cover was tightly fastened on with a plainly written address, and Papa promised to have it sent off at once.

"I wonder what will come of it?" said Mamma, as they stood looking at the heavy box.

"I predict that you'll never get a word of thanks," answered Aunt Jane, as if to atone for her generosity.

"You will probably get a letter asking for more," added Mr. Field, half regretting his ten dollars now that it was too late to change it for a five.

"I know the dear little boys will be awfully glad to get it, and I shall like my goodies better because they have got some too," cried Bertie, untroubled by a doubt and full of happy satisfaction at having shared his comforts with those poorer than himself.

It was Christmas Eve, and far off in Iowa, people were making merry all through the small town of Washington. Even down among the shabby streets, some small festivity was going on, and the shops were full of working people buying something for tomorrow. But up in one room of an old house sat a woman rocking a sick baby to sleep and trying to sing while tears ran down her cheeks.

It was a very poor room with little in it but a table piled with work, a cold stove, one lamp, and an almost empty closet. In the bed were two black heads just visible under the shawl spread over them, and the regular breathing told that Jimmy and Johnny were sleeping soundly, in spite of the cold and hunger, and the prospect of no Christmas presents tomorrow.

As she rocked, poor Mrs. Adams glanced at the unfinished work on her table and wondered how she should get on without the money she hoped to have earned if baby had not fallen ill.

Then her eye wandered from two small socks hung up on either side of the fireplace to the two little, red apples on the mantel overhead. They were all she could get for Jimmy and Johnny, and even these poor gifts could not go into the stockings until the holes were mended, for neither had any toes left.

"As soon as baby drops off, I'll mend them, and maybe I can finish a couple of vests, if my oil holds out. Then I can get a bit of candy for the poor little lads. Christmas isn't Christmas to children without sweets," said the mother, looking tenderly at the black heads under the shawl she was shivering without.

As if anxious to help all she could, baby did "drop off," and being tucked up at the foot of the bed, slept nicely for an hour, while mother's fingers worked as fast as cold and weariness would let them.

No answer to my letter. Well, I hardly expected it, being a stranger and everyone so busy at this time of year. But it would have been such a comfort just to get a trifle for the poor dears, thought Mrs. Adams, as she sat alone, while the bells rang Christmas chimes and a cheery murmur came up from the wintry streets below.

Just then a bumping was heard on the stairs, a loud rap came at her door, a rough voice said suddenly, "Something for you, Ma'am—all paid," and a hurried express man dumped a big box just inside her door and was gone before she got her breath.

For a minute she thought she must be dreaming—it was all so sudden. Then she was sure that it was some mistake, but there was her name on the muddy lid; and she clasped her hands in speechless delight, feeling that it *must* be the answer to her letter.

Down went the work, and catching up the poker and a flat-iron, she had that cover off in about three minutes, and, astonishing to relate, not one of those dear children woke up in spite of the noise.

If the Fields, Aunt Jane, and Bertie could have seen what went on for the next hour, they would have had no doubts about the success of their present, for Mrs. Adams laughed and cried, hugged the bundles, and kissed the kind note Mamma had slipped in. She put on the warm wrapper and purple shawl at once, and felt as if comfortable arms were around her. But when she put her hand in the pocket of the gown, where something rustled, and found the money, she broke down entirely, and, dropping on the floor, fairly hugged the box, sobbing:

"God bless these dear people and keep them safe and happy all their lives!"

Many presents were given that night, and many thanks returned, but none was a greater surprise than this one, and none more gratefully received. Its coming was like the magic of fairy tales, for everything seemed changed in a minute; and poor Mrs. Adams felt warm, rich, and happy, with comfortable clothes on her back, ten dollars in her pocket, and in her bosom the kind letter that proved even better than the box that she had generous friends to trust and help her. That cheered her most of all, and when her lamp went out after an hour of real Christmas work and a touching letter to Mrs. Field, she crept to bed with baby cuddled close to a glad and grateful heart.

"What's that?" said Jimmy, as he woke next morning and heard a roaring in the stove where usually no fire was kindled until a late hour, to save fuel.

Popping up his head, he gave one astonished stare 'round the room, and then dived to the bottom of the bed where they usually burrowed to keep warm.

"I say, Johnny, it isn't our room at all. Something's happened, and it's just splendid," he whispered, pulling his brother's hair in his excitement.

"Go 'way! I ain't coming up yet," was the sleepy answer, as the elder boy curled himself up for another nap.

"There's a big fire, and something smells real nice, and there's new clothes all 'round, and baby's sitting up in a red gown, and mother's gone, and our stockings are crammed full—really, truly!"

The last piece of news roused Johnny and sent both scrambling up to sit staring in speechless wonder for several moments.

It was as Jimmy said. A good fire made the air comfortable, something nice sizzled on the stove, a big loaf, a piece of butter, and six eggs appeared upon the table where mush and molasses were usually seen day after day. On the curtains were pinned little coats and trousers, hats hung on the bedposts, and a row of half-worn boots seemed ready to prance off the window seat. Baby sat bolt upright, as gay as a parrot, in a red, flannel nightgown and blue socks, with an orange in one hand and a rubber horse in the other. But, most joyful sight of all, two long, gray stockings dangled from the mantelpiece, brimful of delightful things that bulged mysteriously and came peeping out at the top.

"Is it heaven?" whispered Jimmy, awestricken at such richness.

"No; it's Santa Claus. Mother said he wouldn't come, but I knew he *would*, and he has. Isn't it tip-top?" And Johnny gave a long sigh of pleasure, with one eager eye on his stocking and the other on a certain pair of blue pants with steel buttons.

"Let's get up and grab our presents," proposed Jimmy, and up it was, for out both went like two monkeys, giving baby a glimpse of their funny nightgowns made out of an old, plaid shawl, bright but warm.

Each seized a stocking and a handful of toys and flew back again to rejoice over the new treasures until Mother appeared with her arms full of bundles. She, too, was changed, for she wore a gray gown, with a purple shawl and red hood—so comfortable! Her face shone, and her lips smiled as if all her troubles had flown away. The sad old mother was gone, and a pretty, happy one ran to hug them, saying, all in one breath:

"Merry Christmas, my darlings! See all the good things that dear lady sent us; and the blessed little boy helped and gave the clothes off his back, and played Santa Claus, and all thought of us. Oh, thank 'em! Thank 'em! And kiss me quick, for my heart is full."

Then a grand cuddling went on, with baby in the midst of it, and no one thought of breakfast till the kettle boiled over and reminded Mrs. Adams that her flock must have something more substantial than sugarplums to eat.

Such fun getting into Bertie's old clothes! They just fitted eight-year-old Johnny, and Jimmy didn't mind if the trousers bagged and the jackets lapped on him. They were new and beautiful to the shabby little fellows, tired of darns and patches; and when both were dressed, they strolled about as proud as two small peacocks.

The poor mother had no fears about dinner, for in the magic box was a pie, a cake, tea, oranges, figs, and nuts, and her morning purchases had laid in a bit of meat with potatoes. So the Christmas feast was safe, and for one happy day, all should have enough.

When breakfast was over and the excited family was about to return to their treasures, Mrs. Adams said, with what the children called her "Sunday look," "Boys, come here and put your hands in mine and say with me, 'God bless our dear little Santa Claus and send him many Christmases as happy as the one he has made for us!' "

Johnny and Jimmy said it very soberly, and then, as if the bottled-up rapture of their boyish hearts must find a vent in noise, they burst out with a shrill shout, to which baby added a squeal of delight:

"Hurrah for Bertie Field, and the jolly box he sent us!"

A New Way to Spend Christmas

Adapted by Stephen W. Hines

*I*n spite of rain and fog, our party met at the appointed hour on board of the boat bound for Randalls Island.

This is one of the three islands that lie in East River that are used for charitable purposes. Blackwells Island is full of hospitals, alms and workhouses; Wards has a hospital for immigrants, a mental asylum, and the Potter's Field; but Randalls is devoted to children.

On it is a nursery in which children over two years old are placed and kept until parents or guardians are able to provide for them. If not claimed, they are bound out at a proper age to respectable citizens to learn some useful trade. There are now in the nursery six hundred and forty-two boys and three hundred and twenty-one girls. A school for retarded children is also on this island as is a hospital for sick babies.

For thirty years has the lady who led our party (a worthy daughter of good Isaac T. Hopper) visited the poor children in their various refuges, taking upon herself the duty of seeing that this holiday is not forgotten but kept as it should be, with goodies, gifts, kind words, and a motherly face to make sunshine in a shady place.

The mayor and a commissioner went also, but the heartiest welcome was given to Mrs. G. For hardly had we landed, when several excited boys, after one look at the boxes piled up in the carriage, raced off in various directions to spread the glad tidings: "She's come, she's come!"

To the chapel first, and there, seated on the platform draped in flags, we looked down upon rows of children, who looked up, smiling and nodding at their good friend, who nodded and smiled back again as if she had been the proud grandmother of every one of them.

The big boys in gray suits sat back, the little fellows in white pinafores, with cropped heads and clean faces, came next on one side, and a flock of girls in blue gowns and white aprons sat on the other side.

They were nearest me, and I observed them carefully, thinking at first what a pretty group they made with gay ribbons in their hair, and an innocent look, which they seemed to keep longer than the poor little men who so early begin to "see life."

But among forty girls, I counted fifteen with defective eyes, nine who were deformed in some way, and seven lame ones—all from the blight of poverty. The effects of neglect and impoverished parentage were on nearly all, if one examined closely. Here and there a smiling little face shone out like a daisy in the grass, and I longed to take these young creatures into some safe corner to grow up in the sunshine and pure air they needed.

Singing followed a very brief speech from the commissioner, who vanished immediately afterward, leaving Mr. and Mrs. G.

and a young reporter and myself to enjoy the simple exercises offered us.

It was touching to hear the small boys stand up and sing away with all their might a song about a "little white angel," whom they begged to leave the gates of heaven ajar that they might get a peep in, if no more, when some of the poor dears looked as if they had never known a home, or expected to till they got back to the heaven so lately left.

I love to hear white-robed choirboys chanting as they pace demurely to and fro in handsome churches; but on this Christmas morning, the song of these small orphans in white pinafores sounded through that charity chapel with a sweeter music to my ears than any Latin hymn I ever heard, even from the Pope's choir in St. Peter's.

The girls alternated with the boys in songs and recitations, the former showing most ease of manner and the best memories, the latter gesticulating with great energy, and stumbling manfully through their tasks as if bound to do or die.

I felt highly complimented and much pleased when a bullet-headed orator of twelve or thirteen gallantly gabbled a Christmas hymn of my own, coming to great grief, however, over some of the lines; for "chanting cherubs" were evidently unknown animals to him, and "mistletoe and holly" a trial to his feelings. But the last line met his views exactly, and Richard was himself again as he stretched out two grimy hands with a hearty "Merry Christmas, everyone!"

As the children labored under the delusion that I was the mayoress, I could clap with the rest and enjoy the joke in private.

Mrs. G. made a speech which ought to have cheered their little hearts, for she assured them that as long as she could she should always come to see them on that day, and when she was gone, her own children would still continue the pleasant custom in memory of her for another thirty years, if need be.

It was not necessary for the teacher to give the signal for cheers and clapping of hands after *that* speech; "it did itself"; and as the girls passed us to go to dinner, the touch on the shoulder from the old lady's hand, with a kindly word and a motherly smile, was evidently considered an honor worth hustling for.

We had a look at them in the first rapture of dinner, and it was a sight to remember, especially the small boys, who fairly swam in soup, and cheered the banquet by a chorus of happy voices with a lively accompaniment of drumsticks.

Then we went to the hospital, and I have rarely passed an hour fuller of the satisfaction that is made up of smiles and tears than the one spent in dealing out gifts to these afflicted children. It was good to see a whole room full brighten as we went in, nurses and all. *They* knew Mrs. G., and the poor babies understood at a glance the mission of the dolly woman and the candy man; for the young reporter lent a hand like a brother, and lugged 'round a great wooden box of sweets with a goodwill which caused me to forgive all the wrongs suffered at the hands of his inquisitive race.

"Dolly!" "Tandy!" "Me, me!" was the general cry, with every manifestation of delight the poor things could show. Some hobbled on their little crutches; half blind ones groped their way as if by instinct; sick babies sat up in their beds, beckoning with wasted hands, while others could only look beseechingly from the corner where infirmity imprisoned them.

Alas, how sad it was to see such suffering laid on such innocent victims and to feel how little one could do to lessen it! No Christmas sermon from the most eloquent lips could so touch the heart and teach the tender lesson of Him who took the children in His arms and healed their ills.

One tiny creature, cursed with inherited afflictions too dreadful to describe, lay bandaged on its little bed, and could only move its feet impatiently, with a pleading sort of moan, as its one dim eye recognized the gay dolls in the laps of its mates. I wanted to give one, but there was no hand to grasp it. Even the bonbons must be denied, for in that poor little mouth even sweets were bitter; and all we could do was to prop up a brilliant dolly at the foot of the bed, leaving baby to lie contentedly blinking at it, with the moan changed to a faint coo of pleasure.

She was never to see another Christmas here, but, as I hurried away, with eyes so full that I could not tell the pink candy from the white, it was a comfort to think that thanks to a good woman's faithful pity, I had given poor baby one hour of happiness in her short life that was all pain.

As if this wasn't heartache enough, we ended by visiting the home for the retarded, the memory of which will supply me with nightmares for some time to come. "All ready and waiting, Ma'am," said the matron, whose bonny face cheered me at the first glance. And as we went up, outstretched heads and eager hands verified her words.

Rows of big boys and girls were ranged on either side of a long hall, with a table full of toys in the middle. They were all innocents, as I prefer to call them, yet all wise enough to turn with one accord and give a good shout of welcome as the little lady hurried in, waving her handkerchief and crying heartily: "Merry Christmas, children!" She was like a fairy godmother in a Quakerish bonnet and brown waterproof.

She had brought some gay pictures as an experiment, and dropping the doll and candy business for a time, the rosy-faced reporter helped me show these brilliant works of art.

On holding up two white kittens lapping milk, all the girls went into ecstasies, mewing, laughing, and crying, "Cat, Kitty, O, pretty, pretty!" in the most gratifying manner. A ship with a display of canvas that would have carried a man-of-war clean out of the water in the gale that was blowing had such an effect upon the boys that they fairly howled, and when I changed the toy to a big spotted horse with three legs in the air and a fierce-looking Turk holding on for dear life, every boy that could see it pranced as rampantly as the Arab steed.

A fresh relay of dolls was unpacked for the girls, and it was pathetic to see how tenderly young women of as old as eighteen embraced the poor counterfeits of the only children they could ever know and love.

The boys waited patiently while the ladies were served and appreciated the dolls so highly that several requested to be supplied with interesting families likewise. But they were invited to choose from the toys instead; and one didn't know whether to laugh or cry when these bearded babies picked out painted dogs, nine-pins or blocks and went proudly back to show their treasures. One dwarf of thirty-five got a Noah's Ark and a squeaking lion, and sat brooding over the wooden family with a vacant smile, too feeble to comprehend how the squeak was made in the brown beast, which he hugged and patted fondly.

We saw their schoolroom, the neat copy books and drawings, various methods for teaching form and color, and heard many interesting facts from the gentle teacher, whose devoted life seemed blest to her, since, in spite of the sad imprisonment she freely endured, she was as fresh and cheerful as if Heaven's sun and dew found her out even there.

The tidy dormitories were kept in order by the girls themselves, and the boys worked at other tasks well and willingly, we were told. Several seemed intelligent enough, but each had a mental weakness of some kind that unfitted them for self-help and self-government; so one could not but be truly grateful that men and women were ready to give, as some had done, twenty-five years of life to this work of Christian charity.

We got some splendid cheers as we departed, and, leaving boxes here and there on our way, drove at last to the boat, tired and hungry, but well content with the day's work.

To my eye there seemed to be a sort of halo 'round the little black bonnet that had led us to and fro all these hours, and it was not difficult to believe that the serene old couple who folded their empty hands with a sigh of satisfaction and sat cheerfully telling over new charities with the soft "thee and thou," which made the sad words "poverty" and "loss" almost sweet, were really Christmas angels in disguise.

I shall always think so, and I fancy the young reporter never will regret that he did not return *early* with the mayor and the commissioner, since by staying he saw scenes far better worth recording than brutal executions or vain hunts after the great swindlers who escape detection.

For my part, though I missed my dinner, I felt as if I had feasted sumptuously on the crumbs that fell from the children's table; and though the smiles, broken words, and simple gratitude of orphans, handicapped, and babies were the only gifts I received that day, they were precious enough to make forever memorable the Christmas spent at Randalls Island.

Tilly's Christmas

"I'm so glad tomorrow is Christmas because I'm going to have lots of presents," said Kate, glowing with anticipation.

"I'm glad as well," Bessy chimed, "though I don't expect any presents but a pair of mittens."

It was Tilly's turn to speak, and she startled them with her words, "I'm very glad tomorrow is Christmas, even though I shan't have any presents at all."

These sentiments were spoken as the three little girls trudged home from school, and Tilly's words struck a cord of pity in the others. Kate and Bessy wondered how she could speak so cheerfully and be so happy when she was too poor to receive even the smallest of gifts on Christmas Day.

"Don't you wish you could find a purse full of money right here in the path?" asked Kate, the child who was going to have lots of presents.

"Oh, don't I! If I could keep it honestly, that is," said Tilly, her eyes glowing at the prospect.

"What would you buy?" asked Bessy, rubbing her cold hands and longing for her mittens.

"I've worked it all out in my mind," Tilly responded. "I'd buy a pair of large, warm blankets, a load of wood, a shawl for mother, and a pair of shoes for me. If there was enough left, I'd give Bessy a new hat so that she would not have to wear Ben's old felt one."

The girls giggled at that, but Bessy pulled the funny hat down over her ears and said she was much obliged but she would rather have candy.

"Let's look, and maybe we can find a purse. People are always going about with money at Christmastime. How do we know someone has not lost it here on this path?" said Kate.

So the three little girls went along the snowy road, looking about them, half in earnest, half in fun. Suddenly, Tilly sprang forward, exclaiming loudly, "I see it! I've found a purse!"

Kate and Bessy followed quickly, but sputtered with disappointment as they realized that there was no purse lying in the snow but only a little bird. It lay upon the snow with its wings spread and feebly fluttered, too weak to fly. Its little feet were benumbed with cold and its once bright eyes were dull with pain. Instead of a chipper song, it could only utter a faint chirp now and then as if pleading for help.

"Nothing but a stupid old robin. How maddening!" cried Kate, sitting down to rest on a nearby tree stump.

"I shan't touch it. I found one once and took care of it until it was well. The ungrateful thing flew away the minute it was able," said Bessy, creeping under Kate's shawl and pulling her hands up under her chin to warm them.

Tilly heard not a word. "Poor little birdie!" she crooned. "How pitiful you look and how glad you must be to see someone coming along to help you. I'll take you up gently and carry you home to Mother. Don't be frightened, dear. I am your friend." Tilly knelt down in the snow, stroking the bird with her hand and the tenderest pity in her face.

It was only then that she realized Kate and Bessy were laughing.

"Don't stop for that thing," they chided. "Now come along. Let's continue looking for a purse before it gets too cold and dark."

"You wouldn't leave it to die!" cried Tilly. "I'd rather have the bird than the money we might find in a purse. After all, the purse would not be mine, and I would only be tempted to keep it. But this poor little creature will thank and love me for my trouble. Thank goodness I came in time."

Gently lifting the bird, Tilly felt its tiny, cold claws cling to her hand and its dim eyes brighten as it nestled down with a grateful chirp.

"Now I've a Christmas present after all," she said smiling. "I've always wanted a bird, and this one will be such a pretty pet for me."

"He'll fly away the first chance he gets and die anyhow," said Bessy. "You'd be better off not to waste your time with him."

"He can't pay you for taking care of him, and my mother says it isn't worthwhile to help folks that can't help us," added Kate.

"My mother said, 'Do to others as you would to be done to by them,' and I'm sure I'd like someone to help me if I was dying of cold and hunger. I also remember the little saying, 'Love your neighbor as yourself.' This bird is my little neighbor, and I'll love him and care for him, just as I often wish our rich neighbor would love and care for us," answered Tilly. She leaned forward slightly, breathing her warm breath over the tiny bird, who looked up at her with confiding eyes, quick to feel and know a friend.

"What a funny girl you are," said Kate. "Caring for that silly bird, and talking about loving your neighbor in that serious way. Mr. King doesn't care a bit for you, and he never will, though he knows how poor you are. So I don't think your plan amounts to much."

"I believe it, and I shall be happy to do my part," answered Tilly. "I must bid you good night now, and I hope you'll have a merry Christmas and receive lots of lovely things."

As she left her friends and walked on alone toward the little old house where she lived, Tilly's spirits began to sink. Suddenly, she felt so poor. Her eyes were filled with tears as she thought of all the pretty things other children would be finding in their stockings on Christmas morning. It would have been so pleasant to think of finding something for herself and pleasanter still to have been able to give her mother something nice. So many comforts were lacking with no hope of getting them. The little family was pressed enough to simply find food and firewood.

"Never mind, birdie," whispered Tilly. "We'll make the best of what we have and be merry in spite of our lack. You shall have a happy Christmas, anyway, and I know God won't forget us, even if everyone else does."

Tilly stopped a moment to dry her eyes and lean her cheek against the bird's soft breast. The tiny creature afforded her much comfort, though it could only love her, not one thing more.

"See, Mother, what a nice present I've found," she cried, entering the house with a cheery face that was like sunshine in the dark room.

"I'm glad of that, dearie, as I have not been able to get my little girl anything but a rosy apple. What a poor little bird it is. Here, quickly, give the poor thing some of your warm bread and milk."

"Why Mother, this bowl is so full. I'm afraid you gave me all the milk," said Tilly, smiling over the nice, steaming supper that stood ready for her.

"I've had plenty, dear. Sit down and warm your feet. You may put the bird in my basket on this cozy flannel."

After placing the bird tenderly into the basket, Tilly peeped into the closet and saw nothing there but dry bread.

"Oh dear," Tilly exclaimed to herself, "Mother's given me all the milk and is going without her tea because she knows I'm hungry. I'll surprise her by fixing her a good supper while she is outside splitting wood."

As soon as her mother left the room, Tilly reached for the old teapot and carefully poured out a part of the milk. Then from her pocket, she drew a great, plump bun that one of the school children had given her. She had saved it for just this purpose. She toasted a slice of the bun and set a bit of butter on the plate for her mother to put on it. When her mother came in, she found the table drawn up in a warm place, a hot cup of tea ready, and Tilly and the birdie waiting patiently.

Such a poor little supper, and yet such a happy one, for love, charity, and contentment were welcome guests around the humble table. That Christmas Eve was a sweeter one even than that at the great house, where light shone, fires blazed, a great tree glittered, music sounded, and children danced and played.

"We must go to bed early," said Tilly's mother as they sat by the fire. "We must save the wood, for there is only enough to last through tomorrow. The day after, I shall be paid for my work, and we can buy more."

"If only my bird were a fairy bird and would give us three wishes," Tilly said quietly. "How nice that would be! But, the poor dear can give me nothing, and it is of no matter." Tilly was looking at the robin, who lay in the basket with his head under his wing, nothing more than a feathery, little ball.

"He can give you one thing, Tilly," her mother said. "He can give you the pleasure of doing good. That is one of the sweetest things in life, and it can be enjoyed by the poor as well as the rich." As Tilly's mother spoke, she softly stroked her daughter's hair with her tired hand.

Suddenly Tilly started with surprise and pointed toward the window. "I saw a face—a man's face," she confided in a frightened whisper. "He was looking in. He's gone now, but I truly saw him."

Tilly's mother stood up and went to the door. "Some traveler attracted by the light perhaps," she said.

The wind blew cold, the stars shone bright, the snow lay white on the field and the wood, and the Christmas moon was glittering in the sky; but no human person was standing within sight.

"What sort of face was it?" asked Tilly's mother, quickly closing the door.

"A pleasant sort of face, I think, but I was so startled to see it there that I don't quite know what it was like. I wish we had a curtain there," said Tilly.

"I like to have our light shine out in the evening, for the road is dark and lonely just here, and the twinkle of our lamp is pleasant to people as they pass by. We can do so little for our neighbors. I am glad we can at least cheer them on their way," said Tilly's mother. "Now put those poor, old shoes to dry and go to bed, dearie. I'll be coming soon."

Tilly went, taking her birdie with her to sleep in his basket near her bed, lest he should be lonely in the night. Soon the little house was dark and still.

278

When Tilly came down and opened the front door that Christmas morning, she gave a loud cry, clapped her hands together, and then stood still, quite speechless with wonder and delight. There, near the stoop, lay a great pile of firewood all ready to be burned. There was also a large bundle and a basket with a lovely nosegay of winter roses, holly, and evergreen tied to the handle.

"Oh, Mother! Who could have left it?" cried Tilly, pale with excitement and the surprise of it all. She stepped out to bring in the basket, and her mother, a few steps behind, stooped down to scoop up the bundle.

"The best and dearest of all Christmas angels is called 'Charity,' " Tilly's mother answered, her eyes welling with tears as she undid the bundle. "She walks abroad at Christmastime doing beautiful deeds like this, and never staying to be thanked."

It was all there—all that Tilly had imagined. There were warm, thick blankets, the comfortable shawl, a pair of new shoes, and best of all, a pretty winter hat for Bessy. The basket was full of good things to eat, and on the flowers lay a small note saying, "For the little girl who loves her neighbor as herself."

"Mother, I really do think my little bird is an angel in disguise and that all these splendid things came from him," said Tilly, laughing and crying with joy.

It really did seem so. As Tilly spoke, the robin flew to the table, hopped to the nosegay, and perching among the roses, began to chirp with all his little might. The sun streamed in on the flowers, the tiny bird, and the happy child with her mother. No one saw a shadow glide across the window or ever knew that Mr. King had seen and heard the little girls the night before. No one ever dreamed that the rich neighbor had learned a priceless lesson from his poor, little neighbor girl.

And Tilly's bird was a Christmas angel, for by the love and tenderness she gave to the helpless little creature, she brought good gifts to herself, happiness to an unknown benefactor, and the faithful friendship of a little friend who did not fly away, but stayed with her until the snow was gone, making summer for her in the wintertime.

THE EDITOR'S NOTES

Tilly's Christmas—

Louisa May Alcott's great gift as a writer revealed itself in her deft characterizations of her heroes and heroines. Sometimes using but a few words of dialogue, she could lay out the essential nature of a boy or a girl whose special thoughtfulness marked them out for praise and reward.

While Miss Alcott was not the only writer for children who believed that the kindly child would ultimately find kindness, and that generous children would surely find generosity returned, she may have been one of that philosophy's most convincing proponents.

Miss Alcott's own fairy tale life was characterized by early poverty and desperate illness, followed by unparalleled success as a writer. By the tender age of thirty-six, she had delivered her father, her mother, and her sisters from the utter penury of their early existence.

At the close of *Tilly's Christmas*, it is said of the main character, "For by the love and tenderness she gave to the helpless . . . she brought good gifts to herself." Such was true of the amazing Louisa May Alcott. And such is true of her kind heroine.

The Virtues of
Louisa May Alcott's Characters

Louisa May Alcott was undoubtedly the most beloved children's author of her time, yet words such as "old maid" and "spinster" have been used to describe her. To some admirers who asked for a photograph, even she herself wrote: "You can't make a Venus out of a tired old lady."

How can such a self-deprecating woman have achieved such heights of literary fame and have accurately depicted the yearnings and aspirations of her youthful audience? Why did young readers sense in her such a friend and confidante when she had no children of her own? I believe we must look for our answers to these questions in the background of her family life.

Louisa May Alcott loved children and believed them capable of great moral maturity because she had parents who loved her and believed her capable of such attainments of character. The daughter of a schoolmaster father and a mother who was one of the first paid social workers in the United States, she had grown up in a household of high expectations.

Character and moral rectitude were everything in the Alcott household. The children were encouraged to speak about their feelings and aspirations, not with the purpose that these thoughts and feelings be indulged, but that they be molded and directed toward virtuous actions.

Father Bronson Alcott made it clear that he expected his little women to aspire to attributes of courage, loyalty, kindness, self-control, and sweet temper. Mother Abba Alcott made it clear that although she shared her husband's views on character development, she also understood that her children must be nurtured and allowed the freedom to have fun and be themselves—even if that meant they were less than little angels.

This may all seem like a tedious kind of goodness that reigned supreme in the Alcott home, but the Alcotts were not out of step with their times in these matters. Moral education was not something newly minted in America. Rather it had its origins in a Europe where French and German philosophers taught that goodness could be acquired through intuition and self-examination and that such pursuits were the whole goal of life.

In general, Louisa May Alcott felt blessed to have had such parents and responded well to such serious nurture. She developed a special love for her mother, who kept the family together when Father was out of work.

Out of this background, Louisa May's own aspirations became quite high. In a diary, she listed Love, Patience, Industry, and Generosity as among her life's goals. This diary was available to her parents, who regularly read it in order to encourage their daughter to aim high and believe in her perfectibility.

Is it any wonder that, though Louisa May Alcott's stories are entertaining, they are also earnest and instructive? This quality made her stories immensely popular with parents, and the children didn't seem to mind the dose of moral medicine that came with the stories, coming as it did from an "old maid" who loved boys and girls so well.

About the Author

LOUISA MAY ALCOTT is the beloved author of one of the world's great classics of literature, *Little Women*. First published in 1868, *Little Women* has captured the imaginations of countless generations of young adults who thrill to read the seemingly real-life adventures of Meg, Jo, Beth, and Amy of the impoverished March family.

A groundbreaking work at the time, Miss Alcott's story is one of the first books to treat children as real people, with real feelings and varied motives, in a realistic setting. Miss Alcott's characters hope, sorrow, and strive in a way that makes readers care for and believe in them.

With the success of *Little Women*, Louisa May Alcott became established as one of the leading lights of American literature and one of the most successful authors of her time. Although her fame was sudden, it did not come easily.

Born in 1832, Louisa May Alcott's fairy tale life did not have a fairy tale beginning. Her father, Bronson Alcott, was an earnest, impractical man who, without much formal education, decided to become a schoolteacher and educational reformer. He failed in the educational profession several times, and with each failure came further poverty for his family. It was left to Louisa's mother, Abba Alcott, to give the family some semblance of emotional and financial stability.

Abba Alcott had to demonstrate a practicality that did not seem to dwell in the deep philosophical and educational recesses of Bronson Alcott's mind. Most assuredly the model for the character Marmee in *Little Women*, Abba became one of Boston's first social workers and, with her meager income, kept the family supplied as well as she could with material necessities.

Abba's example of self-sacrifice affected her daughter. From a very early age, Louisa May began to act the role of an adult and took it upon herself to do what she could to pull her family out of genteel, and sometimes not so genteel, poverty. She took any menial job to help out and was very aware of the fact that friend and neighbor Ralph Waldo Emerson had made them gifts of money over the years.

From very early on, Louisa Alcott was able to help the family by publishing short articles, poems, and stories in the various magazines that fed the voracious reading appetite of the Boston public. While these efforts never paid great sums of money, they did provide a little relief for the family and a lot of experience for Louisa.

Ironically enough, it was the Civil War that gave Miss Alcott her freedom to step out of the family shadows and into her own limelight.

In 1862, Louisa May Alcott volunteered to become a nurse in a Union hospital. The experience, though short, changed her life. After the briefest of training, she found herself caring for desperately ill and dying men. She discovered new strength in herself as she fed her charges, helped alleviate their sufferings, and ministered words of comfort to those who would not see home nor sweetheart again.

The work was exhausting, the conditions for the nurses themselves appalling, and Louisa nearly died. Bronson Alcott had to go to Washington, D. C., to rescue her, and although she recovered rapidly, her health was never quite the same.

Out of this tragic experience came her war book, *Hospital Sketches*. In itself not a great success, the book did give evidence of a new maturity in Louisa's writing. This maturity was appreciated by her Boston publishers who became increasingly supportive of her work. Writing as much as thirty pages of copy a day, from this time forward, Miss Alcott never lacked an outlet for her writing.

Then, in 1868 came *Little Women*, instant fame, and the enormous sum of $8,000 in royalties. The family's financial worries were at an end. The very happy conclusion of *Little Women* really did mirror that of her own dear family except for one thing: Louisa May Alcott never married as Jo March did. That was a dream that was never to be.

Instead, Louisa May remained faithful to her family, nursing her mother through her last illness, and finally passing away herself in the same year her father died. From 1832 to 1888, it had been a short but eventful life.

About the Presenter

STEPHEN W. HINES is a writer, researcher, and editor who has worked with words on a professional basis for twenty years. His book, *Little House in the Ozarks: the Rediscovered Writings* (of Laura Ingalls Wilder), rose to the *Publishers Weekly* best-seller list in 1991. Since that time, he has  devoted himself to the rediscovery of other worthy but overlooked efforts by famous authors.

Following several successful books on Laura Ingalls Wilder, Hines discovered *The Quiet Little Woman: A Christmas Story* by Louisa May Alcott in a long-forgotten children's magazine. This book appeared on the CBA best-selling hardcover fiction list for several months in 1999 and 2000.

Stephen lives with his wife and daughters near Nashville, Tennessee, where he continues his research and writes a column for a local paper. His books have sold more than one million copies.

About the Artist

C. MICHAEL DUDASH, the artist for this collection, has been an artist and illustrator for the past twenty-four years. His oil paintings have won him a national reputation and numerous awards  from the Society of Illustrators (NYC & LA), the Society of Publication Designers, Communication Arts, and HOW Magazine. Much of his time in recent years has been focused on collaborative projects with several Christian publishers where he has been able to express his personal faith through fine-art, prints, books, and gift products.

Additional copies of this book and other
titles published by RiverOak Publishing
are available from your local bookstore.

Kate's Choice
The Quiet Little Woman
The Quiet Little Woman (family gift edition)

If you have enjoyed this book,
or if it has impacted your life,
we would like to hear from you.
Please contact us at:

RiverOak Publishing
Department E
P.O. Box 55388
Tulsa, Oklahoma 74155

Visit our website at:
www.riveroakpublishing.com